Broader, Bolder, Better

Broader, Bolder, Better

How Schools and Communities Help Students
Overcome the Disadvantages of Poverty

Elaine Weiss and Paul Reville

HARVARD EDUCATION PRESS
CAMBRIDGE, MASSACHUSETTS

Paperback ISBN 978-1-68253-348-2
Library Edition ISBN 978-1-68253-349-9

Cataloging-in-Publication Data is on file with the Library of Congress.

Published by Harvard Education Press,
an imprint of the Harvard Education Publishing Group

Harvard Education Press
8 Story Street
Cambridge, MA 02138

Cover Design: Ciano Design
Cover Photo: Dimitri Otis/DigitalVision/Getty Images

The typefaces used in this book are Weiss and Helvetica Neue.

Elaine Weiss:

This book is dedicated to Kayla and Maya,
who are wise enough to appreciate all the
enrichment and support they have enjoyed, and
to Lizzie, whose future will shine brighter
the more of those she receives.

Paul Reville:

To the children whom our school system
and our society have failed for far too long.

"Equality is giving everyone a shoe.
Equity is giving everyone a shoe that fits."

—NAHEED DOSANI

"Genius is evenly distributed across zip codes.
Opportunity and access are not."

—MITCH KAPOR, ENTREPRENEUR
AND PHILANTHROPIST

Contents

PART I

Poverty, Education, and the Need for Systems of Support

1

Why Integrated
Student Supports?

How many of you have started off your day, sometime in the past few weeks, on the totally wrong foot? You woke up fifteen minutes late and couldn't make a cup of coffee, so you arrived at work kind of cranky. Your kids were scrambling to make it to the bus, one forgot her lunch (which you realized as the bus pulled away), and you argued with your spouse about who had to be late to work to take the lunch to the forgetful one. How much did that throw off your morning or the whole day?

With these words, former Joplin, Missouri, school superintendent C. J. Huff opens his presentation to dozens of audiences every year. And his description of the scenario always elicits a strong response from the crowd, whether it's a dozen people in a small workshop at one of his Bright Futures conferences or a big room of 250, where he's a plenary speaker. People nod in recognition, turn to their neighbors to find similar smiles on their faces, and laugh about the disastrous days those inauspicious mornings prompted.

But then he strikes a more serious note:

Now put yourselves in the shoes of a child who is having this kind of morning. A child whose morning is a continuation of the night that preceded it. Forget the coffee—this kid didn't have breakfast. And not because he didn't have time to make it, but because there wasn't any food in the house. And he was already hungry, because he also didn't eat dinner. Or maybe there was dinner, but there wasn't a table to eat it at (which is also why he had a hard time doing his homework). Or maybe there is a table, and he was hiding under it because there were bullets flying outside the window and that was the best place to take shelter.

You all just agreed that not having coffee—or milk or sugar to put in it—could throw your morning off track. Yet we expect kids whose mornings start off like this to come to class, to sit down quietly, to ignore the rumbling in their stomachs and in their minds, and to listen, take in what their teachers are saying, and do great work. Really?

We begin this book with this short soliloquy by our colleague because it illustrates the degree to which schools and teachers across the country—a fair share of them, at least—are playing an inevitably losing game. They are ignoring what we have learned about children and learning in recent years—as well as common sense.

This book is about changing our collective disregard of what research says about educational advancements. It shines a light on two parallel sets of gaps that jointly drive achievement gaps: disparities in support and in learning opportunities. It aims to connect the dots between what we know about human motivation and how children learn (and why many students in the United States are not learning to their potential). In so doing, we hope to make a case for radically rethinking the design of not only our schools but also our communities and their policies and practices affecting children and education. Specifically, the book advocates helping schools and communities come together to create systems of integrated student supports (ISS) for all children. Throughout these pages, we identify leading initiatives, advocates, organizations and networks working toward the common goal of providing a pipeline of supports from cradle to career across a variety of settings throughout the United States.

Importantly, this book highlights how twelve diverse communities in a dozen states are making progress in doing just that: designing child development and education interventions and systems to meet children's needs inside and outside school. All the communities employ ISS in service of whole-child education. These supports free children up to engage in the type of critical thinking and deeper learning to which our schools and education systems aspire, as psychologist Abraham Maslow illustrated in his well-known hierarchy. And these communities ensure that rich learning experiences are available to every student, not just a lucky minority of them. While the bulk of the book is devoted to highlighting the unique practices and strengths of these ISS initiatives, which can serve as models for other communities and school systems, we also feature other examples of promising initiatives.

These diverse ISS efforts, while admirable, are by no means perfect. This book does not wave a Mission Accomplished banner, nor do the initiatives' leaders suggest that their work is complete. Indeed, the headway these districts have made in boosting achievement, tackling chronic absenteeism, meaningfully engaging students, and narrowing race- and income-based opportunity and achievement gaps are intentionally described as indicators of progress, not successes. Moreover, while all these initiatives put schools at the center (with community partnerships playing key roles), other ISS models divide the task differently. In many models, schools are only one of several bodies or agencies that drive community initiatives to foster child development and well-being. And besides offering inspiration and guidance, these case studies also present caveats about the challenges these communities have faced and the limitations to scaling up and expanding their efforts.

This book illustrates how communities (or school districts)—the level at which many important education decisions are made—can shift their focus toward a comprehensive, support-based set of strategies designed to enable all children to come to school every day, genuinely ready to learn. By providing wraparound support to students in need, communities ensure enhanced learning and school effectiveness and diminish gaps in opportunity and thus achievement. They effectively make the case for unifying and building the ISS field, so that policies are enacted at the federal, state, and local levels to support the growth of such services and their availability to children all across the country.

DISPARITIES IN SUPPORT: MASLOW'S HIERARCHY VERSUS CHILDREN'S REALITIES

Maslow posited that, to achieve full potential, every human being needs to have certain needs met.[1] At the most basic level, those needs include food, water, warmth, and rest. Just above that are needs for security and safety. With those fundamentals in place, people can focus on their innate need to be part of something larger—which Maslow characterizes as "belongingness and love needs" and which include friendships and other intimate relationships. People who have all those needs met can then work toward fulfilling higher-order needs related to esteem and, at the apex, self-actualization: achieving one's full potential, including creative activities (figure 1.1).[2]

Life's realities, however, pose high barriers for a growing share of our children to viably reach for that pinnacle. Indeed, data paints a stark picture of a country whose failure to attend to children's fundamental needs has guaranteed that schooling, despite all our costly education reforms, will also fail for many of these children. Decades of education reform efforts have yielded modest if any improvements in most places where poverty is prevalent. To be sure, there are outliers, schools and individuals defying the odds, but on average, we still have an iron-clad correlation

FIGURE 1.1
Maslow's hierarchy of human needs

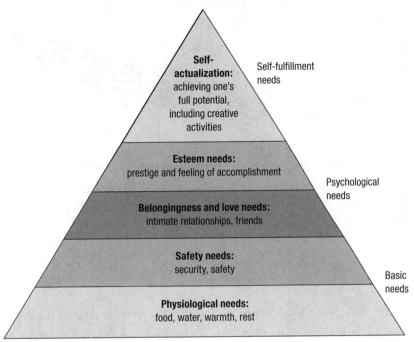

between socioeconomic status and educational achievement and attainment (figure 1.2).

Poverty and its attendant stresses matter profoundly to a child's odds of succeeding in school. The data shows that on average, schooling is an insufficient instrument for overcoming the disadvantages of poverty. This observation is borne out by the diminishing social mobility in our society, but few have figured out what to do about it. The communities featured in this book have made a start.

POVERTY: TROUBLING TRENDS

The fiftieth anniversary of President Lyndon Johnson's 1964 declaration of the War on Poverty sparked substantial debate. Many conservatives

FIGURE 1.2

Academic achievement and socioeconomic status: US school districts, 2009–2013

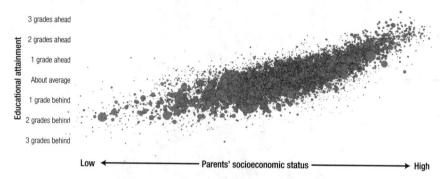

Source: Sean F. Reardon, "School District Socioeconomic Status, Race, and Academic Achievement," Stanford Center for Education Policy Analysis (2016), https://cepa.stanford.edu/content/school-district-socioeconomic-status-race-and-academic-achievement. Copyright © Sean F. Reardon. Used with permission.

declared the war a total failure, noting that the share of Americans deemed poor by federal standards has barely changed and that the poor are now more dependent on government handouts than they were in 1964. Progressive voices counter that those so-called government handouts keep many American families out of poverty but that this assistance is both insufficient to meet the high demand and politically contentious. In reality, the enactment of safety net programs such as cash welfare and food stamps, along with help from older social insurance programs like social security and unemployment insurance, made a major dent between 1964 and the late 1970s.

But the poverty rate has since climbed back up. Decades of stagnant wages, increasingly regressive tax policies, and declining support for safety net social policies, all exacerbated by the major recession of 2008, have pushed millions of American children back into poverty. In 2013, the Southern Education Foundation reported an alarming tipping point: for the first time since data on school meals has been collected, over half of all US public school children qualified.[3] And the rise in poverty had been rapid. Just seven years before that report, the national rate was 41 percent (versus 51 percent in 2013).

A 2014 report by the American Federation of Teachers dives into this data state by state and county by county, illustrating the alarming trend from the academic generation that began school in 2000 to its 2012 successor cohort. Aptly titled *Child Poverty: Moving in the Wrong Direction*, side-by-side maps of the fifty states and the District of Columbia reveal that by 2014, twenty states had no counties with a low poverty rate (with less than 10 percent of its children living in poverty) (figure 1.3).[4]

An increasing number of children are also growing up in very deprived circumstances. Currently, 11 percent of young children live in households with annual incomes below 50 percent of the federal poverty line—that is, $10,210 for a family of three—up from 9 percent in 2008. The number of children living in areas of concentrated poverty—areas in which 30 percent or more of their neighbors are also poor—likewise grew rapidly. In 2012, some 21 percent of all children were poor, and of those, 36 percent, or more than one in three, were living in concentrated poverty.

POVERTY: INCREASING IMPACTS

Rising poverty over the past few decades is associated with several factors that directly and indirectly impede children's readiness and ability to learn and teachers' abilities to be effective instructors. In 2016, one in four US children was sufficiently *food insecure* to qualify for food stamps, and the number of homeless children was a whopping 1.3 million in the 2013–2014 school year, double the number from a decade earlier. Some of the country's largest cities have discovered unsafe lead levels in water, the most basic of basics, with children in poverty disproportionately at risk.

Other, more common health problems also put low-income students at particular disadvantage. Asthma, which affects less than 8 percent of US

FIGURE 1.3

Percentage of children living in poverty, from birth to seventeen years, in 2000 and 2014

The United States has one of the highest child poverty rates among industrialized nations. Many American households are struggling, creating a real educational challenge for far too many students.

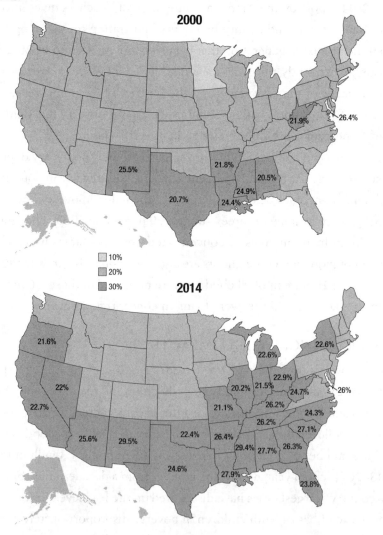

Source: American Federation of Teachers, "Growth in Child Poverty Mapped by County in the 50 States," American Federation of Teachers, www.aft.org/growth-child-poverty-mapped-county-50-states. Used with permission.

children overall, has much higher rates among black children, Puerto Rican children, and low-income children living in urban centers. Triggers like pests and dirty air cause acute attacks that make it hard to focus in class and can lead to chronic absence from school. Cavities are so prevalent and are so frequently left untreated among poor children that studies suggest that dental problems may be the second-most significant cause, after asthma, of children's loss of multiple school days. Other research documents the frequent misdiagnosis of children living in poverty as learning disabled when, in fact, they have unidentified vision problems. When these children receive eyeglasses, their ability to learn can dramatically improve.

Many students also lack second-rung safety and security needs. Their public housing complexes are the frequent sites of violence, or their routes to school require navigating hostile gang territory. In sum, a significant share of children are not having many of their most basic needs met.

Living in poverty, especially in deep or concentrated poverty, also takes a heavy toll on parents in ways that reduce children's ability to learn and achieve in school. A parent's inability to survive day-to-day, put food on the table, ensure children's physical safety, and keep a roof over the family's head induces massive parental stress, which can lead to depression, addiction, and other forms of dysfunction. Exacerbating these problems, especially for children of color, is the sharp rise in the number of adults being sentenced to prison, often for nonviolent offenses. As two education economists report in a recent study, up to 10 percent of African American students have a parent in prison, and one-quarter have a parent who has been incarcerated.[5]

Living with these dire daily realities leads to a condition that scientists call *toxic stress*, which we now know impedes healthy brain development, reduces the ability to focus, and increases impulsivity.[6] It also drives high levels of the stress hormone cortisol, which can cause the deterioration of bodily systems, increase vulnerability to disease, and even negatively affect genetics and heredity, generally lowering people's prospects for success.[7] And like the other impediments to effective teaching and learning described here, toxic stress is heavily concentrated in certain neighborhoods and schools, adding to the other burdens felt by those schools' teachers, principals, and students.[8]

These are the realities facing millions of American students and the teachers and schools that serve these children. And increasing stratification by social class and resulting segregation of children concentrates the country's highest-needs students in some districts, schools, and even classrooms. Anthony Bryk, who founded the Consortium for Chicago School Research, described a critical minority of the high-poverty Chicago public schools that he and his colleagues studied as "truly disadvantaged" because of their high share of students living in "extraordinary circumstances." They assessed schools in which one in four children have been reported to social services for abuse or neglect, meaning that in a classroom of thirty students, a teacher might have seven or eight students experiencing that level of trauma.[9] Not coincidentally, academic performance in such schools is abysmal.

While the schools described by Bryk and his fellow researchers are extreme examples, they are by no means isolated. Moreover, it does not require this level of dysfunction to make a teacher struggle to have all his or her children reading, adding, and subtracting at grade level, let alone attaining higher-order thinking. In other words, students' and schools' realities are increasingly butting up against the human needs in Maslow's hierarchy, and meeting those needs is proving an insurmountable obstacle.

OPPORTUNITY GAPS: PERVASIVE AND PREDICTIVE

Disparities in learning opportunities compound the gaps in support for disadvantaged children, forcing these students even further behind their more privileged peers. And just as Huff describes in personally identifiable terms the challenges posed to children who lack the basics, upper-middle-class people's experiences with their own children illustrate this second set of gaps.

Take a typical week in the lives of such children. After a day at school where teachers appreciated the children's intelligence and abilities and created experiences to support and enhance them, the kids spent their afternoon at (pick one) chess club, music lessons, soccer practice, or doing homework in a quiet, orderly space. If it was nice out, they walked or biked to a safe, well-maintained neighborhood park. On the weekend, one of the parents or a grandparent took them to a movie, a museum, or, if they were really lucky, a theater production in the city. This fairly normal week in upper-middle-class children's lives is replete with opportunities to build on what they learned during class, explore things they are curious about, spend quality time with adults who care about them and are imparting knowledge, and broaden their horizons.

Now contrast that week with the life of a "typical" child living in poverty. The school is much less likely to offer chess club or robotics, and if it does, those extras might cost money or public bus fare that parents cannot afford. Or the activities might require the child to walk home through a dangerous neighborhood. Music lessons and organized sports are out of reach financially and pose logistical challenges for parents working multiple jobs or odd hours. There may or may not be space to do homework, and such a space is unlikely to be quiet or stocked with snacks that make thinking more constructive. There is little or no access to the kinds of technology tools and devices that infinitely enrich the lives of affluent peers. Weekends are not time off, but often periods of boredom interspersed with rushed trips to the grocery store and other errands that are frustrating with only one parent and little money. Movies and museums are rare indulgences, and travel may be nonexistent.

By the time typical low-income and middle-income children finish elementary school, the cumulative difference in learning opportunities has become enormous. Fully half of the 6,000-hour learning gap (by eighth grade) that scholars report is due to disparities in after-school activities. The next biggest chunk is attributable to preschool, with summer camp costing another 1,000 hours. Day trips and family reading time round it out.[10]

These numbers point to serious flaws in the argument that schools alone can be the great equalizer in our society. They belie the assertion that schools, even though they account for only 20 percent of a child's waking hours between kindergarten and graduation, can somehow miraculously overcome the enormous and growing inequalities in income, wealth, opportunity, and social mobility that characterize our society. Schools alone, as currently constituted, are inadequate to the job of becoming society's "great balance wheel" as envisioned by that celebrated founding father of American schooling, Horace Mann. When children from backgrounds of poverty compete with affluent suburban students in school, the playing field is starkly uneven because of vastly unequal supports and opportunities. Moreover, the unfairness begins early, far before school, in babies' earliest days and months.

One widely cited study documents that by age three, children of very poor parents already lag far behind their wealthier counterparts in knowledge and use of vocabulary—elements that predict their subsequent readiness and capacity to read and learn unless these early deficits are addressed.[11] Those early gaps are then compounded by the lack of access to high-quality preK programs. Together, these early disparities in experiences, relationships, and stimulation drive enormous gaps in children's readiness to learn at kindergarten entry. Whether they measure children's math or reading skills, the gaps are larger than a full standard deviation. And while they are smaller in absolute terms, similar gaps are revealed with respect to noncognitive skills like persistence and the ability to communicate with peers and teachers.[12] To comprehend the impact of these gaps on children's odds of school success, the What Works Clearinghouse estimates that in the context of education, a gap of one standard deviation would require at least four, independent, highly effective interventions to close. So it isn't hard to imagine the barriers these early achievement gaps pose for low-income children and their teachers and schools.

As described above, health and mental health problems, and insufficient support to address them, push low-income children further behind, causing them to lose focus in school and miss days from preventable illnesses. At the same time, opportunity gaps exacerbate the impediments to learning. For example, when poor children have limited access to enrichment and learning opportunities in the summer, their learning is impeded during the school year. Mountains of data indicate that summer learning should be an entitlement, not an accident of birth, yet we continue to ignore this need and thereby resign ourselves to continuing "failure" in education. As *Freako-nomics* author Malcolm Gladwell sums it up, "Virtually all of the advantage that wealthy students have over poor students is the result of differences in the way privileged students learn when they are *not* in school . . . America doesn't have a school problem. It has a summer vacation problem."[13]

These multiple and cumulative support and opportunity gaps point clearly to the need to radically rethink our delivery systems for child development and education—when and where it takes place, by whom, and the various partnerships required for that to happen meaningfully and consistently. Indeed, this rethinking and redesigning is what the best ISS communities are engaged in.

BRINGING MASLOW AND MATH CLASS INTO ALIGNMENT

Neither the impact of poverty nor disparities in learning opportunities are unknown. What is newer, however, is the growing recognition that decades of efforts to improve schools without tackling those impacts have fallen far short. Prior insistence by a prominent camp of education reformers that schools must take a no-excuses approach to poverty, and their call to focus narrowly on raising standards and holding schools accountable for doing so, have given way to increasingly widespread acknowledgment that we need to treat poverty for what it is—the largest obstacle for a significant and growing number of students.[14]

We are thus at a pivotal moment in education policy-making. Evidence shows that the prior generation of school reform efforts had only modest impacts in boosting achievement and narrowing gaps, although a few states, Massachusetts and New Jersey in particular, achieved quite a bit.[15] Indeed, one of us (Paul) points to his state's major progress in raising scores on the National Assessment of Educational Progress but its failure, despite those gains, to substantially shrink race- and income-based gaps in those scores and in other metrics of academic proficiency as an urgent reason to rethink how we design school reform efforts.[16]

The Every Student Succeeds Act (ESSA), the most recent iteration of the federal Elementary and Secondary Education Act, delegates much of the authority and responsibility to improve schools back to the state and local levels. This shift reflects popular sentiment, but because many states are divided and have limited capacity, much of that responsibility will fall on local communities. ESSA also encourages states to consider a broader set of metrics of student progress but provides little guidance on how they should do so. And the current US Department of Education under Secretary Elisabeth "Betsy" DeVos is showing little inclination to step into that breach. So what do we do?

Now is the time for communities to step up on behalf of children, a time for a promising "new localism." Two Brookings scholars point to a path forward: "Power is shifting globally. With national governments challenged, cities in the United States and beyond have assumed increased responsibility for addressing many of our biggest policy challenges. Cities are able to act because their power rests not in government alone, but in market and civic strengths that emanate from the concentration of valuable economic, physical and social assets . . . The emerging framework of multi-sectoral governance and networked problem solving is what might be called 'new localism.'"[17]

It is in the spirit of this new localism that, in this book, we present these examples to local officials who, with their communities, have the most direct and immediate stake in the future of our children. A growing number of leaders—political, academic, and educational—are now calling for a community-driven whole-child education system, to complement high-quality school reform. By *whole-child*, these advocates mean systems that work intentionally to nurture the full range of children's developmental domains—academic, social, emotional, behavioral, and physical. These leaders are asking for communities, districts, and individual schools to design policies and practices to realize such a vision. The ISS communities described in this book give a glimpse of what's possible.

We describe a more complex and ambitious set of goals than what most schools have historically sought. For the millions of children whose basic needs are not consistently met, we join the growing chorus calling for a broad, integrated set of student supports that bring together schools, communities, and social programs. Such a comprehensive approach could enhance school-parent-community working relationships, expand student learning opportunities with respect to both time and quality, and ensure attention to urgent social, emotional, and physical health needs that often prevent children from learning.

A good ISS system requires multiple moving parts to operate effectively. It asks schools to reach out to parents and the broader community for engagement and support, something that few schools have a track record of doing, especially in high-poverty neighborhoods. It means not only offering preschool, after-school enrichment, and summer learning, but also expanding the school day and year and making sure that those extra hours, days, and weeks are qualitatively better than what many schools currently provide. An ISS approach asks schools to become curators, but not necessarily providers, of the services and other supports needed to ensure that all children can come to school ready to learn. When it comes to health care, mental health needs, nutrition, safety, housing, and other matters, communities must step up to take responsibility, working with schools as partners to help solve the problems that prevent their students from learning at high levels.

WIDESPREAD GROWTH OF INTEGRATED STUDENT SUPPORTS IN THE UNITED STATES

Embracing these challenges, communities across the country have taken on this complex endeavor and are making comprehensive systems work. These communities recognize that schools cannot possibly do this alone, nor should they. They see that many of our schools are drowning under the burdens of meeting children's in-school and out-of-school needs. Naturally, schools filled with compassionate adults are ready to step up and do this work when no one else does, since our education system implicitly assumes that schools should solve these problems. But schools weren't built to address many of these challenges. They don't have the capacity. Children's well-being is a 24-7 job, 365 days a year, and it must be a family and community responsibility. We now need a new social compact, one in which every member of a community assumes responsibility for building the platform of support and opportunity necessary for children to succeed. This new social compact is what the leaders in our example communities are trying to invent.

In these places, school and city leaders have come together to declare that poverty, rather than being an excuse, is a root cause of problems in both their schools and their communities. They have reached out to government leaders (in housing, public safety, and public health), to other leaders (in business and in faith- and community-based organizations), and to parents to help design systems of supports that meet students' basic needs. These communities have taken inventories of unmet needs, mapped out the available resources to meet these needs, worked to coordinate those resources, and developed new resources to plug holes in existing services. Such efforts are under way in hundreds of communities in every state.

Dozens of district-level initiatives employing comprehensive approaches call their strategy *community schools*, and many of these schools receive technical support from the Coalition for Community Schools in Washington, DC, or the National Center for Community Schools in New York City (or both).[18] More recently, as community schools have gained momentum, both of the national teachers unions and other organizations are also advancing this strategy. In twenty-five states, hundreds of school districts, including many that house community schools, partner with the national nonprofit organization Communities In Schools (CIS) and its state affiliates to deliver a targeted set of health, enrichment, and other services supporting nearly 1.5 million students in 2016.[19]

As of late 2017, more than three hundred communities in forty-two states and the District of Columbia, plus Puerto Rico and the Virgin Islands, were affiliated with the Campaign for Grade-Level Reading and had implemented one or more components of an ISS strategy.[20] Fifty-eight districts and counting across eight states are affiliates of Bright Futures USA, another ISS-aligned initiative that has a strong presence among small- to medium-sized and rural districts.[21] Distressed zones of cities (and a handful of rural areas) designated by the federal government as Promise Neighborhoods are using their federal grants to provide comprehensive education and health support for students and their families.[22] And other community programs are using the term *Promise* in their names to describe philanthropic pledges of free college tuition for students who meet specific criteria. These programs have used this commitment to provide ISS that enables more students to take advantage of those scholarships. The most widely known and most researched of these programs is in Kalamazoo, Michigan (www.kalamazoopromise.com).

More intensive ISS efforts are under way in various cities under the auspices of City Connects (a Boston College–based initiative), Say Yes to Education, Harvard Graduate School of Education's By All Means campaign (operated by the school's Education Redesign Lab), and others. In some of these efforts and others, such as districts that are working with StriveTogether, schools play only one of many leadership roles. Community leaders come together in collective-impact initiatives featuring *children's cabinets* and other broad-based, representative boards that set goals, develop strategies, measure progress, and hold partners accountable for making progress on key indicators of children's well-being.

BACKGROUND ON ISS COMMUNITIES, AND OUR AIMS FOR THIS BOOK

Both of us work in the areas of ISS and whole-child education and are convinced of the importance of scaling them up. One of us, Elaine Weiss, led an education policy campaign, the Broader, Bolder Approach to Education

(BBA), which called attention to the many ways that poverty impedes effective teaching and learning and advanced strategies to alleviate those impacts. As part of that work, she collaborated with communities across the country to write about the community efforts featured in this book. As former Massachusetts secretary of education, the other of us, Paul Reville, was one of the architects of the education reform efforts that helped propel the state to the top of the pack in student achievement. He sees the large, stubborn achievement gaps that persist as evidence of the critical need to think more broadly about improving school systems so that equity goes hand-in-hand with excellence. Paul launched the aforementioned Education Redesign Lab at the Harvard Graduate School of Education to explore this issue. He is also leading the lab's By All Means project, a six-city pilot of mayoral-led ISS efforts, to create and study some new on-the-ground efforts that can ultimately be replicated and scaled up.

Convinced of the importance of ISS and whole-child education in advancing better outcomes in education and learning, BBA spent two years studying and documenting the efforts of communities that have employed ISS for this purpose.[23] Our selection of the twelve communities that form the basis of this book was based on recommendations from colleagues, on stand-out examples from national ISS networks, and on community leaders' self-nominations. To be eligible for study, the community had to provide a range of student supports, advance whole-child school improvement strategies, and engage parents and educators in the effort. Finally, it had to demonstrate not only that these efforts were boosting student achievement, but also that the district was narrowing gaps in social class, racial and ethnic status, and/or other aspects of disadvantage for its students.[24]

These communities have built on conversations spurred by community and school leaders to tackle poverty head-on. They draw on the assets, public and private, of a range of agencies and other service providers to meet every child's basic needs and enable effective teaching and learning. Wrapping basic nutritional, physical health, and mental health supports around disadvantaged students' school experiences, the communities are plugging holes in their early-childhood, after-school, and summer opportunities.

These programs' approaches vary according to each community's unique needs and assets, but all of the communities have designed systems to close gaps in both support and opportunities. And all have seen substantial boosts to student outcomes, school outcomes, and, in some cases, community outcomes because of the ISS work.

This book is organized into three parts. Part 1 provides the rationale for making an ISS system a common feature in communities. It also introduces the communities where this work is bearing fruit in the form of improved student outcomes. Part 2—the bulk of the book—describes the strategies that these and other communities have employed to advance whole-child education through the use of ISS and examines the challenges of doing so. Finally, part 3 explores the history of efforts that now make up the nascent ISS field. We look at where it stands today and what must happen for ISS and whole-child education to become the norm that we believe is needed, given current economic, demographic, and political realities and trends. In addition, we note that if it is to fulfill its true potential, the ISS movement must do more than address issues related to poverty and lack of opportunity. Segregation, structural racism, and related economic exploitation act as potent barriers to future success for far too many of today's students. We envision an ISS movement that breaks down those barriers and makes thriving and success meaningful options for every one of our children.

2

Integrated Student Support Communities

Models of Progress

The twelve communities we studied, and the others described in this book, are by no means the only school districts in the country to apply ISS. Nor was the search for them exhaustive. We did intentionally work to identify a set of communities that are diverse in many respects, but there are many more that are making progress through use of ISS, and still others now starting similar efforts. Indeed, in talking with these districts' leaders and others connected to their efforts, we have come across other people who would be likely to provide additional lessons and guidance. We hope this book will not only inspire more communities to create similar strategies, but surface others that are already doing so. We expect that future research will expand on the work presented here.

This chapter briefly describes each of the case study communities to give readers a basic sense of the work these communities have done and continue to do. It then summarizes commonalities across the dozen communities.

These communities have used a variety of approaches to provide ISS and create whole-child systems of education. And this diversity makes sense; supporting students well requires understanding their unique needs and strengths and those of their families and communities and tailoring a system of services, based on local assets, to meet them. Given the range of demographic, geographic, political, and other factors characterizing these communities, it is no surprise that leaders in each community identified specific challenges that students and their parents faced in engaging with and succeeding in school and that the leaders designed and aligned services that met those challenges.

Successful ISS initiatives provide wraparound services that attend to the early-childhood years along with nutritional support, physical and mental health care, and enriching after-school and summer activities in children's K–12 years. The term *wraparound* is used in multiple ways, including, sometimes, as a synonym for ISS. In this book, we use it mainly to describe services and supports that compensate for a lack of basics in children's lives—such as healthy food, health care, and mental health support. By wrapping supports around children, we ensure that the children do not slip through the cracks because of the failure of one or more of the settings in which they are served to attend to these needs. In the early-childhood context, wraparound services could refer to such supports as mental and emotional health care as well as services that target the whole family, such as parenting education and child development information. These communities also work to enhance students' experiences in the classroom and to develop systems that advance not just their academic, but also their social, emotional, academic, and behavioral development. Effective school improvement efforts involve parents and other community members from the start, meeting students' and families' express needs by using those families' and communities' talents and assets to address the challenges that students face within and outside schools. Importantly, these efforts do more than just try to reform existing systems of education. They are family- and community-designed, enhanced systems of child development, support, and enrichment that go far beyond the school.[1]

While we could categorize the communities in many ways—by size, region, political ideology, and so forth—in this book, we define them by type of ISS strategy employed. We thus describe how communities used various ISS approaches: community schools, Promise Neighborhoods, Bright Futures USA, and Promise scholarships. An additional two communities, by far the largest of those studied, are using multiple types of ISS approaches, but they still have a way to go to support all their students.

COMMUNITY SCHOOLS

Two of the oldest and most well-established initiatives studied, Children's Aid (formerly Children's Aid Society) community schools and City Connects, are in two of the country's largest urban districts, New York City and Boston. These initiatives serve heavily low-income populations and student bodies that are racially, ethnically, and linguistically very diverse. Both Children's Aid and City Connects are members of the Coalition for Community Schools, and both view the need for ISS through that lens, though City Connects operates under its own unique model. A third, much smaller city, Vancouver, Washington, is the only district in the country to have created full-service community schools that serve every student.

The Coalition for Community Schools describes the community-school approach as "both a place and a set of partnerships between the school and other community resources. Its integrated focus on academics, health and social services, youth and community development and community engagement leads to improved student learning, stronger families and healthier communities."[2] Community schools focus heavily on wraparound physical and mental health and nutrition supports for students, often through the use of school-based health clinics. In districts that employ this strategy, district-level leaders and coordinators in each school also partner with numerous local agencies and nonprofits to offer enriching after-school and summer options, and all prioritize parent/family engagement.

Across its twenty-two community schools in four of the city's five boroughs, Children's Aid offers comprehensive support for some of the city's most struggling schools, many of them in immigrant communities. The flagship Salome Urena de Henriquez School campus, for example, serves students in Washington Heights, the heavily Dominican "upper" Upper West Side neighborhood that is the basis for Lin-Manuel Miranda's first Tony Award–winning Broadway musical, *In the Heights*. For over a decade, the school has taken advantage of the fact that many parents walk their children to school in the morning. It has aimed to bring those parents into the building, starting with a parents' room where they can drink coffee and often take classes on relevant subjects. That room is across the hallway from the school's health clinic, which houses, among things, the country's only in-school orthodontic clinic. There, students who would otherwise never have access to braces can get them free or at reduced cost through a monthly payment plan.

For more than twenty years, Children's Aid's partnerships with state and city agencies and with a wide range of nonprofit service providers have gradually enhanced the support it gives students who have no other way to receive these services. When he was first campaigning for mayor, Bill de Blasio ran on a platform dedicated to leveling an increasingly inequitable playing field in the city. He drew on the successes of the Children's Aid efforts to promote a key component of that platform: converting many of New York's most troubled schools into community schools. Four years later, his goal of creating one hundred new community schools has been surpassed: today, there are over two hundred such schools in the city, and Children's Aid has offered key guidance on implementation and other issues, as well as taking the lead in a few of those new schools.

On the other coast, Vancouver, Washington is just across the Columbia River from Portland, Oregon. The medium-sized school district (Vancouver Public Schools) serves twenty-four thousand students, with a growing share of them from low-income, racial and ethnic minority, and immigrant families. In response to resulting challenges, school and community leaders formulated a plan to convert all thirty-five schools in the district to Family-Community Resource Centers (FCRCs), the district's term for full-service community schools. As of 2017–2018, that goal has been realized through a combination of eighteen in-school FCRCs and two mobile FCRCs. Each of the mobile centers serves multiple lower-poverty schools through regular weekly visits.

Vancouver has capitalized on its success in building strong community partnerships and delivering districtwide support to focus on nurturing students' social and emotional skills. Understanding that the foundations for both these and more traditional academic skills are laid in children's earliest years, the district has invested in several early-childhood development and education programs and integrated them with its elementary schools. For example, in Fruit Valley Elementary School, the cite of the first FCRC, Head Start and preK programs also serve young children from the most disadvantaged families, in addition to the school's K–5 classrooms. By working closely with kindergarten teachers and discussing strategies to build on children's early gains, these programs ensure a seamless tradition into kindergarten and sustained academic progress. Vancouver Public Schools has also pioneered efforts to ensure that more students are prepared to succeed after high school, whether they go to college or start a first job, and that students will become engaged and contributing citizens in their community and country.

Though it is a member of the coalition, City Connects in Boston operates wholly independently and does not consider its schools actual community schools. Through a model developed by the Boston College Lynch School of Education's Center for Optimized Student Support, City Connects uses *whole-class review* in its approach to ISS.[3] This review of every individual student's strengths and needs distinguishes City Connects in two key respects. First, it intentionally shies away from the deficit model that initiatives responding to poverty often inevitably adopt—a focus on unmet needs. City Connects emphasizes instead the assets that every child brings to the table and works to strengthen them. It reviews these assets as well as the child's specific needs to customize a set of enrichments, resources, and other supports that are unique to each child and that draw on the rich variety of resources available. For example, in Boston, the resources include museum-associated arts classes and dance instruction and world-class health care.

Whole-class review also enables City Connects to place students within tiers of strength and need. A given student, for example, might fall into a high-needs and high-strengths tier and thus be supported through a combination of one-on-one counseling for the child's emotional needs and an advanced dance class to boost the student's talents in that area. And through sophisticated data collection (see chapter 3), school-site coordinators can track the supports delivered to each child, assess how well they are meeting target needs, and adjust them as necessary while bringing on board new partners and resources when they are useful.

These comprehensive approaches to education are paying off in big ways. In addition to having children who are more likely to attend school regularly and score higher on standardized tests, parents from Children's Aid community schools are substantially more engaged in the schools. Vancouver has seen impressive increases in the share of students who are taking and succeeding in advanced high school courses, with the biggest increases among low-income students and students of color. Since 2010, there has been a 167 percent increase in enrollment in Advanced Placement (AP) and International Baccalaureate courses among Vancouver students living in poverty. Similarly, Boston City Connects high school students are substantially less likely than their comparable peers to be chronically absent, and they are disproportionately enrolled in one of the city's three prestigious high schools that have competitive admissions processes.

PROMISE NEIGHBORHOODS

Three of the other study communities implement ISS through a Promise Neighborhoods framework. The approach is modeled after the Harlem Children's Zone, which marries education, health, and other supports through a third-party coordinating agency. This place-based strategy was a priority of the Obama administration and Secretary of Education Arne Duncan.[4] Two communities—a string of counties across the Appalachian region of eastern Kentucky and a distressed area of North Minneapolis—received federal Promise Neighborhoods grants. The third community, in East Durham, North Carolina, applied for a grant but did not obtain one. This group now operates entirely on private funding.

In the Appalachian region surrounding Berea, Kentucky, the vast majority of students are white, but there are also multiple Native American communities, and the Native culture influences how Partners for Education (PfE) has leveraged its Promise Neighborhoods grants. PfE, a department within Berea College, has grown over the past fifty years from managing the college's Upward Bound program to working with communities to provide a range of social, economic, and other supports across the region. Arts—especially the rich tradition of Appalachian art—plays a major role in PfE-supported schools. As detailed later in the book, the schools are exposed to the arts at various levels through enriching programs like artists in residence, arts nights featuring student masterpieces, and Homesong, an annual musical theatrical production that brings together neighbors of all ages to reframe a regional narrative that has tended to emphasize stark poverty while neglecting the rich cultural heritage children are now learning.

To improve education in one of the most isolated regions of the country, PfE has also developed innovative ISS approaches that are uniquely suited to rural communities. Faced with a lack of space in the few existing early-childhood centers and families too far away to send their small children by bus, it solicited grant money to retrofit two school buses into roving Readiness Buses that visit children and parents weekly at their homes to provide early education and parent support. And PfE takes excellent advantage of technology. For example, high school students can explore beating human hearts in real time and a school nurse can work with a remote doctor to transmit information and diagnose students' illnesses so they don't have to miss school. These pioneering initiatives help explain why PfE was the first rural recipient of a federal Promise Neighborhoods grant and has since received two more grants so that it can expand to more counties.

In 2009, community leaders exploring data from Duke University's Children's Health Initiative found that East Durham's children suffered disproportionately from exposure to violence, poor health care, and lack of access to early education. A coalition of neighborhood residents thus initiated a series of kitchen-table meetings that spurred a visit to the Harlem Children's Zone and, the following year, a commitment to create a similar cradle-to-career system of supports for East Durham children and their families.

Nine years later, the East Durham Children's Initiative (EDCI), incorporated as a nonprofit corporation, is a robust, far-reaching effort that integrates parent input and other key community data to guide implementation and expansion. In response to the residents' lack of access to exercise and other healthy activities in this high-poverty, distressed community, EDCI has established free Zumba classes; collected bicycles to distribute, for free, to neighborhood children; and brought in a farmers market. And while the state provides extensive access to high-quality early-childhood education, Spanish-speaking parents were having trouble finding options that worked for them. So in 2016, EDCI collaborated with the Latino Educational Achievement Partnership to launch LEAP Academy, which now serves 30 three- and four-year-old students and their parents in the area. The academy also reflects the area's changing demographics; though still heavily African American, East Durham is now home to a growing number of immigrant families from Central America.

Like EDCI, the Northside Achievement Zone (NAZ) operates in a racially and economically isolated part of a city, in this case, North Minneapolis. Serving a population that is almost entirely African American and that earned an average of just $18,000 per household in 2012, NAZ is grounded in the belief that getting more area children to graduate from high school and succeed in college starts with engaging and empowering their parents. When a family joins the program, it is thus connected to a family achievement coach, often a neighborhood resident, who works with the family one-on-one to explore its unique needs and set specific academic and economic goals. These family achievement plans are the basis for students' progress in school and the family's progress with respect to employment and housing.

The initiative's cradle-to-career approach also includes targeted classes for NAZ parents, who, soon after their children are born, learn about child development and strategies to prepare their children for school and to support them once they are there. This strategy is complemented by scholarships, funded over the past few years by a federal Race to the Top Early Learning Challenge Fund grant, that enable zone children to attend high-quality early-childhood education centers, as certified by the state's quality and rating and improvement system. As NAZ continues to evolve, CEO Sondra Samuels believes that laying these strong foundations and empowering parents will continue to improve children's academic success, ultimately ensuring that many more students will enroll in and succeed in college.

Young children in these eastern Kentucky, East Durham, and North Minneapolis communities are much better prepared for school than their peers outside these communities. In 2013–2014, for example, half of NAZ "scholars" were fully ready for kindergarten, compared with just one-third of their peers, and since 2015, around 95 percent of LEAP Academy children have been assessed as kindergarten ready. And those gains are sustained. Although the students are much poorer than their counterparts across the state, students in Clay, Jackson, Knox, and Owsley Counties served by PfE have made bigger gains than students have on state language arts and math tests. Between 2012 and 2016, the share of those students who were deemed "proficient" increased from just over one-fourth to 40 percent in math and from around one-third to roughly half in English language arts. Parents in all three communities—PfE, EDCI, and NAZ— also became much more engaged, with their new sense of empowerment reflected in their participation in committees, task forces, and even running for school boards.

BRIGHT FUTURES USA

C. J. Huff recounts that when the school board hired him in 2009 to lead the Joplin School District in Missouri, he contrasted the board's mandate to raise graduation rates with his assessment of the burdens that increasing poverty was placing on educators and principals. The Joplin School District serves a regional hub of a quarter million people in the southwest corner of the state across a mix of semi-urban, suburban, and rural areas. He also perceived a sharp disconnect between schools and the community. Absent a frank conversation about poverty's impacts and a strong effort to engage the community to mitigate them, he knew he could not satisfy the board. So he created a team to survey key community members about their expectations of the schools, to talk face-to-face with parents, and to explore the connections between schools and the city's workforce and businesses. The resulting three-part strategy eventually became the foundation for Bright Futures USA, a nonprofit that Huff founded. Bright Futures aims to provide ISS through a triage system to meet each student's basic needs; to gradually build community engagement in, and ownership of, schools; and to embed service learning in every classroom. The framework for Bright Futures in Joplin and in the dozens of affiliates created since is individualistic: it aims to leverage "every community member's time, talent, and treasure."[5]

This goal makes sense, given the demographics of most of these affiliate communities. One of them, Pea Ridge, Arkansas, serves just around two thousand students, virtually all of them white, in a mostly rural region of "Walmart Country." Many students' parents work in and commute to the corporation's headquarters in Bentonville. Like many other Bright Futures affiliate districts, both Joplin and Pea Ridge are situated in what Huff, who retired in 2015, describes as "the buckle of the Bible Belt." In these districts, residents tend to see addressing poverty as an individual, not societal, responsibility.

The category 5 tornado that ripped through Joplin in 2011, killing 161 people (including 7 students) and wreaking nearly $3 million in damage, also strengthened Bright Futures and illustrated the program's power. With the luxury of substantial money to rebuild several schools that had been destroyed, Huff made some key investments. First, the district built a combined K–8 elementary and middle school that incorporated design elements recommended by teachers. There are pull-out rooms between classrooms with glass walls for students who need some extra attention. An outdoor classroom that can be used most of the year sits in the middle of a cluster of classes. Smaller touches like fidget chairs in all classrooms help students who struggle to focus do so without the need for disciplinary action. Knowing, too, that like the low-income children in most districts, Joplin's low-income students had been enrolled in the oldest and most dilapidated school, Huff redrew boundary lines to put them in the state-of-the-art building. He also invested in a new high school with five college- and career-readiness wings, including a voc-tech wing and an arts-and-theater wing that houses the city's main venue for live productions.

Another issue that Bright Futures districts address is child nutrition. Many ISS communities fill backpacks with nutritious snacks and shelf-stable meals to keep children fed over weekends and to ensure that they can focus when they return on Monday morning. Others provide snacks and even dinner in after-school homework clubs. In Bright Futures districts like Joplin and Pea Ridge, one of the first things new affiliates establish is food and school-supply pantries. Stocked with donations from local supermarkets and other stores, these resources are available to teachers and counselors who recognize a need. A whole-child approach also includes one-on-one relationships with caring adults. Strategies can be as simple as the car and bus buddies who greet children in Pea Ridge as they arrive at school, or approaches can be more intensive, like volunteer lunch buddies who meet weekly to eat lunch with Joplin students, talk about school, and offer help with homework.

In Frederick County, Virginia, where superintendent Dave Sovine began to team up with Bright Futures in 2015, one of the highest priorities he and his teachers cite is unmet mental health needs among the district's students: "Five or ten years ago, we saw this level of trauma among our middle-school students. Now we see second graders and even kindergartners coming to school unable to focus and acting out in the classroom."[6] Pea Ridge's partnerships with three regional mental health providers give students access to services such as emotional support, crisis intervention, and even in-patient care.

This attention to students' emotional and health needs has delivered concrete benefits. Pea Ridge students who could not otherwise have participated in extracurricular sports have been able to do so, thanks to a local doctor who provides the required health exams. Teachers in Joplin report improved morale as their students' mental health and behavioral needs are addressed by school and other partners, and recognition that the needs they had been shouldering alone are now a community-wide responsibility. Over the first four years of Bright Futures implementation in Joplin, the average ACT score among students who qualify for free and reduced-price lunches rose from 17.74 to 20.19; low-income students went from lower scores on a critical test of college readiness to scores above the national average. This improvement occurred over a period in which the share of students taking the test increased by nearly 250 percent.

PROMISE SCHOLARSHIP COMMUNITIES

Across a growing network of other communities, ISS has emerged as a strategy to bolster the value of commitments by philanthropists or public institutions, or both, to pay for the costs of college for students who graduate from their high schools and are accepted into college. So-called Promise initiatives have brought into stark relief the reality that many of the students who would benefit from these generous offers are unlikely to do so.[7] While such initiatives remove a major financial barrier to postsecondary education, students may still lack the academic and other skills needed to succeed in college. Two very different communities—the Tangelo Park neighborhood in Orlando, Florida, and the city of Kalamazoo, Michigan—showcase the power of ISS approaches to complement and greatly boost Promise scholarship programs and make college enrollment and attainment a viable reality.

The African American residents of Tangelo Park had already organized to take back their neighborhood from the drug dealers who threatened to overrun it when hotelier Harris Rosen identified this community as the recipient of his intended Promise commitment in 1994. Indeed, the community's capacity for self-improvement was part of what made Rosen believe his donation could make a real difference. Unlike many other philanthropists, however, from the start Rosen took the community's lead in deciding how and where to invest, rather than bringing his own list to bear on these decisions.

That approach influenced his support for neighborhood women who were running childcare centers from their homes. Recognizing that strengthening this community asset would both improve young children's school readiness and further boost neighbor-to-neighbor bonds, he worked with the providers to improve their skills and help them gain accreditation, while also supporting social workers, nurses, and specialists to enrich the curriculum and children's daily experiences. Today, children continue to get support as they progress through school. Support includes church-based homework help programs, after-school enrichment at the local YMCA, and school counseling geared to help students prepare for success after high school, including guidance on course and major selection and interventions for students who struggle after they get to college.

While suffering from many of the same maladies that its peer cities face across the Rust Belt, Kalamazoo, which sits halfway between Chicago and Detroit, also has long benefited from a local institution—the Upjohn Company (which merged into the Pharmacia & Upjohn Company in 1995)—and associated wealthy residents with a personal stake in the community's well-being. In 2005, several such local benefactors came together anonymously to announce the establishment of a scholarship fund that would ensure that all Kalamazoo Public Schools graduates who are accepted to any of the state's public colleges or universities would receive full payment of their tuition.

Pam Kingery, who has been leading Kalamazoo's Communities In Schools (CIS) affiliate since before the inception of the Promise, describes the announcement of the scholarships as a galvanizing moment for not only the schools, but also the community overall. Business leaders who had kept their involvement at arm's length began to embrace their potential to support students and teachers. Agencies such as the public library and the city's symphony stepped forward to offer enrichment opportunities that would enable more students to take advantage of the scholarships, and churches organized to provide homework help and test preparation sessions. And as described later, a prominent local economist who had long sought to boost local families' access to preschool found a new opening to advance that objective that has proven fruitful. Although there is still a long way to go to provide system-wide student support, the Promise has also spurred changes within schools—changes that substantially boost disadvantaged students' odds of being able to take advantage of the Promise.

Both the Tangelo Park Project and Kalamazoo Promise show progress toward the goal of having all students graduate and succeed after high school. A rigorous study of the Kalamazoo Promise finds that students are 14 percent more likely to enroll in college within six months of graduating from high school, and 34 percent more likely to enroll in a four-year college than they would have been, absent the Promise. Such improvement is particularly critical for the city's low-income students and students of color.[8] An analysis of college success rates in Tangelo Park estimates that, according to its demographics, the community would have been expected to produce 50 college graduates between 1994 and 2014. Instead, it produced 196 total degrees, including 118 bachelor's degrees and three doctorates.

EMERGENT MULTILAYER INITIATIVES

The last two of the twelve communities studied by BBA are somewhat different from the others. They are the largest—one serving a midsize Southwestern city and the second the largest county and school district of a mid-Atlantic state—and the most complicated. Both communities have evolved over several decades to provide a growing share of their students with ISS and whole-child education through multilayered efforts. Like all these communities, Austin, Texas, and Montgomery County, Maryland, are works in progress, but supports and enrichment are less consistent in these two than in the others, and ISS initiatives are still ramping up.

Montgomery County, the nation's seventeenth-largest school district, spans rural, suburban, and semi-urban areas. It educates students who come from 157 countries and who speak 150 languages in its 204 schools. Its family engagement and support mechanism, Linkages to Learning, is also a community-school strategy. However, Montgomery County Public Schools is distinguished from the other case study communities by its use of several other initiatives that, together, work to deliver ISS. For example, with eligibility rates for subsidized school meals ranging from the low single digits in wealthy areas of the district to nearly 100 percent in the poorest, in 1999 the district began to provide breakfast to every student in higher-poverty schools, expanding to seventy-nine schools by 2015. For the same reason, the district has placed school-based health clinics in its highest-poverty schools.

District investments in school-based Head Start, other preschool programs, new higher academic standards, and a series of curriculum enhancements complement long-standing county housing policies that encourage racial and economic integration and ensure that many students attend diverse schools. More recently, Joshua Starr, superintendent from 2011 to 2015, led the development of a new curriculum and a series of other systemic changes to district policy and practice that advance social and emotional learning. Nurturing students' social and emotional skills—resilience, self-management, and relationship-building abilities—is core to a whole-child education.

In Austin, similar investments in embedding social and emotional learning, along with a growing community-school movement, have their roots in parents' organizing efforts in the 1990s. Austin Interfaith's hard work to empower parents and teach them to become involved, vocal advocates began with their success in securing district funding for needed healthcare support and has continued to pay off. Schools with many immigrant parents who do not speak English at home benefit from those parents' involvement in pushing for high-quality teacher preparation programs and supporting the teachers' authority to design innovative curricula. These efforts help put their children on a more even playing field with their higher-income, nonimmigrant counterparts.

As is true of the other ISS communities featured here, Austin has also recognized the importance of giving disadvantaged children a better early start. Like Michigan, the state of Texas funds preK for all low-income children, but unlike Michigan, its program is of low quality. The Austin Unified School District thus supplements state funds to expand to a full day and to provide an enriching, hands-on curriculum. The local investment also enables Austin to serve three-year-olds, along with the four-year-olds supported by the state program.

A DIVERSE MOVEMENT WITH A COMMON GOAL

As these brief descriptions make clear, communities that are using ISS to advance whole-child education improvement efforts are doing so in a broad range of ways and are themselves diverse with respect to demographics, political leanings, and other characteristics. At the same time, they are all grounded in a common understanding of the challenges facing their most disadvantaged students and of the supports needed to close the opportunity and enrichment gaps that drive achievement gaps.

The impacts of poverty are felt everywhere—in big cities, where the challenges have long been well known; in isolated rural areas, where the impacts are sometimes less visible; and in suburban areas and smaller cities, where poverty may raise new issues for previously more affluent and homogenous communities. Conversations about poverty are initiated differently from one place to another, but when school and community leaders have the will to make them happen, those discussions lead to the conclusion that if an area's children are to succeed, the entire community must unite behind them. The communities we've described show that ISS is feasible in diverse contexts. And as the outcomes illustrate, all these communities are finding that meeting students' needs helps students learn better, helps teachers do their jobs more effectively and with more satisfaction, and helps schools run well. The benefits even spill over to the community at large.

These communities take a broad view of ISS to advance whole-child education. While we embrace the definitions of ISS used by groups like CIS and the researchers at Child Trends (a nonprofit organization conducting child development research), we expand that definition in our book. We want to address the enrichment gap that we believe is parallel to and closely intertwined with support gaps that ISS is designed to close. For this reason, we emphasize that these communities have adopted ISS in service of a whole-child approach to child development and education, and we urge readers to consider this aspect of community and school system improvement a central one, and not an extra or add-on.

The following chapters describe in detail some of the most interesting and promising ISS strategies that communities have embraced. We hope that the strategies will inspire you to get involved in local efforts in your own area, to encourage your community leaders and school district to explore new approaches to educating the whole child, and, where relevant, to scale up existing strategies for a regional and even state-level impact. Ultimately, we will need to substantially step up advocacy, policy, and funding efforts if ISS is to grow to the scope and scale that we know our country needs to achieve equity and excellence in the twenty-first century.

PART II

Integrated Student Support Strategies

3

Personalizing Support to Meet Every Child's Needs

Communities adopt ISS strategies in response to a range of unmet needs associated with growing up in poverty. These include a lack of adequate nutrition (students may come to school not having had breakfast—a common impediment to students' focus and effective instruction); acute physical and mental health problems; eviction and potential temporary homelessness; onetime needs for specific articles of clothing; and many others. To remove such impediments to student learning, education leaders are seeking to build systems that quickly and efficiently meet these needs while minimizing embarrassment or stigma for students.

No single system can serve as a template for how to mitigate these problems, because the needs and resources of students, families, and communities vary so widely. To help other communities understand the variety of options available for ISS, we describe how four very different communities have developed such systems both for the short term and for the longer term. Solutions vary widely. From the development of a Facebook page to inform Bright Futures community residents and businesses about unmet student and family needs to providing checkbooks (now credit cards) for principals in Vancouver, ISS districts are arming their leaders with tools to personalize the supports. In North Minneapolis, the Promise Neighborhoods' cradle-to-career approach drives even more intensive support: coaches help families create unique plans and goals, and specialists connect the families with resources to meet those goals. The most comprehensive of these personalized support systems is City Connects' whole-class review, which uses rigorous data collection to address both academic and nonacademic needs. A 2016 cost-benefit analysis has found that City Connects is a uniquely powerful education improvement strategy because of its ability to tailor an individualized set of services to each student, with whole-class review at the core of the program.[1]

Finally, this chapter describes how comprehensive data systems in several communities assess a broad range of measures of student progress and of child, school, and community well-being. These data systems, another powerful means of individualizing support and personalizing learning, enable schools, social workers, and other service providers to better target the right resources to the right child at the right time.

USING SOCIAL MEDIA TO MEET INDIVIDUAL NEEDS

When a community decides to join Bright Futures USA as an affiliate, the community must first determine how the "time, talent, and treasure" of its residents, businesses, and faith institutions can advance the goal of meeting every student's basic needs within twenty-four hours. Bright Futures leaders then work with district or community leaders to begin to establish food, clothing, and school-supply pantries that school social workers and counselors can utilize to meet teacher-identified student needs, like weekend food backpacks, notebooks, and shoes. They also initiate *angel funds,* to which donors from the community contribute to fill holes when those pantries cannot meet a specific need. These funds are also available to build capacity for meeting longer-term student needs.[2]

District leaders, however, regularly encounter needs that cannot be well addressed by either matching processes or angel funds. For example, in building up Joplin's Bright Futures program, then superintendent and Bright Futures founder C. J. Huff was periodically faced with requests for items not stocked in a pantry and too expensive for a student or parent to purchase.

One of Joplin's high school seniors had no parents to support him and needed a pair of size 13 steel-toed boots to take advantage of a welding program at the Franklin Technical Center. The boots were required for the program and would cost well over $100, far out of reach for the student. Given the lack of human service agencies with the resources to fulfill that request, this unique need was posted on the Bright Futures Joplin Facebook page, on the off chance that a member of the community could help. Within fifteen minutes, a woman responded to the request. She recalled that her husband, who also happened to have feet this size, had bought such a pair of boots the year before, but she was pretty sure he had never used them. Sure enough, she found them in her garage and was delighted to see them put to good use. As a result, the student who dreamed of being a welder was able to report to his first day of class with the required equipment.[3] Other similar requests often involve clothing for job interviews. One young woman, a recent graduate, needed a suit and dress shoes. She received two of each. One resident had found a suit and dress in her own closet, and a second person took the opportunity to visit a department store and make the purchase her annual contribution to Bright Futures. So the young woman not only looked great and nailed her interview, but also wore a second, new suit the first day on the job.

This approach to meeting students' unusual needs was so successful that it ended up being the trigger that transformed Bright Futures from a single-shot strategy in one district to a growing regional and now national ISS movement. In the fall of 2010, Huff received an inquiry from fellow superintendent Phil Cook in neighboring Carl Junction, Missouri. Cook said that his residents were following the Bright Futures Joplin Facebook page and even contributing through it. He had begun receiving phone calls from patrons in his district asking why the Carl Junction schools were not doing what Joplin was doing. That conversation evolved into the creation of the first Bright Futures affiliate in 2010 and four more in the southwest Missouri region over the next six months.

Meeting specific student needs through Facebook has since become a core strategy for affiliates as they come on board. The local Bright Futures program run by the Beaufort County, North Carolina, chamber of commerce enjoys widespread community participation through its Facebook page. As soon as a need is posted on Facebook in the morning, someone has often met the need that same morning.[4] Facebook is also a way for districts to thank their Bright Futures partners, like the local chiropractic office that took a class of Beaufort County students bowling. And while many posts request small items that are just difficult to come by, others can help entire families, like this post in Beaufort County:

> There is a need for a young boy who is living in a family situation where the family has no furniture. The child does not have any furniture in his room—no bed, dresser, anything. There is also no other furniture in the home—the only furniture in the home is one dining room table. The immediate need is a bed frame and mattress and box springs and dresser for the child. A rug would be nice as the floors are plywood floors and are drafty. Other needs would be a couch and other furniture for the home.

Whether it is through Facebook or other social media with broad reach, strategies that inform community members of children's and schools' needs and that encourage people to come together can have a powerful impact on the personalization of ISS.

EMPOWERING PRINCIPALS TO ADDRESS IMMEDIATE NEEDS

Vancouver Public Schools makes ISS accessible to all its students and families through in-house and mobile Family-Community Resource Centers (FCRCs). Dozens of public and private community partners boost the schools' capacities to meet student needs, while several local foundations provide stable funding to support these efforts.

Even so, principals periodically encounter unmet student and family needs. Many of these are addressed in an unusual fashion, thanks to the Foundation for Vancouver Public Schools. The foundation, which was established in 1988 by then superintendent Jim Parsley to meet student needs he saw emerging, had roughly $4.2 million in assets as of its thirtieth anniversary in 2018.[5] Among the ways it supports the district's schools, the foundation supplies every principal with a specially targeted credit card (formerly a checkbook). Since 1998, Vancouver principals have been authorized to make purchases to cover a range of immediate needs that are unique to students and that, like those that Huff posts to Bright Futures Joplin's Facebook page, could not be easily met by the system of supports already in place. Principals have made purchases for various needs, including food; clothing; shoes; personal care items; grocery cards; school supplies; bus passes; health needs like eyeglasses, medications, and dental care; and emergency rental and utility assistance when other resources are unavailable.

Teachers and principals report that the ability to quickly break down barriers to student learning is critical to keeping student learning on track. Moreover, when such student needs can be met through donated funds, teachers and other school staff are spared using their personal money, a problematic reality that is increasingly common in other districts across the country.

Like a Facebook page, the Vancouver strategy requires, first, that a system of supports be in place and, second, that teachers, counselors, and principals know both what the system can provide and where the remaining gaps are. Principals must be sufficiently connected and aware of the needs of their students to act quickly when a student shows up in flip-flops in February or when a student is facing the need to feed two younger siblings for the last two weeks of the month after food stamps have run out (and the principal needs to know that there are no parents at home). District leadership needs enough trust to give principals the autonomy to decide when and how to use foundation money, including large chunks, like a family's monthly rent payment. Such a system also requires transparent accounting and accountability. Perhaps most critical, unlike Facebook, the Vancouver strategy requires a community philanthropic foundation that has amassed and can sustain sufficient assets to provide this level of resources consistently, year after year.[6]

Despite these challenging prerequisites, the Vancouver system admirably tailors its supports to the unique needs of students and families and ensures that those needs are met quickly and respectfully. Because of its success, the system merits exploration by other districts seeking to individualize supports so that all students come to school ready and able to learn.

PROVIDING ONE-ON-ONE SUPPORT WITH COACHES AND SPECIALISTS

The Northside Achievement Zone (NAZ) sees strengthening and empowering families who live in segregated and economically isolated North Minneapolis as central to its goal of getting more of the neighborhood's students to graduate from high school and complete college.[7] But residents in the thirteen-by-eighteen-block zone, where families often live near or below the poverty line, face multiple barriers to stability, let alone to thriving. And while many of those barriers are common across the neighborhood, each family's circumstances are also unique. So NAZ recruits community members, who understand those challenges firsthand, to work with each zone family to set goals, monitor progress, and provide connections to resources to help the family achieve progress.

Nearly thirty *family achievement coaches* work in the neighborhood. Typically, families are each assigned a single coach with whom they will work during their involvement with NAZ. (Each coach serves about thirty families, and each NAZ anchor school houses three or four coaches.) When families join NAZ, they are set up to work toward completing a family achievement plan with goals in key areas—financial, academic, and health. There were just under a thousand NAZ families as of June 2018, and a large majority had fully developed their family achievement plans.[8] Trained to provide guidance to advance families' personal, academic, and economic goals, the coaches meet regularly with families to help set and track progress, share information about parenting and child development, and recommend connections to the zone's services and partner organizations. The coaches also monitor the children's social and emotional competence, identifying delays and other problems and promptly connecting children to any needed supports. A second group of NAZ employees, *family support specialists,* have graduate degrees in social work or human services. These specialists work with families in the areas of housing, career, or finance. In particular, they provide targeted assistance to support progress toward goals.

One major strength of the NAZ approach is the level of personalized support that coaches can give to families. Another key strength, of course, is the NAZ staff's deep understanding of the community. In 2015, around 83 percent of coaches lived or had lived within the zone, 90 percent identified as Northsiders, and 30 percent came from families that participated in NAZ.[9] Because of this deep background, the coaches approach their work with a unique perspective on the challenges facing neighborhood families. Consequently, they can engage families with familiar language and without any of the stigma associated with advice from outside "experts."[10]

Finally, and perhaps most importantly, coaches and specialists reinforce the theme emphasized by the strongest whole-child ISS initiatives. They identify and utilize the myriad assets that exist but that are often overlooked in high-poverty communities, especially low-income communities of color.

INDIVIDUALIZING SUPPORT WITH WHOLE-CLASS REVIEW

At the start of the school year, the school coordinators for City Connects schools in Boston meet with every teacher to explore the academic and personal history of each of the teacher's students. During that hour-plus meeting, the teacher and coordinator work together to identify each student's unique strengths and talents, as well as his or her needs—academic, social-emotional, physical, and family-related. This review forms the basis for an individualized plan of enrichment and support that is tracked and continually updated throughout the year. The plan also provides teachers, parents, principals, and schools with a broad range of data on how a child's needs are being met and the ongoing impact of those services on the student's learning.

This system was developed by City Connects in response to concerns that existing school support systems were inadequate and poorly matched to school and student needs in several respects. Mary Walsh, City Connects executive director, explains: "The typical approach to student support in most schools: 1) is fragmented and idiosyncratic, serving a small number of high-need students; 2) does not address the full range of needs, focusing mainly on risk; 3) does not collect data on the effectiveness of the supports offered students; and 4) in practice, does not operate as a core function of the school, and as a result, seeks minimal teacher engagement."[11] The City Connects model, which uses six characteristics of optimized student support to address these flaws, is customized to each student's unique needs and strengths and comprehensively considers developmental domains and family characteristics.[12]

Whole-class review has several key steps (figure 3.1). The first step, identifying a student's strengths and needs across four domains (academic, social-emotional, physical, and family-related), is followed by the identification of relevant services and enrichment supports, both in school and in the community. Students (and their families, as appropriate) are then connected to those service providers. Site coordinators play key roles in documenting and tracking the delivery of services and following up with providers and students to make sure that the fit is a good one. (If not, adjustments are made.)

During whole-class review, teachers and school-site coordinators group students into three tiers that reflect the children's mix of strengths and risk factors. Tier 1 indicates "strengths and minimal risk"; tier 2 is for students with "strengths and mild to moderate risk" (with subgroups 2a for mild and 2b for moderate risk); and tier 3 indicates "strengths and severe risk." While more than one in ten students are placed in tier 3 each year, comprehensive support and enrichment drives strong progress, so that nearly half of those tier 3 students move into a lower tier during the school year.

Regardless of tier, a student's tailored set of supports might include some combination of prevention and enrichment, early intervention, and

FIGURE 3.1

City Connects whole-class review system

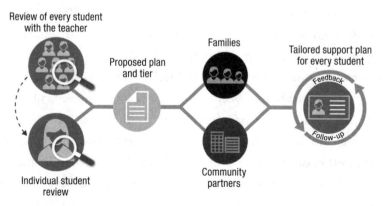

Source: City Connects, "Our Approach," City Connects, Boston College, 2015, www.bc.edu /bc-web/schools/lsoe/sites/cityconnects/our-approach.html. Used with permission.

intensive services. In accordance with the tier system, services are along a spectrum that begins with category I, prevention and enrichment services. These include arts and academic enrichment, traditional extracurricular activities like organized sports, a health and wellness curriculum, and a violence prevention intervention. Even for students who are deemed to be at very high risk, the City Connects initiative emphasizes their strengths and the importance of designing personalized systems to bolster those strengths. City Connects school-site coordinator Jaymie Silverman praises the whole-child aspect of whole-class review and its focus on the many assets that low-income students bring to class, rather than only their needs: "To have the opportunity to sit down and talk about every single student is unique. It also forces us to highlight the strengths of every student. And oftentimes it's just easy, especially with some of our most challenging students, to get bogged down in the things that aren't working well and the challenges that teachers encounter on a daily basis."[13]

This focus on strengths as well as needs means that in addition to tracking the system's progress in meeting student needs, data collection helps the schools assess the students' progress in their areas of strength. (Acknowledging the students' progress boosts their confidence in their own abilities). One powerful example is John Winthrop Elementary School in Boston's Dorchester neighborhood, where more than 80 percent of the 330 students come from low-income families and at least two-thirds live in high-poverty, high-crime neighborhoods. In 2013, the state of Massachusetts declared Winthrop a struggling, level 4 school, basing the designation on "an analysis of four-year trends in absolute achievement, student growth, and academic improvement needs."[14] In 2014–2015, when the school began to work with City Connects, it had ten community partners. Through site coordinator Silverman's efforts to help teachers identify student needs and strengths, the school was connected with several targeted partners that would meet these needs and build on the strengths. By the end of 2015–2016, Winthrop had forty-three partners. In 2016–2017, every student received at least three services, and a total of 2,756 services were delivered to the school.[15]

In another Boston elementary school, information gathered from whole-class reviews led the City Connects site coordinator to develop a Health and Wellness Committee, which has brought the school, among other things, Healthy Family Fun Nights, bike helmets, fresh-food trucks, a Cooking Challenge, and a garden where students work with staff to clean up beds, plant seeds, and observe the growth of flowers and food. In the Bronx, whole-class review has enabled some of New York City's highest-poverty Children's Aid–managed community schools to ensure that children are connected to supports many have long lacked, like enriching after-school opportunities, and has empowered teachers to address social, emotional, and behavioral barriers they know impede their students' ability to learn.

Research has documented that whole-class review not only helps City Connects boost student achievement but is highly cost-effective as well. Six experts who researched the initiative and assessed its total costs relative to the benefits found that City Connects is successful because of the initiative's ability to identify every student's strengths and needs and to target "the right services to the right student at the right time." Screenings are more comprehensive and systematic, and needs are more consistently met. And the relationships established across the city enable City Connects to draw on a much broader range of service providers than might otherwise be available absent such an intensive, student-by-student assessment.[16] These benefits point to the advantages for ISS initiatives that draw on comprehensive data systems to advance the personalized, student-centered learning that scholars deem uniquely effective.

USING DATA SYSTEMS TO INDIVIDUALIZE ISS

While its whole-class review system is impressive, City Connects is not alone in its development of a sophisticated data system to tailor supports and enrichment to students and schools. Vancouver Public Schools collects data from several sources to shape programming specific to each FCRC and to identify individual students and families needing additional support. School performance data guide FCRCs' annual action plans, and site coordinators use data to identify students who are chronically absent and enroll them in attendance programs. And each center collects and reports data related to program attendance, resources, in-kind contributions and grant awards, connections to agencies, and other metrics and then uses the data to evaluate its work. In addition, internal and external stakeholders also use data from student, family, and community needs surveys to build programs for their schools.

These systems were developed in response to a question that stakeholders raised during the district's strategic planning process: "How would you measure the success of the [FCRC] initiative?" Superintendent Steve Webb says while barriers to student success are often beyond a school's or district's control, measuring near-term outcomes at the school level, like attendance and evidence of learning, can help the school and district mitigate those out-of-school factors.[17] For example, the FCRC team has explored how strengthening connections between resource coordination, family engagement, and partnership growth can reduce barriers to consistent attendance. And linking FCRC strategies to the top known causes of chronic absence—such as mental health problems, lack of transportation, and family dysfunction—helps the district understand the reason for, and measure the value of, its investments. In turn, these strategies help the district assess how much those investments are helping schools achieve their goals.

Vancouver's unusual approach to holding itself accountable, as a district, for student and school progress also uses the data collected by each center to continually track support and enrichment so that these services can be continuously improved. To follow progress and help the centers base their strategies on data, Vancouver developed a district performance scorecard. Similar to a student or school report card, it keeps track of data for every benchmark and indicator that the district established in its 2012 strategic plan.[18] Program data measures access to resources (type and quality of basic needs to be addressed and resources recommended); level of and change in parent involvement (e.g., attendance at school-based activities and parent education opportunities); and extent of partnerships (type and growth of direct services provided by partners to support the students and their families). Together, the scorecard's twenty-five key performance indicators tell a richer story of the district's performance than do the A–F report cards employed by some states. The scorecards also present a more informative and useful profile of student and school success than that offered by state assessment measures.

Other organizations, in addition to the twelve ISS communities highlighted in this book, are in various stages of planning and piloting similar data systems. Probably the most intensive of these has been created by Say Yes to Education, a nonprofit organization founded by millionaire George Weiss in 1987 to encourage a group of Philadelphia sixth graders to attend and finish college. The organization began to develop its postsecondary planning system in Syracuse, New York, the first city where Say Yes implemented large-scale ISS efforts grounded in a comprehensive overhaul of the district's public school system. Drawing on input from teachers, service providers, Say Yes school-site facilitators, parents, and students themselves in its second city, Buffalo's postsecondary planning system tracks all the district's students against thirteen indicators (and thirty subindicators) across academic, social-emotional health, physical health, and financial support domains. The sophisticated system overcomes many privacy issues often cited as barriers to collaboration across sectors and enables leaders from schools, counseling services, social services, after-school programs, and other agencies to target personalized supports to individual children. Its user-friendly interface encourages parents, students, and other important groups to provide timely data, and its various filters permit different users access only to the data that pertain to them.

From this data, stakeholders can receive periodic progress updates on each student's personalized growth plan. The postsecondary planning system is designed to act first as an early warning system to flag students who may be veering off track. Say Yes also plans to produce postsecondary planning reports for individual schools and for subgroups of them to identify trends in areas of need and to better coordinate different services. By focusing on broad areas of child development and the students' growth in them, the system helps teachers advance whole-child education. As a report tracking the evolution of Say Yes from Syracuse to Guilford County, North Carolina, notes, the postsecondary planning system "encourages educators to think about students beyond test scores and supports schools and communities in developing students holistically."[19]

Say Yes has invested large sums in, and devoted extensive research to, its postsecondary planning system, which is now in its initial stages of implementation in its second citywide effort, in Buffalo, New York.[20] (Say Yes describes the system as "fully operational" but notes that although data is being collected for every student, the school- and system-level responses to the data are taking longer to happen.) The system is in even more preliminary stages in Syracuse, where Say Yes encountered several obstacles to work that it started in 2006, and in Guilford County, where Say Yes began to implement ISS in 2017. The organization also plans to begin to implement postsecondary planning in Cleveland in the 2019–2020 school year, where the system will be an integral part of the Say Yes program's work from the start.

Sondra Samuels, Northside Achievement Zone CEO, points to NAZ Connects, a similar collaborative data system, which has been part of NAZ's work from its inception, as critical in several respects. First, the information from a range of partners enables the initiative to target the right supports and enrichments to the students who need them. Second, the data provide NAZ with feedback on how those programs are helping students make progress toward their academic and related goals, so that supports can be tweaked and improved as needed. Finally, Samuels says, "it is the only way we can prove that the model is working." Indeed, the most recent report from Wilder Research, the initiative's contracted evaluator, draws on system data to find that overall, more intensive use of NAZ services leads to better student outcomes. For example, children who attended four-star early-childhood centers and whose parents participated in the College-Bound Babies parent education class were better prepared for kindergarten than were their peers who had only participated in one of the two programs, and NAZ "scholars" enrolled in schools with achievement coaches had statistically significantly higher test scores than did those not enrolled in NAZ.

A much more recent addition, Harvard's By All Means initiative, tracks *measures of success*, benchmarks against which to gauge communities' progress toward building effective systems of opportunity and support for their children. Working through their respective advisory boards, or children's cabinets, cities report on indicators of committed leadership, investment and sustainability, collaborative action, access to services, and child/youth impact, among other indicators. Together, these measures tell a story about the progress of systems-level work to better serve children across multiple initiatives.

UNDERSTANDING A COMPLEX SYSTEM

Whole-class review, like the use of Facebook in Bright Futures districts and checkbooks for principals in Vancouver Public Schools, is only one part of the complex system of supports and enrichment opportunities in ISS communities. Schools must invest time and resources—financial, human capital, and so forth—to design and implement such systems. The most intensive of these systems, for example, Say Yes to Education's presecondary planning system and City Connects' whole-class review, provide particularly helpful data to a wide range of actors and require much more than such lighter-touch efforts as the creation of a Facebook page. Lighter-touch efforts include more modest, less systemic interventions with potentially broader reach but usually less effect than more intensive interventions. As these examples illustrate, however, individualizing support for students and families pays off in myriad ways. It might help in the short term, for instance, by removing an immediate obstacle to a student's ability to get to class or focus on a critical lesson. It can have a longer-term impact by building both students' confidence in themselves and trusting relationships between families and school staff.

Personalizing supports and thereby eliminating impediments to learning enable more students to express their interests, unlock their curiosity, develop motivation, and fully engage in class, key prerequisites for boosting achievement and cultivating lifelong learners. Systems like those explored in this chapter—from less to more intensive—that help schools personalize both intervention and enrichment opportunities could benefit other districts with similar goals.

4

Harnessing the Power of the Faith Community

Faith institutions are in many ways natural partners of school improvement efforts grounded in ISS. Like the public schools in their communities, churches, and other religious institutions across the country are on the front lines of efforts to counter the impacts of poverty. They are the community institutions to which families turn in times of need, and they are where Americans seeking to help their most vulnerable neighbors go to do so. In the past few years, pastors, ministers, rabbis, and imams have also joined school principals and superintendents in welcoming immigrants and refugees to their congregations and in countering the hostility directed toward those and other vulnerable populations.

Not surprisingly, many communities that employ ISS point to faith institutions as key providers of some of those supports for students and their families. In more politically liberal communities, like Vancouver, churches have been important partners in the district's work to establish Family and Community Resource Centers in a growing number of the district's schools and to make FCRC services available to all students and families.[1] Faith institutions also play a role in more conservative areas, like Berea and the surrounding eastern Kentucky counties served by Partners for Education. Churches in that region have launched weekend backpack programs to ensure that children are fed between Friday afternoon and Monday morning. Other churches provide Christmas gifts.

Partnerships with faith institutions are not necessarily a consistent feature across ISS communities, however. This inconsistency stands in contrast with the social service agencies, health and mental health providers, after-school and summer enrichment programs, and YMCAs and Boys & Girls Clubs that support students across the diverse communities studied by the Broader, Bolder Approach to Education (BBA) campaign. This distinction may be due in part to a history of political and legal barriers to the involvement of faith institutions in schools. Engaging these leaders, and their congregations' members, requires careful attention to these issues and ensuring that as faith leaders enter schools as tutors, mentors, and volunteers, they understand their roles and the boundaries while also feeling fully welcomed by the schools.

The services and supports provided by the faith community are not necessarily offered at school sites. In fact, some of the vital services, like care for younger children, are provided at churches or other institutions. What's most important is that these efforts be interwoven into a strategy to provide children and families with the supports and opportunities needed for students to come to school every day, ready to learn. Faith leaders can help whole communities reconsider the communities' "social compact" with children and families. While the faith community can and should be a welcome partner to the school system, faith institutions have enormous power and leverage, which can be used in the community to build an integrated system of supports for all children.

Faith institutions and their millions of members thus represent a potentially untapped (or undertapped) resource in many ISS communities. As such, their central role in two communities studied—Joplin and Pea Ridge—and in the dozens of Bright Futures USA affiliate districts now in operation, offers a model for capitalizing on this resource that can further deepen and strengthen not only school-community bonds but also the community-wide response to the needs of children.

This chapter describes how Bright Futures in particular has utilized faith leaders, faith institutions, and the institutions' members as core components of their strategies to mobilize community time, talent, and treasure to mitigate poverty-related barriers to teaching and learning. We also explore less intensive ways that communities can tap the resources of the faith community.

BRINGING IN FAITH COMMUNITIES AS A RESOURCE FROM THE BEGINNING

As discussed, the ISS communities we highlight in this book are diverse in many respects. For example, their geographical locations and political cultures vary widely. Bright Futures was launched in Joplin, a medium-sized city in the southeastern corner of Missouri, adjacent to its borders with Arkansas, Oklahoma, and Kansas. C. J. Huff's description of the region as "the buckle of the Bible Belt" suggests the prominent role that churches, most of them Baptist, play in Joplin and many neighboring communities. It also helps explain the strong alliances that Bright Futures affiliates have cultivated with faith institutions.[2]

When Huff describes the community outreach his team engaged in during his first nine months as superintendent, faith leaders get top billing, along with the city's business leaders, social service agencies, and parents. Huff's team viewed faith leaders as key players in the school improvement agenda, a determination that turned out to be spot-on and that has helped shape the development of the sixty-plus Bright Futures district affiliates across eight states by the spring of 2018.

Overcoming Challenges to Engaging Faith Institutions

Huff recounts the perspective he developed while training to be a school leader, emphasizing the benefits as well as the potential dangers of bringing a religious group into a school for any purpose. Among his concerns are legal and constitutional barriers, both real and perceived, and the sense among religious leaders and faith members that they would be unable to drop their religious identity at the door, as required. These common reservations explain why many spiritual leaders often feel removed from their community's public schools. Nonetheless, Huff believes the risks can be overcome and that school-church partnerships can deliver substantial benefits to students, families, and the schools.

Perhaps most critically, principals are wary of the legal issues that seem to stand in the way of a faith community's involvement in the schools. No education law class is complete without a thorough review of the separation of church and state. This constitutional issue, in particular, has been embedded in educational leadership training programs in the form of case studies and shows up routinely on assessments educators must pass to gain certification to become a principal or superintendent. All of which leads principals to believe that it is easier to play it safe and keep religious institutions out of schools. Another clear component of legal policy is that if you let one group into your school, you cannot deny access to another. No one wants to be accused of discrimination, so this area of law poses another barrier to allowing faith institutions into schools. These legal realities also make superintendents like Huff acutely aware of the very real danger of lawsuits. This fear has worked both ways: faith institutions have stayed out of schools, and walls have been built up over time. Indeed, faith leaders share a similar perception that schools and religious institutions cannot work together without violating the Constitution.

Huff describes the unfortunate outcome of this failure to understand the nuance that actually exists in the law: "It really just becomes easier to give all the reasons why you can't work together as opposed to finding solutions that open the doors to people of faith. At the end of the day, it's not so much about separation of church and state so much as we are just looking for good people to work with kids and support our schools. Churches are another entity that can do so . . . just like human service agencies and businesses."[3]

These barriers and fears were starkly visible in Joplin in 2009. Huff's team struggled at the outset to even get faith leaders to talk with them about plans for school improvement, let alone become engaged in the work. The strategic action plans that gave birth to Bright Futures drew on the resources of a full range of community constituents—including local businesses, social service agencies, and faith institutions. When the team sent out invitations to the kickoff breakfast in April 2010, however, no one from the extensive Joplin faith community showed up. Huff and his colleagues concluded that the walls had been built up high and wide and would require much more work to be bridged.

Bright Futures scheduled a second meeting and another series of conversations at the district's administrative offices. A small group of faith leaders came this time. Initial discussions about what a school-faith community partnership might look like ensued, and faith leaders weighed in on what they would like to see in such a partnership. Having made little concrete progress, however, Bright Futures scheduled a breakfast for the faith leaders with an agenda developed specifically for them. The turnout was much better, with fifteen to twenty churches represented in the room at a local restaurant. District leaders worked through the agenda, but Huff, seeing the body language among church leaders, felt that Bright Futures was still not making much progress. So he stood up to speak on behalf of the district, expressing its desire to work together with the faith community. He remembers that when he finished, the response did not seem promising:

> Still no luck. But as I sat down, Steve Patterson [a youth minister] stood up and said something I'll never forget. "Fellas, we have our school superintendent here inviting us into our schools. We know the need exists. We are

not here to test the Constitution. That has been tried and we are not here to try it again. But even though we know we can't be the voice of God in our schools, we *can* be the hands and feet of God by serving our children and our schools as volunteers, mentors, and tutors." The tone in the room changed immediately. The faith community got on board and quickly became the biggest advocate for that work.

Patterson, the director of missions for the Spring River Baptist Association, now sits on the national Bright Futures advisory council. He recalls first being recruited during an early survey of area churches when Huff was looking for "safe adults" to fill the large gap between the demand that school-based counselors reported for mentors and the capacity of the local YMCA to deliver them. The first time Patterson heard about Bright Futures, he doubted that schools would actually welcome members of his congregation into their classrooms. In his experience, Joplin's schools had always had a "hands-off approach."[4] He also was skeptical that members who were inclined to volunteer—who saw the work to support high-risk students as part of their duty as good Christians—could viably keep that powerful feeling of faith sufficiently separate to satisfy the church-state "wall" that he understood to be required. Much to his surprise, however, when he gave it a shot, the school made Patterson feel right at home. School staff and students alike expressed their gratitude at the churches'— his and others'—ability to quickly fill an important need that other city institutions had not been able to do. Perhaps most important, Patterson found that leaving his pastor hat in church and counseling students without preaching or proselytizing to them felt natural, rather than an insurmountable problem. In other words, respecting church-state boundaries without building an actual wall between the two was eminently viable.

Building Balanced, Respectful Church-School Partnerships

Over time, Patterson has become an enthusiastic advocate for Bright Futures. Since his seminal role at the 2010 faith breakfast, he has been leading workshops at the organization's national conferences about the important role faith institutions play in their communities' schools. Moreover, as he tells his peers when he urges them to recruit their own members to serve in Bright Futures affiliate district schools, leaving your ministerial hat in the church doesn't turn out to be a problem.

His efforts have proven to be quite effective. Other faith leaders and parishioners have followed his call to get out of their pews and into their communities to serve others. Whether they are mentoring students in the lunch buddy program, battling food insecurity by donating food and stuffing snack packs, volunteering at local human service agencies, supporting school events and parent events, or just stepping in to help a family in need, churches now have a direct link to families and children. And this link enables them to support community members in need, whether they do so through in-school or through community-wide activities.

Beyond faith members' individual roles as lunch buddies and bus greeters (in Pea Ridge, a newer affiliate), they and their pastors or ministers also serve in school site councils. In those capacities, they work alongside parents, teachers, and local business leaders to guide the school's work with Bright Futures and its plans for improvement. In Joplin, twenty-two churches are represented on the site councils of the district's eleven elementary schools. Three churches make up the entire council for one of the smaller schools, Royal Heights, and five additional churches serve on the councils of Joplin's four middle schools and its high school.[5] This work has greatly strengthened relationships between schools and the neighborhoods they serve. Patterson describes a wonderful example of faith involvement in the southern region of the district. Before Bright Futures, members of the church would talk about "that school down the hill." After they became partners with Bright Futures, those same members began referring to the school as "our school down the hill." This change of one small word reflected how welcome they felt and the impact they knew they were having.

Church leaders and members also serve in other capacities, including roles in the Bright Futures Advisory Board for the school district and, as Patterson demonstrates, at the organizational level, as well as on a variety of subcommittees as needed. In Frederick County, Virginia, Bright Futures has had representation from the faith community on its advisory board since the affiliate's start in 2013. Winchester Church of God, one of the area's larger churches, engaged its members, although the superintendent Dave Sovine says much of that interaction was behind the scenes. But in 2018, with people's increased awareness of Bright Futures as the go-to organization to pull these supports together, several smaller churches are now reaching out to Nancy Mango, the Bright Futures coordinator, asking how they can support the initiative and the community. Many churches, having long maintained food banks, brought this work to Bright Futures. In addition, church groups work at the program's center along with retirees and student service groups to pack meals to go out weekly from schools. And now one church is looking at sponsoring one of the high schools, James Wood, to provide mentor experiences and other support activities. Recently, Sovine says, the game has changed dramatically: whereas Mango used to spend her time reaching out to churches and businesses asking for their support, "now they are coming to us, asking, 'How can we help you and our schools?' This has emerged and taken hold within the past year."[6]

Ongoing Support for Faith-School Partnerships

At the organizational level, Bright Futures USA advocates for, and provides technical assistance on, engaging faith leaders as core community partners. At its March 2017 Community Engagement Conference in Siloam Springs, Arkansas, one workshop was titled "Back-to-School Bonanza: Engaging Your Faith-Based Community in Helping Make Sure Kids Have What They Need to Start School."[7] A second workshop, "Out of the Pew, Into the Field," was designed to help congregations find the right fit for working with youth in the community, noting that "faith-based organizations across the country are becoming the hands and feet of God by getting out of the pews and into the schools." Another asked participants to explore the school partnership: "What Does it Mean to be a Faith-Based Partner?" And a fourth workshop was titled "Motivating the Movement: How Lay People Reach out to Their Faith-Based Leadership to Encourage Involvement."

The "Motivating the Movement" session, run by Bob Burton, national regional mobilizer of the North American Mission Board, was described this way:

> For a few moments, we'll walk in the shoes of our community of faith leaders. Understanding pastors and other ministry leaders is vital to having an effective Bright Futures school partnership. Come join us for this workshop as we learn together how to encourage faith-based involvement for the first time and/or move into greater levels of involvement for your community of faith. You can become a catalyst for creating a culture of mercy missions and helping ministries through healthy school partnerships. Learn how to tap into this large pool of volunteers for your school.

Evidence of the importance of faith institutions from the start is also seen in a Joplin newspaper's description of Bright Futures USA's first such conference, in 2013. Patterson was among the speakers, as was Jay St. Clair, community outreach minister of College Heights Christian Church in Joplin. Back then, as in 2017, conference participants could attend a workshop on engaging faith institutions and leaders as partners supporting the schools.[8] The first speaker representing the faith community was Matt Proctor, president of Ozark Christian College. He had helped set the stage for church-community collaboration after the April 2010 breakfast.

The initial reluctance of faith leaders to dive into Bright Futures' school improvement plans was overcome through a concerted effort to include them. Once persuaded that their involvement was both viable and valuable, they were all in and their engagement was tightly interwoven into the school improvement efforts. This transformation suggests the potential for other communities to include faith institutions in their ISS work from the start.

OTHER ISS-FAITH PARTNERSHIPS

Bright Futures communities are by no means the only ones working to engage faith leaders and institutions as part of their efforts to provide ISS. School districts that employ community-school strategies or Promise Neighborhoods' cradle-to-career approaches likewise turn to churches (and other faith communities) to enable wraparound supports for students and families. Faith engagement is not necessarily a core component of these initiatives' ISS efforts, however, and may be more a school-by-school strategy than a districtwide one. The following examples indicate that other communities employing ISS can take varying approaches to engaging faith institutions in their work and that all can probably take some pages from the Bright Futures playbook. They also illustrate the range of both within-school and community-wide roles that faith institutions can play in providing comprehensive student support.

In Vancouver, faith institutions have played a fairly central role from the start in the expansion of the district's Family-Community Resource Centers. In an effort to determine how local churches and faith leaders could help enhance their community work, Clark County Public Health initiated grassroots "faith-based coffee" events in early 2013. The first meetings received an enthusiastic response, but faith leaders expressed a preference to work with and through the school system, since that approach offered them the most direct, consistent access to the children they wanted to help. The timing was perfect—Vancouver Public Schools had just developed its strategic plan to expand FCRCs and was eager to join forces with this key partner.[9]

Faith institutions have been wonderful in responding to schools' express material needs—for example, through food and clothing drives. But Anne Johnston of Clark County Public Health sees faith communities' role in filling *relational needs* through initiatives like student mentors and parent-ing classes as even more exciting. Because of their central, trusted role in the community, Johnston says that the monthly faith-based coffees have evolved into larger learning opportunities where the schools, faith part-ners, public health officials, and social service agencies come together. "This really had to be about them putting their faith into action, and loving and serving and not evangelizing. So we had those tough conversations at those meetings as well."[10]

Four eastern Kentucky counties served by Berea College's Partners for Education initiative—Clay, Jackson, Knox, and Owsley—are heav-ily white evangelical Baptist. And churches are helping in several of the region's schools. Tyner Elementary School, for example, gives students nonperishable food to bring home over the weekend, to make sure they have meals between Friday and Monday. A local church initiated the pro-gram of brown bags, and "now they got a lot of people in the community on board."[11] Churches, in other words, can be the catalyst for broader engagement and support. And at Big Creek Elementary School in Oneida, Kentucky, a church in Blount County, Tennessee, has been partnering with the school for six years. Volunteers from the church drive nearly four hours each way to deliver "shoebox Christmas" presents to every kid in the school. Church members enjoy lunch in the cafeteria as kids pose for pictures in their owl-themed hoodies (Big Creek is in Owsley County, so owls are everywhere) and show off their new Slinky toys, fidget spinners, and craft kits to their friends.[12]

Other ISS communities similarly draw on faith institutions and leaders for specific services but have not incorporated them as key partners. An exception is the Tangelo Park Project, where the Tangelo Baptist Church has been a core component of philanthropist Harris Rosen's ISS-oriented support for the community for the past twenty-plus years. As part of its work to help families access educational and social services, the church recently established an instructional center, staffed entirely by volunteers, some of them former teachers, to help students with homework and preparation for important exams.

Both North Minneapolis and East Durham present strong potential for greater involvement of churches. And faith institutions have played an important role in the Northside Achievement Zone, but the role is different from that in many other communities. Although NAZ's Sondra Samuels did not intentionally recruit from area churches, there are several in the neighborhood. Many congregants live in the zone and care about these issues, and several of her staff are local parishioners. Indeed, one of her first recruits, an associate at one of the largest churches, Shiloh Temple, today oversees NAZ's early-childhood education work.

Mary Mathew, a director at EDCI, notes that while some East Durham churches are small and have limited capacity to offer support, over the years, the East Durham Children's Initiative has engaged with the neighborhood's and broader city's faith-based organizations in various ways. Early on, EDCI partnered with a church to provide land for a new KaBOOM! playground, and the initiative's office has been located in three churches so far. Churches have also given volunteer support for EDCI programs and events, hosted community meetings, and offered pantry food, Thanksgiving meals, and school supplies. Other EDCI partner organizations, like Durham Cares, also work specifically around church mobilization to provide student support.

Despite these examples of faith leader engagement, there is more work to be done to make such partnerships an intrinsic part of ISS community work. Beth Brown, who directs PfE's Promise Neighborhoods work, talks about having largely missed the boat with respect to collaborating with faith leaders. She sees the failure to engage them early in work in eastern Kentucky as a squandered opportunity, and she is looking for ways to enhance those relationships going forward, in the second grant cycle.[13] And Mathew says that, notwithstanding the important role of churches in EDCI student and family support, "of course, we could always be doing more to engage them."[14]

In Vancouver, too, Johnston notes that faith leaders "are often that overlooked stakeholder that doesn't get invited to the table when it comes to coalition-building, when it comes to policy development." So programs like faith-based coffees are one key to ensuring that this critical community asset is not overlooked. It also helps faith institutions that want to engage but may not always know how to do so.[15]

REALIZING THE TRUE POTENTIAL OF "UNUSUAL ALLIES"

At the same time, national momentum is growing to harness the power—and credibility—of faith leaders and their members to improve schools and education systems. In the early-childhood field, for example, efforts to recruit "unusual allies" began over a decade ago with projects to engage business leaders. Now these efforts include faith leaders in their ranks as well. Ready Nation, perhaps the best known of the partnerships between business leaders early-childhood education efforts and which began as the Partnership for America's Success (sponsored by the Pew Charitable Trusts), is now part of the Council for a Strong America. The council has grown to serve as the umbrella for advocates among police forces, business leaders, members of the armed forces, coaches and athletes, and, now, Shepherding the Next Generation, which describes itself as a collective of "evangelical pastors and ministry leaders calling for biblically-based and effective approaches to strengthen families and communities."[16]

In September 2016, building on this interest, BBA convened a small group of national and local faith leaders in Washington, DC, to explore their interest in working in the area of education and poverty.[17] Catholic, Baptist, Muslim, and Jewish religious leaders and organizational advocates discussed how their respective groups are already engaged in some of these issues. For example, the Catholic Partnership Project for Better Early Childhood Development is a collaborative effort between Catholic schools and Catholic Charities programs targeting vulnerable young children in

Catholic school settings. Two representatives from the Clapham Group explained their engagement of faith leaders in target communities to advance an agenda for antipoverty social justice policy.[18] Participants noted substantial interest within faith institutions and among interfaith groups to learn more about poverty-related needs in education. They also observed that education and antipoverty advocates must develop resources targeted at faith communities to help inform and activate these communities and to arm them with the information they need to make the case for ISS to policy makers.

Considering both the work on the ground to engage faith leaders in hundreds of communities and the institutions with national initiatives to organize those leaders, there is real potential to bring ISS efforts to greater scale. Faith leaders have enormous power to mobilize communities, drive advocacy initiatives, and organize the provision of opportunities and supports in both schools and their wider communities. They can be highly effective proponents for communities to step up and meet the needs of its children.

And as community leaders, school leaders, and other participants in the BBA convening emphasized, faith leaders are uniquely powerful messengers. Across the political and ideological spectra, they are widely respected and seen as credible. And because the doctrines of all three monotheistic religions preach the need for antipoverty work, these institutions are natural allies of ISS advocates. Communities looking to initiate, scale up, and sustain their ISS work should look to Bright Futures and other strong ISS models to engage faith partners from the start and make them central to their work. Advocates at the regional, state, and national levels should also be considering the important role of faith leaders early on and ensuring that they are represented at the table as strategy discussions evolve.

5

Integrated Student Supports in Rural Communities

Strategies to improve high-poverty schools tend to focus on urban centers. While these districts do face substantial problems that merit attention, thousands of rural communities where residents live in concentrated poverty can be invisible to those living outside of them. They have thus been largely neglected by advocates and policy makers. However, roughly 20 percent of the nation's children live in rural communities and attend schools there. Our failure to educate these children for success has profound implications for the economy and democracy. We must turn our attention to these communities and develop a better understanding of how to make ISS work for rural adults and children.

Two of the communities studied by BBA—Berea, Kentucky, and Pea Ridge, Arkansas—illustrate how communities whose residents live in isolation can effectively integrate student supports by tailoring their efforts to rural areas' unique needs. And while it is mostly nonrural, Joplin, Missouri, another Bright Futures district, also serves a number of rural students. Moreover, all three areas are predominantly white, belying the common perception that poverty, and concentrated poverty, are minority problems.

These communities and many others across the country provide helpful models of how some strategies can ensure that students in rural areas have the comprehensive support they need to learn effectively. Some of these communities are in small towns; others in some of the most remote regions in the United States. We also explore a few other strategies that might be effectively adapted from nonrural settings to rural communities.

Across the United States, millions of families and children are living in poverty in small towns, on farms, and in remote and often isolated areas. Over the past few decades, as coal mining and manufacturing jobs in these communities have disappeared, as family farms have been absorbed by large corporations, and as small towns have emptied out, a growing share of high-poverty regions are rural. Many of these, including the eleven-state region of Appalachia, which stretches from Ohio all the way south to Alabama, are marked by intensely concentrated poverty.[1]

These areas also have low levels of adult educational attainment and high rates of unemployment, mobility (transience), teen pregnancy, single parenthood, and drug and alcohol abuse. A *New York Times* article on Mc-Dowell County, West Virginia, assessed the impacts of President Johnson's War on Poverty at the program's fiftieth anniversary. The piece describes an area that was largely untouched by that effort: as the coal industry declined, towns hollowed out, families fell apart, and drug abuse and imprisonment rose sharply.[2] The eastern Kentucky region around Berea looks much like McDowell. The poverty rate was roughly 27 percent in 2015, nearly twice the national average, and it climbed above 40 percent in some counties. In 2013, more than one-third of children lived below the federal poverty line.

On the one hand, students growing up in these areas face many of the same obstacles that their counterparts in distressed urban neighborhoods face. Both groups of students are disproportionately likely to be raised by young, single mothers with low levels of educational attainment and thus few job options, suffer from food insecurity and hunger, be in poor health, live in substandard housing conditions, and attend under-resourced schools. On the other hand, meeting children's needs in rural areas poses unique challenges. Not only is poverty intense, but resources such as mental health providers can be hours away and hard to access, so care is less available and consistent.[3]

These rural communities tend to have few assets and resources and have weak support systems, typically far below the those in most urban communities. Tax dollars, philanthropies, higher education, nonprofit partners—all are in short supply. It is hard for schools to find qualified teachers to hire in such small isolated districts, and inequitable school funding systems put rural schools at particular disadvantage. When the American Federation of Teachers committed to improve McDowell County Schools as part of a larger community-building strategy, one of the first challenges it identified was the lack of decent housing, which impeded schools' capacity to attract and retain good educators.[4] The dearth of good jobs is compounded by the long distances people must travel to take advantage of scarce employment options; the lack of public transportation exacerbates these challenges.

In the past few years, the dire circumstances in many of our rural communities have spurred a growing opioid crisis. Addiction is among the mental health problems that disproportionately affect distressed rural areas, and now an overdose epidemic means that children are losing their parents to jail or death in large numbers.

STRATEGIES FOR SUCCESS IN RURAL ENVIRONMENTS

Two communities that have achieved some success in mitigating poverty's impacts through the use of ISS are rural, one of them situated in one of the nation's most remote, impoverished regions. Both offer strategies that other rural schools and communities could learn from and adopt, for example, improving early-childhood care and education and cultivating a college-going culture and making postsecondary education a realistic possibility. Other communities, such as Joplin, illustrate how comprehensive initiatives can serve rural as well as nonrural students, and some nonrural communities employ strategies that could be adapted to rural contexts. As communities and school districts across the country develop such strategies and build new systems of instruction, support, and accountability under the Every Student Succeeds Act, these examples offer timely and relevant guidance.

Early-Childhood Education

Center-based childcare and preschools tend to provide higher-quality care and education for young children, but such providers are more expensive than the friends and family or neighborhood providers who serve most low-income children. Moreover, parents may be uncomfortable placing infants and very young children in center-based care, and those providers may also be less convenient for parents who need coverage beyond the outdated nine-to-five workday. These factors pose even larger impediments in rural areas, where parents earn less, on average, than do their urban and suburban counterparts and where many commute long distances.

Further obstructing a strong, early start for children is the difficulty in practicing nurturing parenting habits that are key to healthy child development. Buying books is financially out of reach for many rural families, and the closest library is often far away, making parents' goal of reading to their children regularly a challenge. And with distances long and transportation options few, getting to parenting classes that promote positive child development practices is similarly difficult.

The state preK program Arkansas Better Chance doesn't reach Pea Ridge, a heavily rural district with some suburban characteristics, so superintendent Rick Neal sought a grant from a local philanthropic foundation to create a small preK center. He also recruited higher-income families so that their children's payments could subsidize the twenty low-income children. The result is a high-quality preK program that enables children in the 2,000-student district to enjoy the high-quality early-childhood education they would have received from the state's preK program. And it offers the added benefit of a socioeconomically diverse early education setting. While rural districts are at a disadvantage to obtain grants from national foundations, local and community foundations that support rural regions can provide this kind of support for smaller districts.

As part of its formation of Bright Futures, Joplin School District established an early-childhood commission. That body began by surveying services and supports already being provided by regional agencies and nonprofits, with the goal of aligning and enhancing them rather than creating new programs. This approach—of serving as a hub for existing services—could be particularly effective in rural areas where services are scarce and where providers may find it difficult to connect with one another to serve families efficiently. The commission identified as its core goal the improvement of early literacy, a major challenge for rural children. It then raised funds to create new-parent kits and to deliver them to area hospitals. The kits include information on how reading regularly to young children supports their healthy development, age-appropriate books, and bibs with the message "Read to Me: 30 Minutes, Every Child, Every Day."

Fund-raising like Joplin's may be more difficult in a rural context, but communities can look to regional and national organizations like the United Way and work with the Dolly Parton Imagination Library, which gives books to children in partner communities, and with local libraries. This kind of collaboration can enable local staff to develop informational material at low or no cost. Recounting his experience with very small rural communities, Huff says that "in extreme rural areas, you have to get more creative and go a few more miles to engage regional resources, but with the right partnerships, these opportunities start to present themselves."[5]

In partnership with local United Way groups, Bright Futures has promoted the Little Blue Bookshelf project, placing bookshelves filled with age-appropriate books in places where low-income families and their children visit, so they can build home libraries. United Way also operates a toy library out of its Joplin office, where children whose parents are visiting can socialize and where parents can check out toys and books to use at home. These efforts are complemented by public service announcements that emphasize the importance of reading to children every day, so that every child has at least a thousand hours of reading experience by the time he or she begins kindergarten.

In eastern Kentucky, Partners for Education, a Berea College initiative that is the first rural recipient of a federal Promise Neighborhoods grant, has had to be particularly creative. Low-income children in Kentucky benefit from the state's high-quality preK program, which serves one-quarter of the state's four-year-olds and nearly one-tenth of its three-year-olds. The rural nature of the counties served by PfE, however, means parents have limited access. Owsley County, which serves only a few hundred students in all, has just one elementary school. Lack of space for preK classrooms is thus a challenge, and many children whose families want to enroll them cannot get slots. Transportation poses a second challenge; schools may be thirty or even forty minutes away, and some parents are reluctant to put small children on a bus for such a long time. Other families live in such remote locations that preK is not an option, or they face so much stress that they cannot manage the preschool application, let alone getting their children to school.

In Clay County, PfE obtained a grant from the Kellogg Foundation to serve the young children most in need of preschool enrichment and who cannot get to schools. As described earlier, the program used the funding to retrofit two buses—the Readiness Buses—as preschool classrooms serving young children and their parents. The buses arrive at targeted families' homes each week for a one-hour session that is divided in half. During the first half hour, parents, children, and two early-childhood specialists work together using the games, toys, and mini libraries that each bus was outfitted with. In the other thirty minutes, the children learn with a teacher while the parents (mostly single mothers) work on family goal-setting, child development, and parenting skills—three areas that help both the parent and the child move toward kindergarten readiness and family well-being. Parents who initially had to be persuaded that preschool was a good idea often become so committed after these bus visits that they go on to sign up their three- and four-year-olds for daily preschool at the area school or other sites, making it much more likely that their children will be fully ready to learn when kindergarten begins.

The Readiness Buses strategy also enables PfE to act as a liaison between parents and schools if parents are uncomfortable directly contacting the school. In addition, the program connects the most vulnerable families to other critical social and financial supports, thus stabilizing the whole household and further advancing children's school readiness. And so-called community storywalks in Joplin and Clay County offer parents opportunities to learn together with young children through interactive, nature-based activities. Such programs take advantage of the natural resources and beauty that are abundant in rural areas but that parents are often unable to access or put to good use.

The Tangelo Park neighborhood in Orlando is not rural, but its residents' physical and social isolation from the city's tourist sector and other resources poses challenges that are similar in some respects.[6] Neighborhood-based early care and education providers, in particular, offer a model that is highly relevant to rural communities. Hotelier Harris Rosen, who has sponsored the community since the early 1990s, understands that families in Tangelo Park want a system of early care that is both culturally responsive and logistically convenient. This observation led him to fund training, resources, and other support to enhance the quality of the neighborhood's home providers. Today, nine or ten home-based early-childhood centers, each of which serves no more than six children, provide high-quality early education for children ages two to four years. Parents walk just a block or two to drop their children off at the homes. The consistency of quality education through their children's early years not only benefits their children but also enables the adults to develop close, helpful relationships with the caretakers.

In rural and isolated areas, this model could support small groups of children in settings that are tailored to those children's unique characteristics—like a Tangelo Park provider who cares for children with special needs—and are responsive to parents' cultural preferences. And as in Tangelo Park, coaches could visit once or twice a week to enhance program quality and provide in-service professional development, nurses from across the region could rotate among providers to address children's physical and mental health needs, and computers and other technologies could supplement lessons from teachers. For example, PfE places early-childhood specialists in Berea area preschool classrooms to enhance the quality of instruction and help teachers improve classroom climate and relationships with students.

The biggest challenge for rural communities would be identifying funding sources to get such systems off the ground and to sustain them. Few rural communities have such wealthy philanthropists to turn to. Consequently, they would need to draw on a combination of smaller grants from regional and community foundations, state and federal early-childhood grants, and other resources. The Tangelo Park Program's preK model is not particularly expensive, however, and so could probably be adapted elsewhere.[7]

Native American reservations face some of the biggest barriers to student success. They experience family and concentrated poverty rates that are among the highest in the country. The reservations mostly exist in extreme isolation, a factor in parents' high rates of drug and alcohol addiction and low levels of both educational attainment and workforce participation. As in Appalachia, opiate addiction is a growing problem; an estimated one in ten pregnancies on reservations are affected by prenatal opiate use.[8] As a result, achievement gaps between Native American students and their white peers start early and grow wider. Tribal and school leaders have responded with new investments in early-childhood development initiatives. A combination of state and federal early-childhood funds and tribal resources enables the construction of centers like the Wewinabi Early Education Center on the Mille Lacs Reservation in central Minnesota.[9]

Attention to issues of cultural relevance and parent engagement spurred the community to build the space so that every room—classrooms, meeting rooms, and hallways—face toward the building's center, where families gather for a monthly powwow. Parent education programs can be tailored to the unique needs and assets of Native American families, as model initiatives like the Family Spirit program in Minnesota and Positive Indian Parenting, a program developed by the National Indian Child Welfare Association, demonstrate. Many preK programs also incorporate Native language immersion to further embed community culture in early-childhood education.

Parent Engagement

In rural areas like tight-knit Appalachia, the engagement of parents or other family members could help offset the often-long distances between school and home. But educators wanting to get parents or other caretakers involved face many challenges. Chapter 6 describes some of the challenges in detail and how various initiatives have tackled these difficulties.

Even isolated rural areas can often secure funding to support key initiatives. A subgrant from the Morehouse University School of Medicine enables PfE to implement Safe and Secure Children, a birth-to-five program that focuses on successful transitions to kindergarten. Parents from the community become leaders, each recruiting five or so families for teams. The ten-week relationship-building program uses a curriculum that addresses issues like effective grocery shopping and healthy eating while connecting parent graduates to the parent task force. Even though there is a wide range of ability and stability across families, parent liaison Sue Christian believes that all families benefit, especially the parents who come in doubting their own capacity to be good parents. It is especially gratifying for specialists like Christian to see parent graduates go on to lead school PTAs or even run for seats on the school board.

The arts have proven to be a particularly effective family engagement tool in Appalachia. Though widely known for its poverty and isolation, the region has a rich history of music and arts and crafts. As will be described in chapter 6, under the auspices of Berea College, PfE works with schools to celebrate this aspect of Appalachian history through various programs that engage both students and other members of the community.

PfE is also bolstered by Family Resource and Youth Services Centers that have been established in low-income counties across the state as a result of the 1990 Kentucky Education Reform Act. While each center is tailored to the specific needs of the community, all the centers provide health and education services, such as care for expecting mothers and crisis counseling. They also serve as hubs of parent and community involvement, and in Promise Neighborhoods counties, they house parent involvement task forces that enhance school-family connections by assisting students with math, supporting teachers, and helping families with students who have special needs collaborate more effectively with schools. Some centers also host workshops that help families build skills, arrange visits to colleges with their children, and offer financial management classes.

Health Support

Poor health is also pervasive and difficult to address in rural communities. Widespread food insecurity, poverty-driven stress, and lack of access to healthy food and opportunities for regular exercise make unmet health needs common. Pediatricians are fewer and farther away than in high-poverty urban and suburban areas, and dental and mental health care providers can be even harder to find. In isolated, poorer communities surrounding ultrawealthy Telluride, Colorado, for example, so many children were arriving at kindergarten with rotted teeth from untreated cavities that the Telluride Foundation funded a mobile dental truck and subsequently a school-based dental program.[10]

Promise Neighborhoods–supported early-childhood councils give oral-health training for new parents, helping to avert cavities and tooth decay. PfE also supports Save the Children's Healthy Choices program, which offers healthy snack options and a half hour of daily physical activity. The program collaborates with school and community partners to provide run or walk clubs, summer fitness programs, community gardens, and food preservation education to advance healthy lifestyles. The creative use of technology is also evident: at Owsley High School, the nurse uses her laptop to electronically transmit to area physicians the temperature, pulse, blood pressure, and reported symptoms of students who don't feel well. The physicians use the information to diagnose the illness and to write a prescription and, if necessary, a referral to the hospital. Before the school adopted this strategy, sick students whose parents lacked the time, car, or money to take the child to a doctor often went without medical care, and many more missed school.

When Pea Ridge's Neal saw extensive unmet health needs among his 850 students, he reached out to the city's physician and dentist, who collaborate with the district's four nurses to provide eye exams, flu vaccines, and other basic health care. The district's social worker goes to schools to address students' and their families' mental and emotional health needs. Three area agencies offer individual, family, and group therapy, and several regional mental health agencies offer therapeutic day treatment for students with severe emotional and behavioral issues.

After-School, Summer, and Other Enrichment Opportunities

Unicoi County, Tennessee, high school principal Chris Bogart describes the challenge he faced when he first assumed leadership of the school and wanted to provide out-of-school enrichment options for his students in one of the country's most isolated rural regions. "[One new staff member] suggested just giving the kids bus tokens to get home from after-school activities, like in her prior district. 'Sure,' I said, 'that would be great if Unicoi had buses.'"[11] So Bogart worked with his staff to design a program tailored to the community's reality. They expanded the lunch period from a half hour to a full hour and opened the entire school to students during that time. The change enabled students with a passion for books to eat lunch while reading in the library, let art students consult with their teacher about projects and do artwork, and made it possible for the school to launch a theater program.

In eastern Kentucky, one of the best resources PfE can assemble to help more students graduate from high school and enroll in college is current Berea College students. Many of them grew up in Appalachia and understand personally the challenges that area middle and high school students face. They are thus uniquely effective mentors, helping with math and reading, providing guidance in choosing high school courses, and navigating the college admissions and scholarship processes. But long distances make face-to-face contact difficult. So PfE created a Skype mentoring system, using technology to connect high school students with Berea College mentors on a regular basis.

Technology is also enabling innovation in schools. In Owsley County's Big Creek Elementary School, a three-year grant has provided every student with a Kindle and digital access to ten thousand books. Principal Nadine Couch says teachers are pleasantly surprised that students take good care of the devices and remember to bring them to school and that the children are reading on snow days and after school, valuable learning time that used to be wasted. High school principal Charlie Davidson's investment in zSpace machines and 3-D glasses at Owsley County High School gives biology students access to realistic digital human hearts that they can "examine" and dozens of other STEM (science, technology, engineering, and mathematics) activities. In the 2017–2018 school year, eleventh-grade biology students got to participate remotely in real time in an open-heart surgery and pose questions to the surgeons, and the 2018–2019 class will work with medical students in Lexington, Kentucky, to dissect a cadaver.

Such uses of technology enable students in a remote, high-poverty school to engage in the kinds of enriching activities normally limited to wealthy private schools. It also demonstrates the major power of technology in rural settings, in particular—to enrich classrooms and children's lives in this way, along with improving health, as the school nurse testifies, and support students through Skype mentorships.[12] These examples and others highlighted here should prompt leaders in other rural districts as well as urban districts to consider adopting and expanding creative uses of technology—uses that enhance learning, rather than purporting to personalize learning by simply adding more computers to classrooms.

PfE also overcomes barriers to summer learning. It mails books to students who live in remote regions and hosts online book clubs that engage students in teacher-led discussions. Pea Ridge has a similar program; the Pea Ridge Book Bus, which is stocked by teachers from the district's elementary and intermediate schools, has delivered books to children within the district since 2015. Both programs keep children learning during the summer months, when low-income children tend to experience learning loss while their wealthier peers, awash with opportunities, surge ahead.

As noted before, schools in Native American reservations face some of the greatest barriers to student success. Compounding problems of concentrated poverty and various types of family dysfunction is a history of systematic neglect and even intentional stripping of the rich cultural history that binds families and communities together. Disengagement from school is thus a common problem among students, but one school district in South Dakota has taken an innovative approach to addressing it. Red Cloud High School on the Pine Ridge Reservation is among a handful of US schools that are using art as a tool to better connect with and engage struggling students.[13] From hallway murals that celebrate their community's culture and their elders' practices to dance classes that bring in those revered leaders to work with students and projects that focus on tribal traditions, students learn about and build on their unique heritage as a way to acquire broader skills that prepare them for higher education and adult life.

College Readiness

With low rates of college attendance and college graduation, and thus fewer college-educated role models, rural communities face unique challenges not only in getting their students ready for college, but also in persuading them that college is a worthwhile and viable option. Appalachia has the lowest share of residents with bachelor's degrees of any area in the country: just 23 percent of adults have a four-year degree, but even that ranges from a high of 25 percent in southern Appalachia to less than 14 percent in central Appalachia, in the area around Berea.[14] In Unicoi County, a district with remote "hollers" so isolated that buses struggle to reach them in snowy winter months, Bogart and his teachers describe parents who are deeply skeptical of the need for postsecondary education. Most of Unicoi High School's teachers grew up in the area, and they recall family members responding to their own suggestions that they might want to go to college with admonitions that they were "getting above their raisin'."[15]

Many children in this region, and even their parents, have never ventured far outside the immediate area, so the prospect of visiting a city, which school leaders see as an important way to broaden their students' narrow views of the world, can be daunting. Bogart recounts a field trip to Nashville, Tennessee, in which one girl's parents were so anxious about her first trip to a big city that they drove the entire five hours alongside the bus, texting every few minutes to maintain constant contact. Teachers therefore begin to introduce their students to the idea of college in kindergarten by wearing T-shirts from their own colleges and posting pennants in their classrooms. They are also working to secure a grant that would let them expand field trips to area colleges and, ultimately, Washington, DC. The hope is that by making college an expectation from an early age, rather than an exception, and by having more students attain it, subsequent students will begin to change their parents' attitudes about postsecondary education.

Though Joplin School District is mostly nonrural, its approach to creating a college-going culture is relevant to such communities. As in the Unicoi County School District, the lack of discussion among many Joplin parents with their children about going to college impedes teachers' ability to get their students thinking about it. As described in detail later in the book, Operation College Bound has helped to cultivate a college-going culture and expose students to post-secondary options from their first school years.

In remote communities, career day might look different, with regional rather than local business leaders—the president of the area bank, the manager of a manufacturing plant in a nearby city, or the owner of the regional farming supply store—coming to talk to students. Even in isolated areas, however, local community colleges encourage students to visit and expand their horizons, and local chambers of commerce are likely to be eager to cultivate interest among the next generation of residents, workers, and taxpayers.

These strategies are also among those highlighted by a ten-state consortium of educators, social workers, business leaders, and state and local policy makers who have come together to form the Appalachian Higher Education Network. The network's 2016 conference focused on helping schools within the Appalachian regions of their states create a college-going culture. In addition to field trips to colleges like those organized in Berea and Pea Ridge, sessions at the conference explored developing partnerships that allow high school students to accrue college credit in their schools, at a local college, or online. As Berea's Skype mentoring program highlights, making reliable internet available to rural residents is a critical step toward boosting educational attainment. The Reconnecting McDowell initiative also made reliable internet a high priority, leveraging a public-private partnership to bring broadband to 90 percent of the area's homes in 2012.[16] A growing number of Appalachian schools have also described hosting college and career festivals, which provide a forum for teachers and principals to talk with students about how they overcame their own fears of being the first in their families to make it past high school.

Berea College offers a particularly creative response to challenges rural and other low-income communities face in encouraging their students to enroll in and finish college. Berea was established before the Civil War by ardent abolitionists. Its first teachers were recruited from Oberlin College, and Berea's founders envisioned the institution as the Oberlin of Kentucky, a place where men and women, both black and white, would learn together. Berea charges no tuition and is the only leading institution of higher education in the country to guarantee debt-free college degrees to every student. A small liberal-arts college, it admits only academically promising students from low-income backgrounds. Most are from Appalachia, and many are the first in their families to attend college. Instead of paying tuition, and in keeping with its founders' goal of dignifying manual labor at a time when it was seen by many as synonymous with slavery, Berea students engage in extensive service learning projects as part of their college experience.[17]

While it has never been replicated, Berea's well-tailored strategy to help more of the region's students obtain a postsecondary education could be adapted to other high-poverty rural contexts. Some of the country's other most isolated areas—Native American reservations, immigrant Hispanic communities in the Southwest, and African American hamlets in the Southern Delta—could benefit from the Berea model.

CAPITALIZING ON RURAL STRENGTHS

Although they share with their urban and suburban counterparts many of the poverty-related impediments to teaching and learning, rural communities also face different and often more challenging barriers because of their dearth of assets—financial, structural, and human capital—and patchwork support systems. When the closest pediatrician or dentist is two hours away, school districts must identify new strategies to ensure that students are immunized, that cavities and ear infections are treated before they become harder-to-treat problems, and that asthma is properly monitored. Health-care issues that might not even surface in better-resourced districts can pose real problems in isolated communities. Forming partnerships with local doctors is key to ensuring that students come to school genuinely ready to learn and undistracted by medical issues.

On the other hand, one advantage enjoyed by many rural communities is that people know one another and are joined in networks of close relationships. These relationships are a type of strength often lacking in urban and suburban communities and can be used for the benefit of students. Bright Futures rural affiliates' use of social media to engage community members in meeting students' basic needs shows how communities can combine smart use of technology and of relationship networks to help out children. When social service agencies and private partners cannot immediately address an urgent request, Bright Futures coordinators put out a call on the district's Facebook page. The social media platform enjoys a record of rapid and effective responses from individuals and families. This strategy is especially critical in high-need situations in which social services are stretched thin or virtually nonexistent.

From providing quality early-childhood education and enriching children's after-school hours and summer months to nurturing a college-going culture, rural schools and communities are designing unique strategies to deliver ISS and advance whole-child education. The examples described here offer a range of models that small towns, farming communities, and even isolated "hollers" can adapt to help their schools, educators, and students overcome those barriers.

6

Empowering
Parents to Improve
Student Well-Being

It is often said that parents are children's first and most important teachers, and extensive research backs this up. Parents take the lead in children's earliest formative years, of course. And even after children begin
preschool or kindergarten, they spend more time out of school than in
it. Mothers and fathers can provide learning opportunities in many more
contexts, and they serve as important role models not only with respect to
what they teach their children, but also how they act. For example, parents
who read for pleasure tend to have children who are more likely to do so.
And parents who value education and let their child know that they do
boost their child's odds of achievement and attainment. Parent engagement
in children's education has also been found to provide substantial benefits
at the school level; parent volunteers, strong parent-teacher organizations,

and parent advocacy on behalf of the schools, and their demands of their schools, tend to improve those schools' quality.

But many parents struggle to stay engaged in their children's education and schools. This is especially true today, when in many households, all the available caretakers work outside the home, and schedules are packed with errands and extracurricular activities. Schools serving low-income, largely minority, and immigrant communities face particular barriers. Many of these parents have low levels of formal education themselves and may have had bad experiences as students, making them reluctant to get involved in their children's schools. Because they often struggle to make a decent living, they are more likely to work hourly, multiple, and irregular jobs. It is not easy for them to attend parent-teacher conferences, let alone volunteer at the holiday party or chaperone a field trip. Immigrant parents, especially those whose first language is not English, often struggle to communicate with school administration and their children's teachers, and some may fear an increased risk of deportation, whether or not they are documented.

Several of the communities highlighted in this book, however, have made not only parental engagement, but also parental empowerment, a core component of their work to integrate student support. These examples, across urban, rural, progressive, and conservative districts, illustrate how diverse communities struggling to tackle poverty-related issues can support parents as partners with schools in their children's education. They also show how communities can build up parents' leadership skills. These strategies have yielded not only better outcomes at the family level, but also extensive benefits for schools and the community as a whole.

Despite serving disproportionate shares of low-income, minority, and non-English-speaking students, schools in communities that employ ISS have a leg up when it comes to engaging the parents. Because their school improvement efforts are grounded in identifying and meeting students' needs and strengths, ISS communities understand much better than do most other districts the different circumstances in which families live. Moreover, their whole-child approach to education inherently considers the contributions of parents and families among the factors that must be supported for school to work well. Indeed, these communities not only stand out for strong parent and family engagement, but also encourage parent empowerment—building parents' confidence and ability to be advocates for themselves, their children, and their schools—which has led to deeper and longer-term impact.

COMMUNITY SCHOOLS: PARENTS AS PARTNERS

While parent engagement is not necessarily a core component of an ISS initiative, it is central in schools that characterize themselves as community schools. Parent engagement is, in a sense, baked into the definition, as described by the Coalition for Community Schools: "A community school is *both a place and a set of partnerships* between the school and community resources . . . Using public schools as hubs, community schools bring together many partners to *offer a range of supports and opportunities to children, youth, families, and communities.* Partners work to achieve these results: Children are ready to enter school; students attend school consistently; *families are increasingly involved with their children's education;* [and] *schools are engaged with families and communities.*"[1] Most of the schools that describe themselves as community schools fail to achieve that full definition. Nonetheless, when a school begins the process of becoming a community school, one of the first actions its leaders take is to survey parents about their desires and needs for their children's education.[2]

Parent-school coordinators are embedded in many low-income schools in the Montgomery County School District in Maryland as part of the Linkages to Learning family engagement initiative. These district staff use multiple strategies to connect families with schools and with a range of local resources. At the basic level, the coordinators work with principals and PTAs to encourage parents to attend parent-teacher conferences, because such parental participation increases the benefit their children derive from school. Among the activities the coordinators host are mock sessions where parents learn how to interpret report cards and what key questions to ask. In other cases, the work is more intensive. In one elementary school, where a child of a parent involved with Linkages had cancer, the coordinator collaborated with the PTA to get grocery and gas gift cards and free babysitting vouchers for the family's younger children, so they could regularly visit the child in the hospital. Such outreach builds trust with parents who may be wary of the school leadership, and the support gradually cultivates a corps of parents who take on leadership and even advocacy roles in, and on behalf of, the schools.[3]

Across the large district, however, the Linkages to Learning initiative's resources are spread thin, with many schools that could benefit from them not well served. Partly for this reason, parent engagement remains much weaker in Montgomery County than in most other community school districts studied by BBA.

In addition to full-time community-school coordinators, program co-ordinators, and part-time education coordinators—all of whom work together to ensure that academic, extracurricular, and school-based student supports are aligned—most Children's Aid community schools in New York City also have full-time parent engagement coordinators. The coordinators who work with parents help the schools offer multiple avenues for parent engagement, including adult education classes and programs to help parents support their children's education, as well as cultural events. These schools also provide other services that boost family well-being more broadly. They help parents sign up for benefits for which they might be entitled but don't know how to access, such as health insurance, the earned income tax credit, or immigration assistance. In most schools, parent coordinators also staff a room that has been designated as a family resource center, where parents can relax and interact with each other as well as receiving training or other services. The goal of all these strategies is to make schools attractive places for parents to visit, to become comfortable with, and to gradually grow to see themselves as the schools' partners.

The evolution of that space in one school in Washington Heights illustrates the school's potential power to engage and empower parents. At first, teachers and school leaders at Salome Ureña de Henriquez School were struggling to get parents from the neighborhood, most of whom are immigrants, and many from the Dominican Republic, to engage in even basic ways, like attending parent-teacher conferences. The community-school coordinator noted that discomfort with the school seemed to be a primary barrier and that many of those parents were walking their children to school in the morning. Perhaps the school could take advantage of this morning ritual to get the adults physically in the door. She suggested dedicating a room near the front door as a parents' room and serving coffee as an incentive for parents to step inside.

Soon, the idea evolved into coffee and doughnuts at drop-off time and a space for parents to get together and chat. So the school decided also to use the room to host classes and other events, in response to parents' express needs and interests. One year, a resident from the neighborhood who was a filmmaker taught a class on how parents could use videos to tell their life and community stories. More recently, the room has been used to develop, rehearse, and present jointly produced student-parent plays. (It is also across the hall from the school-based health clinic, giving parents another avenue to be involved.) Perhaps the most powerful sign of how engaged and empowered parents have become, however, is reflected in a local catering business started by several mothers. The school employs the moms to cater school events when possible, giving them not only an additional source of revenue but also exposure to potential clients they would have been unlikely to reach without that help.

Having already established several Family-Community Resource Centers, in 2008 Vancouver Public Schools further enhanced its capacity to engage and empower parents through its new strategic plan. The ambitious vision for increasing equity and excellence across the district involved six elements: instructional quality, flexible learning environments, programs of choice, early learning, safe and supportive schools, and family engagement.[4] (While FCRCs are the key vehicle for family engagement, they play important parts in several other elements as well.) Over the subsequent five years, Vancouver built out resource centers into all thirty-five schools through a combination of expanding in-school centers to seventeen schools and funding two mobile centers that serve the other eighteen schools on a rotating, regular basis.

Site coordinators in each FCRC focus intensively on assessing the needs and strengths of not only their students but also those students' families. Consequently, the coordinators are well positioned to reach out to families and, as coordinators at the elementary, middle, and even high school levels report, they have established deep, trusting relationships with many parents. When a site coordinator who learns that a parent cannot attend an evening meeting gives that family a gas card, the action sends a clear message that the school cares and that the parent's input is important. Likewise, assistance with finding housing or a job, both common forms of support provided by site coordinators, removes stigma from social supports and make parents feel at home in schools. At Fruit Valley Elementary School, a group of mothers, all immigrants from Central America, recount their transition from new arrivals who were intimidated by teachers and principals to frequent volunteers at, and strong advocates for, those schools. These women say that the schools have become their home away from home and their children's path to a bright future. The school's site coordinator proudly describes the key role these *madres* play in recruiting fellow moms (and dads) to volunteer in classrooms and otherwise engage with the school in a variety of ways.

Central-office FCRC staff who work with homeless and chronically absent students add another layer of parent engagement with some of the districts' most vulnerable and disconnected families. Early education programs such as 1-2-3 Grow and Learn bring parents and their young children together to strengthen early bonds, and the early-childhood literacy packets distributed to thousands of new parents help them be excellent "first teachers" to their children. Such initiatives also tend to increase parents' engagement in children's education as children enter and progress through formal schooling.

An especially strong example comes from Austin, Texas, where parent organizing in the city's heavily Hispanic immigrant schools laid the foundations for what has evolved into plans for a districtwide community-school strategy. In the fall of 1991, Austin Independent School District schools were resegregating after desegregation orders were lifted, students in the highest-poverty schools were struggling to raise their test scores, and many students were failing to graduate from high school. In response to these problems, the nonprofit organization Austin Interfaith reached out to Zavala Elementary School, setting in motion a decade-long organizing effort.[5]

By December, Austin Interfaith organizers had been invited to a PTA meeting at Zavala to discuss that work, and in April 1992, members of the nonprofit organized a neighborhood walk to hear parents' perspectives on what was working in their children's schools and what changes they wanted to see.[6] The public assembly that Austin Interfaith held the following month to bring together people who wanted to help improve the city's schools—the Rally for Success—drew about three hundred school district officials, board members, state education officials, and even members of the police department.[7] And with parents' priorities in mind, the organizers decided to first take on the issue of student access to health services, notching an early win when the city committed resources for student immunizations and a new school-based health clinic.

This initial win helped Austin's east-side schools organize into a local network called Alliance Schools. At its height, the movement counted sixteen schools: thirteen elementary schools, along with Kealing and Webb Middle Schools and Johnson High School.[8]

Once the foundations were laid for parent organizing, leaders turned their attention to specific strategies to improve school function and outcomes for students. During the second year of parent organizing work in Zavala, the school's core team introduced several reforms that helped even the playing field for low-income students. Austin Interfaith also worked with district and municipal leaders to create a new teacher pipeline to develop, recruit, and retain more bilingual and special education teachers; create a new position for a parent-support specialist for high-poverty schools; and establish after-school and summer programs and adult English as a second language (ESL) programs.

Through their organizing efforts, Alliance Schools benefited from the teachers' and students' increased awareness of the condition of their school's facilities and from an improved school environment, more student and parent involvement, and stronger school-community relationships. Parents in more-organized schools reported better access to information, better communication with the school and teachers, and more respectful interactions with school staff. Measures related to teacher collegiality, morale, and joint problem-solving were higher in high-involvement schools. The school board was among stakeholders recognizing that this type of reform was very different from and much more effective than others.[9]

The reform was also associated with improved academic performance. Despite serving a higher percentage of low-income, black, Latinx, and English language learner students than the district average, Alliance Schools saw substantial gains, and schools with high levels of engagement in the Alliance Schools network saw greater increases in student test scores than did schools with low levels of engagement.[10]

As discussed next, the Alliance no longer exists in this form. However, the foundations it laid enabled the emergence of two more-recent layers of ISS strategies: efforts to embed social and emotional learning in all Austin Independent School District schools, and community-school efforts that have grown from one struggling high school into a districtwide initiative.

PROMISE NEIGHBORHOODS AND OTHER COMMUNITIES: PARENTS AS LEADERS

In addition to engaging parents in their children's education, many of these districts—like Austin—recognize the importance of empowering parents who have traditionally been ignored or even denigrated by schools. In Orlando's Tangelo Park neighborhood, the Parent Leadership Training program helps parents address their children's academic needs by boosting the adults' decision-making and communication skills. The program, which was launched by the University of Central Florida after consultation with the principal of Tangelo Park Elementary School and the local YMCA, begins by helping parents understand the school system, a common challenge in high-poverty and isolated communities. It then explains the importance of education and helps parents build the kind of leadership skills that help them engage with schools and advocate for their children and their children's schools.[11] (Parents of two-year-old children in the Tangelo Park Program's early education system are also required to take a parenting course, which enables the parents to be more engaged and empowered early in their children's education.)

These programs fill a critical gap in neighborhoods like Tangelo Park. An emerging line of research suggests that public schools are designed to operate effectively for middle-class parents, who are set up to make key decisions for their children, and that most schools thus fail to provide the guidance that less educated parents rely on.[12] Indeed, parents who participate go on to take more active roles in their children's school activities: helping with homework, communicating better with teachers, and volunteering in the classroom. School administrators and YMCA staff have noted parents' increased engagement, and the principal reported that every one of the new School Advisory Council officers was a former participant of the Parent Leadership Training program.[13]

In the distressed Northside neighborhood of Minneapolis, the Northside Achievement Zone uses Promise Neighborhoods grant funds to hire family achievement coaches and family support specialists to work with individual families. Believing that strengthening families is the foundation to children's academic success, parents' abilities to thrive economically, and community revitalization, NAZ puts the family at the center of its work. When a zone family joins the program, it is assigned a coach who works with both parents and children to come up with a family achievement plan and steps to make progress toward it. Coaches also refer families to a range of NAZ and other community resources that help them achieve those goals. Support specialists, who have advanced degrees in relevant fields, are also available to offer additional assistance.

Though it does not receive federal Promise Neighborhoods funding, the East Durham Children's Initiative follows a similar model of parent engagement and empowerment. This commitment is reflected in how the initiative got its start—a 2009 kitchen-table conversation attended by over one hundred community residents launched EDCI—and parents' and caregivers' active participation in their children's education is one of EDCI's six interconnected goals.[14] Early-childhood investments include support for home visits, community story times, and other opportunities to encourage parents as their children's first and most important teachers. And parent advocates serve roles parallel to those of NAZ coaches and specialists—working with families one-on-one to understand their needs, to set goals, and to refer them to resources to help them meet those goals, as well as helping the adults connect with their children's schools in positive and empowered ways. In addition, the Parent and Community Advisory Council, composed of parents and caregivers who are actively involved in EDCI, meets several times a year to discuss identified areas for additional community input.

In Appalachia's tight-knit communities, gaining the support of parents and families is especially critical for children's success. At the same time, the long distances between schools and homes, many parents' limited formal education and discomfort with school administrators, and their lack of understanding about colleges—what and where the colleges are and what they could offer—make parental engagement particularly difficult. Rochelle Garrett, who directs family partnerships for Partners for Education, says that many parents she meets remind her of her own parents: "They are focused on practical outcomes for their kids, meaning getting a job after high school. College might not be on the radar, or if it is, it's more of a distraction than a goal."[15] Her team's work has been made even tougher recently by the growing share of children being raised by their grandparents, and even great-grandparents, because of the opioid epidemic.[16]

To tackle these challenges, PfE hires three family engagement specialists in each county for which it has Promise Neighborhoods funding. The specialists begin to work with parents early in the kids' lives and aim to build relationships that will far outlast the grants that fund their work. In Owsley County, family engagement specialist Sue Christian launched a parent task force to help parents who are like she used to be—intimidated by teachers and principals (people more educated than the parents are) and thus lacking the courage to speak up and ask questions—feel empowered. Christian says her goal isn't for parents to host bake sales; she wants them to embrace their roles as their children's first teachers and as advocates for, and constructive critics of, those kids' schools.

Two programs have proven to be powerful parent engagement tools. In several of its communities, PfE works with the Families and Schools Together (FAST) program, which builds teams of community leaders, school leaders, and parent leaders to strengthen vulnerable and unstable families and connect them to schools.[17] Christian melds FAST funding with a second grant that enables PfE to implement Safe and Secure Children, a birth-to-five program focused on successful transitions to kindergarten. The ten-week relationship-building curriculum addresses issues like healthy eating and grocery shopping, and graduates are connected to the parent task force. Christian believes that despite a big range of ability and stability across families, all the participants benefit, perhaps most of all the parents who come in with little belief in their own capacity. "At the end of the program, parents tell you, 'I'm not as big a muck-up as I thought. There are lots of other parents dealing with the same kinds of things I am.'" She sees evidence, too, that the strategy is working. Recently, the local elementary school announced its plan to stop a weekend food bag program because of concerns that state law limited what students could bring on the bus. A task force parent challenged the decision, pointing out that the school had the authority to clarify the law's intent in its school handbook. As a result, the school's most vulnerable students didn't have go to hungry, and parents recognized their power to get educated and to effect meaningful change.[18]

Parents' discomfort with schools and lack of confidence pose other challenges that are much less pressing in middle-class, suburban schools. So the PfE task force in Owsley County piloted a back-to-school night aimed at stemming parent-child tensions, along with ensuring that parents had a basic understanding of the curriculum and knew who their children's teachers were. Over a hundred parents showed up, bucking the principals' skepticism that anyone would come, and by the fall of 2017, roughly two-thirds of students had a parent participating in the back-to-school nights. These nights are also an opportunity for the task force to check in with schools on supply lists. Christian says that bringing school supplies to hand out at back-to-school night "helps kids show up prepared on the first day. Otherwise, it's three weeks until their parents' next paycheck, and they lose all that time and ground."[19]

Indeed, basic budgeting and money management issues affect family stability and, thus student well-being, now and into the future, especially as these issues pertain to college affordability. Low average family incomes across the region and lack of experience with banks and saving, along with predatory practices in the financial industry, make it important to educate parents about how to spend and save wisely. PfE installed virtual teller machines in several locations and collaborates with a local credit union to teach parents financial literacy. Research shows that a child who has a savings account is more likely to graduate from college, so PfE also works in high schools to teach students how to open savings and checking accounts.[20]

And of course, the physical and social isolation parents experience impedes engagement. Unique strategies developed by PfE showcase the potential for rural communities, in particular, to bridge those barriers to engaging and empowering parents. Two brightly colored Readiness Buses travel across Clay County each week, providing hour-long early-childhood education sessions. As described in more detail in chapter 5, these mobile learning centers offer support to both children and the parents. J. Morgan, who directs communications for PfE, describes the buses' importance: "By working with parents to create their own unique family goals, the early education specialists' design a process that lessens the sense that education is a way to break the family apart."[21]

Schools also bring parents and entire families into schools in the evenings and during the summer. As described earlier, the arts night that showcases students' artwork has become one of Jackson County's most popular events in recent years, with some attendees forced to use overflow parking. At college and career nights, parents can learn about and get help filling out financial aid forms. All Pro Dads brings fathers into schools with their children to read a book each month, while Grilling with Dads and community-wide canning sessions do double duty: engaging families and improving community health.

In tiny Owsley County, Appalachian artist and art consultant Judy Sizemore introduced a new program, Homesong, to help the region's families and communities tell their own stories through theater. English teachers encourage their students to interview family and community members about their lives and histories, which are then woven together by scriptwriters into a play. Berea College student Frankie Jo Baldwin, a graduate of Owsley High School and one of the first students to participate, says that the experience still opens up opportunities for her. At first, she says, people did not believe in the idea or think that anyone would come, but it sold out every night, and now the group does encore performances.

LONG-TERM IMPACTS OF ENGAGEMENT

Over the eight-year period from 1992 to 2000, the Alliance Schools network in Austin grew to involve roughly one-quarter of the district's elementary schools and half of its high-poverty schools. While those efforts faded around 2001 because of pressure from test-based accountability measures, the foundations the network established have helped to surface and strengthen more recent work toward a comprehensive educational approach in the Austin Independent School District.[22]

In 1992, Texas Industrial Areas Foundation (IAF) won a commitment from the state's department of education to direct new funds to low-performing schools through the creation of an investment capital fund. The fund enabled low-performing schools to obtain grants for teacher professional development, parent leadership training, and after-school enrichment activities. The fund also served as an incentive for schools to join the Alliance Schools network.[23] At the same time, parent and community engagement came to be a foundational practice across schools, in part as assistant principals who had been trained at Alliance Schools took the practices they had learned to the schools where they became principals. Austin Interfaith's strong relationship with Pascal Forgione, then district superintendent, also helped spread these practices throughout the district.

IAF organizers came to their work with the goal of using community organizing to help parents, teachers, and administrators jointly reinvent the culture of failing schools. Training in the principles and practices of community organizing helped transform the way each of these groups understood its role in school improvement and how they could work together, as a school community, to achieve shared goals. As Zavala Elementary School parent leader Lourdes Zamarron said: "Reinventing the culture of schools was a radical idea. Before becoming involved in Austin Interfaith, the idea of neighbors changing schools did not make sense. The word *power* was not in my vocabulary."[24] Organizing also helped teachers identify and fight for the academic and enrichment needs they saw in their classrooms.

This organizing ability was channeled into efforts to build community schools starting in 2007, when low test scores brought on threats of closing down first a middle school and then a high school. The threats were met with community resistance and plans to instead bring needed social services and other supports to bear to raise scores and turn the schools around. These efforts have since evolved into a plan to turn thirteen high-poverty district schools into community schools.

Strong parent involvement cultivated by the organizing efforts probably also played a part in making Austin Independent School District the most successful of eight urban districts that participated in a pilot effort to embed social and emotional learning in the schools.[25] Launched in 2010 by the Collaborative for Academic, Social, and Emotional Learning (CASEL), the Collaborating District Initiative aimed to make the nurturing of a much broader set of student skills and abilities a priority for schools. Because they were already engaged in the schools, parents could be more easily informed and involved in that work, and schools that were already connected to the community could draw on those additional resources to make their social and emotional learning work more effective.

The Parent Leadership Training program piloted in Tangelo Park has led the participating parents to take a more active role in their children's school activities, including helping their children with homework, communicating more with teachers, volunteering in classrooms, and even becoming members of the school government. But while these activities have lasting impacts on those parents' children, other influences are even larger. With Tangelo Park solidly successful, in the fall of 2015 sponsor Harris

Rosen began to plan to extend the program into the downtown Orlando neighborhood of Parramore. Parent Leadership Training representatives from Tangelo Park had laid some of the groundwork for the expansion through their earlier training of Parramore parent leaders.[26]

Research shows that such parent involvement and leadership, which is rare in places like Tangelo Park, promotes the advocacy that drives improvements in the schools, from better funding and infrastructure to more effective instruction. And because stronger schools make for stronger communities, the entire city benefits.

7

Using Promise Scholarships to Create Community-Wide Integrated Student Supports

This chapter describes how an unusual motivator—a commitment of college scholarships for all students—can help bring a community together to provide the support that enables more students to attend and complete college. Two very different Promise communities, Orlando's Tangelo Park and Kalamazoo, Michigan, illustrate the power of so-called Promise scholarships to energize the entire community. (Promise scholarships are commitments by either individuals or institutions to cover the costs of college for a specific group of students—a class, a school, or an entire district.)

Key stakeholders who are engaged include city leaders, who see the potential for schools' reputation and success to boost the municipality's financial well-being; business leaders, who stand to benefit from a better-educated and more skilled workforce; social service agencies, whose work is more efficient and effective when supports for students and families are coordinated; faith leaders, who already play supporting roles for families in need and now have more help to do so; and, of course, parents. As this chapter illustrates, there are many ways in which these stakeholders can be engaged through multiple avenues for involvement. These approaches thus vary from one Promise community to another.

This chapter also describes the work of Say Yes to Education, another Promise initiative that incorporates ISS as a core component of its goal of increasing postsecondary success. Say Yes has been in Syracuse for almost a decade and in Buffalo for several years, and it is now starting to implement ISS in Guilford County, North Carolina, and Cleveland. We explore both the parallels and the differences between these and the Promise initiatives in Tangelo Park and Kalamazoo.

Finally, we assess the implications of these example communities for policy and practice. Among other aspects, we examine how the structure of a Promise influences both student enrollment and persistence in college.

WHAT IS A PROMISE, AND HOW DOES IT WORK?

Many low-income students in the United States face a daunting list of obstacles to getting into, and through, college. They are disproportionately likely to attend elementary, middle, and high schools that fail to prepare them for the advanced coursework that many colleges require. Their scores on standardized tests are too low for acceptance to many colleges. These students also typically struggle to navigate the application and financial aid processes and, consequently, lack the means to pay for increasingly expensive higher education. So-called Promise scholarships can remove the latter barrier. *Promises* are commitments to a particular class or school or even an entire school district—usually by wealthy donors or groups of them—to cover the cost of postsecondary education for students who graduate from high school and are accepted to college.

The mechanisms of Promise scholarships vary substantially from one setting to another—for example, they might apply to specific universities; might cover only tuition; or might also include room, board, and other expenses—but the basics look much the same. As described earlier, Say Yes to Education, for example, began as a commitment by millionaire George Weiss to a class of Philadelphia sixth graders. From its start in 1987, Say Yes has evolved into a multicity initiative serving all students in Syracuse and Buffalo (and now expanding to two other school districts).[1] Like their peers in those cities, every student who grows up and goes to school in Tangelo Park is eligible for a full scholarship that has been sponsored for the past two decades by billionaire hotelier Harris Rosen. (This initiative recently expanded to Parramore, a larger Orlando community.) And in Kalamazoo, an anonymous group of local philanthropists made a joint announcement in November 2005 to support the postsecondary education of every student who graduates from the district's high schools.

In all these cases, Promise scholarships address families' and communities' unmet financial needs and remove a key barrier to college attendance for many of their students. Of course, however, Promise financial aid alone does not itself provide adequate preparation and supports for students. The premise of committing to pay for college for every student who graduates prompts concerns about the requisite preparation and achievement among disadvantaged students. These same students, who attend under-resourced high schools, are likely to have been taught algebra and chemistry by uncertified teachers. They probably also attended segregated, high-poverty elementary schools in which the foundations for learning may not have been well established. They were also less likely to have had the advantage of a high-quality preschool. So while Promise scholarships alleviate critical financial barriers to attaining a college education, they do not necessarily address many of the others.

GETTING KIDS TO COLLEGE FROM "DAY ONE"

In some of the most effective Promise communities, scholarship commitments have stimulated greater awareness of, and attention to, prerequisite supports and opportunities necessary for college acceptance and completion. In these communities, the scholarships have spurred community-wide efforts to offer ISS.

Residents of Tangelo Park are particularly lucky that when Rosen first decided that he wanted to invest in the futures of students in that neighborhood, he began by consulting an old friend who is an early-childhood expert. Sara Sprinkle told Rosen that if he wanted his big new investment to pay off, he needed to get kids to school ready to learn from day one. Doing that meant working with local leaders to ensure that every family had access to quality early-childhood education that they could afford— no easy feat.

While the state funds preK for every child, Florida's program is of very poor quality. For this reason, Rosen and his team started from scratch to create a local solution. The Tangelo Park childcare program began in 1995 with two neighborhood home-based providers caring for two-, three-, and four-year-olds. It has since grown to nine or ten providers, depending on how many small children need care in a given year. The providers, who are certified by the state, open their doors at 7:30 in the morning and stay open until 5:00 p.m., Monday through Friday, fifty weeks a year. And all are in neighborhood homes, so parents can walk down the street or around the corner and drop off their child with a neighbor who will be a consistent presence in their child's life from when the child starts to talk until the time he or she enters kindergarten. Nurses and early-childhood specialists who work with providers ensure that the children's health needs are met and that the children reach their developmental milestones.[2] Former Tangelo Park Elementary School principal Diondra Newton remarks on the program's huge positive impact: "This has been so good for the children of Tangelo Park . . . You see a huge difference between kids who did the [early-childhood program] and those who come from elsewhere."[3]

Rosen's commitment spurred a range of other investments by the community in its children and families. Recognizing students' unmet needs with respect to help with homework and mentoring, the Tangelo Baptist Church launched after-school programs to serve students who needed a safe, nurturing space in those hours. Staffed entirely by volunteers, including current and former Tangelo Park Elementary School teachers, the program also offers other support, such as assistance with SAT preparation, to help students take advantage of Promise scholarships. The local YMCA likewise has stepped up, providing enrichment programs as well as instructional support for students who are suspended. And Rosen chipped in, for example, to hire a lifeguard so that Tangelo Park children can take swimming classes.

The Tangelo Park Program's partnership with the University of Central Florida also led to the creation of the parent leadership training program. Designed to help parents partner with schools to boost their children's education, the university program begins by showing parents how to navigate the school system and then helps them build leadership skills so that they can be active supporters of, and advocates for, their children and the children's schools.

Rosen's investment has even drawn in-kind support from far away. Since 2008, Cornell University students have had the opportunity to spend a week in Tangelo Park learning about the program and supporting the community's students. Each spring break, a small group of undergraduates works with Tangelo Park Elementary School teachers to design science and literacy fairs. Rather than going to Daytona Beach or Disney World like many of their peers, the alternative spring break team works with childcare providers to help out for a day. They also are paired up with middle school students to become their mentors for that week, discussing with the teens both the importance of college and the challenges of getting into and succeeding at a school like Cornell, thus building relationships that often continue after the Cornell students return to Ithaca.[4]

In Kalamazoo, the Promise has worked somewhat differently to drive ISS. A midsized Midwestern city halfway between Chicago and Detroit, Kalamazoo has suffered many of the poverty-related challenges of its Rust Belt counterparts, but it also benefits to an unusual degree from the long-standing generosity of local philanthropists. In 2005, an anonymous group of those wealthy individuals came together to announce the creation of a scholarship fund that would operate in perpetuity. The Kalamazoo Promise enables every graduate of the district to enroll, tuition free, in any of fifteen state colleges and universities, including the flagship University of Michigan at Ann Arbor, or to any of dozens of community colleges and technical and vocational institutions.[5] (Other colleges have recently been added.)

Political science professor Michelle Miller-Adams, who has extensively researched and documented the impacts of the Promise, believes that the relative simplicity of Kalamazoo's model—every student who lives and goes to school in the district is eligible for a scholarship—is what makes it such a powerful community development and engagement tool.[6] Its simple, inclusive reach makes people feel that the benefit is intended for their children, not just other people's children (as might be the case, for example, with programs that require minimum GPAs). The specifics of how a Promise is designed—its "dosage," "intensity," "saturation," and other key factors—also influence its impact.[7] The Kalamazoo Promise provides so-called first-dollar scholarships, meaning they are not contingent on students' applying for or receiving other public or private financial aid. Also, the lack of any financial eligibility requirements is likely to render the Kalamazoo Promise particularly sturdy; initiatives that benefit all, like social security, tend to enjoy much greater public support than those, like food stamps and cash welfare benefits, that target the poor.[8]

Pam Kingery, who took the lead of Communities In Schools (CIS) Kalamazoo in 1999, emphasizes the scholarship's power as a catalyst for widespread community engagement. Before the Promise, business leaders that CIS convened to explore how they could help improve Kalamazoo's schools told her, "That's the public schools' issue, not ours." Twelve years later, she says, they embraced their responsibility to help nurture the workforce they want to see.[9] From around 2005 on, as a result, the Kalamazoo Public Schools district has experienced a surge in support from the community. More adults are volunteering in schools, area churches are offering new tutoring and mentoring programs, and the private sector has stepped up to create internship programs that help disadvantaged students gain valuable experience. The Promise also spurred community-wide organizing efforts like the Learning Network of Greater Kalamazoo.[10]

CIS, a national nonprofit that partners with high-poverty schools to provide ISS, had been working in several of Kalamazoo's neediest schools since the early 2000s.[11] Kingery describes the work as having gotten off to a bumpy start, but the creation of the Promise kicked the work into much higher gear.[12] District teachers and principals, who were among the residents most encouraged by the Promise announcement, soon recognized that their many students who were lagging academically would not be able to take advantage of the scholarship program's generosity unless these children received substantial help. So as of 2017–2018, CIS was recruiting over eight hundred volunteer tutors each year, as well as paying "push-in math tutors," who are assigned to freshman algebra classes to work with any students who need extra assistance. CIS also raised funds to run after-school programs and health and dental clinics in several schools and to place social workers—"success coaches"—in both of the district's high schools.

The Promise also prompted the district's schools to step up with a range of supports to help students succeed. Soon after it was implemented, superintendent Michael Rice, who was then new on the job, worked with middle school teachers in several struggling schools to shift their schedules to increase time devoted to core curriculum instruction. The resulting personalized remedial instruction led to improved test scores in language arts, math, or both for most Kalamazoo middle school students. Schools are also working hard to create a college- and career-going culture. Every sixth grader gets a full-day orientation at Western Michigan University, and high schools provide college-readiness classes for every tenth grader. Finally, the district developed a new alternative education program to help students who would not otherwise be eligible for the scholarships, because they would not have graduated from high school, recover credits or learn in a nontraditional environment.[13]

The city's libraries have also gotten involved, supporting both early-childhood and K–12 education. They collaborate with schools to host reading and homework help programs and, because many children lack books in their homes, ensure that all district students have library cards and use them regularly.[14] After the inception of the Promise, the grassroots, church-based After School Homework Center expanded into Pathways to the Promise; it now offers many more kinds of support, all aimed at getting more students prepared for college. Pathways provides teen homework and summer enrichment programs as well as a parent program that helps parents develop plans to better support their children's education. Retired church members and teachers serve as mentors, aides, counselors, and even program evaluators. In addition, small grant funds are used to hire teens as teacher aides and tutors and to provide small gifts to families that have graduated from the program.[15]

As in Tangelo Park, the Kalamazoo Promise also spurred conversations about making sure that young children start school ready to learn and thus the importance of investments in early-childhood education. (Michigan has a high-quality state preK program that serves many low-income Kalamazoo students, but some do not qualify or cannot get slots.) Upjohn Institute economist Timothy Bartik, a member of the school board in the Promise's early years, is a longtime advocate of public investments in preK programs. Bartik's 2007 conversation with Rice about developing a universal preK program in Kalamazoo led to a series of community-wide meetings in 2008 and 2009, culminating in the 2010 convening of a larger committee to develop a plan for a universal preK program.[16] Kalamazoo's Ready 4s, which builds on the state's preK program, has substantially increased the number of children served and the quality of their early education settings.[17] As of 2015–2016, it served 432 children and their families in eleven of the district's seventeen elementary schools.

PROMISE PLUS ISS: A STRONG RECORD OF RESULTS

The combined impacts of Promise scholarships and the wraparound supports they have spurred are impressive. A survey of Kalamazoo students, parents, teachers, and other community stakeholders finds large improvements in school climate, teacher expectations, and student motivation.[18] Detentions and suspensions, which pose major barriers to achievement, have decreased substantially, especially among African American students. More scholarship-eligible students are earning high school credits, and greater numbers of disadvantaged students are taking AP courses. (Both trends suggest that schools' efforts to create a college-going culture is taking hold.) Gains in AP course-taking roughly quadrupled among both low-income (from 53 to 193) and African American students (from 63 to 263). At the same time, the modest enrollment of 8 Hispanic students who had taken such courses in 2007–2008 shot up nearly tenfold, to 78, in 2014–2015.[19]

The benefits of the scholarship funds themselves are also being widely used. Depending on the graduation year, between 80 and 90 percent of Kalamazoo Public Schools graduates are eligible for at least some benefits, and of those, more than four in five students have used them at some point.[20] Moreover, as options for scholarships have expanded, so have both the proportion of students attending college and their odds of postsecondary success. The graduating classes of 2006 through 2014 could have used the Promise scholarship at any one of the state's forty-four public colleges or universities, and starting with the class of 2015, the options now also include fifteen private liberal-arts colleges that are members of the Michigan Colleges Alliance.[21] A rigorous Upjohn Institute study finds large increases in college enrollment, credits attempted, and success. The authors estimate a 14 percent increase in the odds of college enrollment within six months of high school graduation and a 34 percent increase in the chance of enrollment in a four-year college.[22] Scholarship recipients are also substantially more likely to earn a postsecondary credential, with the proportion increasing from a baseline of 36 percent to 48 percent, four-fifths of that increase attributable to the attainment of bachelor's degrees.

In Tangelo Park, early indicators of success of the Promise program and ISS included a marked increase in the share of children who were coming to kindergarten ready to learn across a range of domains—90 percent or above, depending on the metric—and a reduction in mobility (student transience) among students from around 50 percent to virtually none. As Tangelo Park scholarship-eligible high school graduates increasingly came from the ranks of those who had started their academic careers in the neighborhood's early-childhood education program, rates of high school completion and of college enrollment and completion began to rise dramatically. Between 2005 and 2012, as the state's rate for on-time (within four years) high school graduation rose from 59 to 76 percent, the proportion of Tangelo Park students (who are much poorer than their average state peers) graduating with this diploma was at least 90 percent, with a 100 percent graduation rate in both 2011 and 2012. Of Tangelo Park students who enroll in four-year postsecondary schools, over three-quarters attain a degree, and an even higher share—83 percent—who choose vocational programs complete them. And among the small minority who pursue graduate degrees, more than nine in ten obtain them.

These are extraordinarily high levels of postsecondary success for a heavily poor, mostly African American community. To put these numbers

in context, one researcher who produced estimates based on income pre-
dicts, for an average community with Tangelo Park's income level, roughly
50 college degrees since 1994, or 9 to 12 percent of students completing
these degrees. However, in that time, 118 Tangelo Park Program students
have earned bachelor's degrees and 54 have completed associate's degrees
(including 32 students who earned both). Tangelo Park has also produced
24 graduate degrees, including 3 doctorates.

SAY YES AND THE EXPANSION OF PROMISE COMMUNITIES

Disappointingly, most other communities that have designated themselves
as Promise districts have not adopted ISS. And as Noradeen Farlekas, who
conducted her doctorate research on the burgeoning Promise field, says,
this absence of integrated support probably explains the failure of many
programs to translate scholarship commitments into substantial boosts
in high school graduation rates and college enrollment and completion.
Programs that *do* embed ISS, conversely, confer a range of advantages:
"Integrated programs [like Tangelo Park], when implemented successfully,
provide disadvantaged low-income students with the services that help
them to successfully utilize the available tuition benefits. Additionally, the
integrated programs with long histories have the benefit of time and experience to continuously improve the content and timing of the programs
that they offer students."[23]

But the other prominent national Promise initiative we've discussed, Say
Yes to Education, has made ISS a core component of its postsecondary success strategy. Say Yes began like many Promise scholarship initiatives—a
commitment by a millionaire, George Weiss, to a class of 112 sixth graders
that if they graduated from high school and were accepted to college, he
would pay for their tuition.[24] But when many of those Philadelphia students
failed to take him up on it, Weiss recognized that the scholarships alone
were not enough to help elementary school kids who were already far

behind catch up and prepare for college-level work. Successive groups of students in Hartford, Connecticut, and Harlem benefited from tutoring, mentoring, summer enrichment, and other wraparound supports designed to fill those gaps.

In 2007, Mary Anne Schmitt-Carey, CEO of Say Yes, persuaded Weiss that assessing the effectiveness of the strategy to boost college enrollment and completion and proving that it was scalable required piloting it in a full school district. Unlike Tangelo Park and Kalamazoo, the Promise work in Syracuse involved, from its inception, a comprehensive school improvement and student-support effort. To secure the Say Yes program's commitment of scholarships for all its graduates, the Syracuse City School District had to collaborate with the city and other key stakeholders to allow Say Yes to conduct a top-to-bottom assessment of the school system and make the substantial changes that the program believed were needed for boosting student outcomes. In addition to embedding more counselors and social workers in schools, making summer enrichment opportunities available to disadvantaged students, and developing family engagement and support programs, Say Yes dived deep into the details of school structure and operations. It also invested in the development of a comprehensive data collection system—the postsecondary planning system described earlier—that is designed to support individual student assessment and growth plans. Another factor that distinguishes Say Yes from the other Promise initiatives described here is its requirement that the local community match or exceed its investment to receive the organization's support. Say Yes makes substantial demands on the communities for procedures and resources designed to make the data-driven Promise program successful and sustainable.

After achieving some progress in Syracuse but also encountering major obstacles, Say Yes announced its expansion to a second, larger, and more challenging city, Buffalo. Starting in 2014, Say Yes has employed the data system it began to develop in Syracuse to assess every students' needs and strengths and to target a range of academic, physical, mental health, and other resources to address them. It has since begun work in Guilford County, North Carolina, and planned to begin work in Cleveland in the fall of 2018, with the postsecondary planning system at the heart of efforts in both places.

There are now dozens of other privately funded Promise programs across the country, as well as others that are publicly funded. According to a database compiled by the Upjohn Institute, as of 2018, there were ninety programs that met its criteria for place-based scholarship programs, excluding state-based merit scholarships like Georgia's HOPE (Helping Outstanding Pupils Educationally) or Tennessee's statewide Promise program. (The University of Pennsylvania's Graduate School of Education has created a map that shows the locations of numerous Promise initiatives, including the state need- and merit-based programs that Upjohn excludes, as well as scholarships from individual higher education institutions.[25]) Programs vary substantially in terms of saturation (the proportion of students who are eligible in a locality, according to several factors) and intensity (how much the scholarship helps defray the cost of, and thus barriers to, college).[26] As Upjohn notes, these two factors, taken together, largely determine the Promise's impact on enrolling more students in college and the students' success there.

APPLYING WHAT WORKS NOW FOR MODELS OF THE FUTURE

The systemic, up-front embedding of wraparound supports for students' physical and mental health and after-school and summer enrichment opportunities distinguish the Say Yes efforts from Kalamazoo Promise, where ISS has evolved organically, but more unevenly. The ISS work in Syracuse and Buffalo is also different from that in Tangelo Park, where a single philanthropist can effectively support the small, contained, single-neighborhood effort. These examples thus provide a useful range of Promise-driven community-level strategies that can help guide future investments in ISS.

One key consideration is the level, type, and depth of community engagement. In Kalamazoo, the scholarships prompted school leaders to explore reforms to help at-risk students be better prepared to take advantage of these benefits. Other community stakeholders, such as libraries and the city's symphony and churches, followed in developing new programs to enhance support for students. The growth of CIS was likewise a response to this demand by community business and other leaders. And while Tangelo Park's efforts were enabled by Harris Rosen's financial largesse, the team he assembled to lead the effort comprised local education, school, and nonprofit leaders, so those efforts, too, were informed and shaped by neighborhood assets and needs.

Indeed, Tangelo Park had already been an organized neighborhood when Rosen identified it for support. In the early 1990s, when low-income African American communities across the country were being decimated by drug sales, addiction, and disproportionate arrests, a group of neighborhood leaders joined forces to prevent their neighborhood from being destroyed. Rather than relying on police, the residents walked their streets each night and confronted local teens—the children of their friends, in many cases—and largely put a stop to drug dealing in Tangelo Park. As one of those residents, Sam Butler, describes, "We had a nucleus of people who were not willing to accept the crime, the drugs, the 'mischief' that some other neighborhoods sort of laid down for. We wanted a better place for our children, a safe environment to raise them, and we believed that we could do something about it."[27] That cohesion was one reason Rosen believed that the Promise would work. His efforts have intentionally leveraged and enhanced community collaboration and cohesion. For example, building up existing neighborhood, home-based early childcare providers further strengthened community bonds, as has support for the local YMCA and church. All these choices make the Promise something in which the community has a personal sense of ownership.

As previously described, Say Yes came into Syracuse and Buffalo with a plan for providing a range of student support that, while informed by needs assessments, was grounded in the organization's existing theory of action. Say Yes chief operating officer Eugene Chasin believes that the failure of Say Yes both to solicit community input in Syracuse from the start and to clarify plans with school leaders and others who are key to its work were major obstacles to the level of hoped-for success. "In Syracuse, some viewed [Say Yes] as an outsider—'Park Avenue going in, telling them what to do,' said [Chasin]. 'Buy-in and commitment did not get transmitted to mid-level administrators and principals . . . We were much more humble going into Buffalo . . . I met with over 100 community-based organizations before we launched. It was a very different approach.'"[28]

And while all Promise scholarships spurred a range of student and family support, the specific type of support given has also influenced the effort's success. Tangelo Park and Kalamazoo recognized early on that better preparing students for kindergarten would be critical to the students' later success in school, their odds of graduating, and, thus, their ability to take advantage of those scholarships. As a result, both districts have improved their early-childhood education systems to put children on a more even playing field from the start. (Say Yes helped establish committees in both Syracuse and Buffalo to address issues related to early-childhood development and the dearth of affordable, high-quality early-childhood education. However, because their agendas focus on connecting families to existing resources and, in the case of Buffalo, increasing developmental screenings, the committees have not necessarily increased families' access to quality childcare or early education.)

The systematic nature of the Say Yes investment (in contrast to Kalamazoo and Tangelo Park), along with the sophisticated data system it developed to assess student needs and to meet those needs, means that students in Syracuse and Buffalo are more likely than their counterparts in Kalamazoo to have tutors, mentors, and other resources to help them succeed in school. (For Tangelo Park, the combination of its small, contained area and its individual "sponsor" makes it better able to achieve much the same level of support in different ways.)

Given the emphasis that Say Yes to Education places on school-based strategies such as professional development and curriculum reform as part of its comprehensive plan for school and city improvement, communities may want to consider their own roles as well. Moreover, both of those communities also enacted some reforms to school practices, such as the enhanced focus on STEM instruction in Tangelo Park and expanded time for core instruction in Kalamazoo middle schools, although these reforms were not part of Tangelo Park's and Kalamazoo's initial visions for improving student access. We understand, and urge policy makers to acknowledge, that in-school and out-of-school strategies are complementary and mutually reinforcing, affecting one another and student well-being in myriad ways.

Finally, as noted prior, the details of the Promise scholarships themselves affect students' ability to access scholarships and persist in postsecondary education institutions. Both Kalamazoo and Tangelo Park are unusually generous, requiring neither financial need nor academic requirements of their students to fund their full tuition.[29] Tangelo Park's Promise covers not only room and board, but even textbooks and other supplies. Although they may seem like minor costs to middle-class families, the cost of these supplies poses an obstacle to low-income students' abilities to pay for college.

The requirements for Promise-eligible students is perhaps more important. Because the Kalamazoo Promise provides first-dollar scholarships, students need not apply for, or obtain money from other sources, such as federal Pell grants or merit scholarships from the college. Say Yes, on the other hand, requires students to first apply for any eligible financial aid (a so-called last-dollar approach). But Say Yes offers scholarships to more colleges, including several prestigious private institutions, than do Tangelo Park and Kalamazoo. Tangelo Park funds only public colleges, and Kalamazoo just added fifteen private ones in 2015. Like Tangelo Park, Say Yes provides last-dollar scholarships, but unlike Tangelo Park, Say Yes scholarships do not cover room and board or books and supplies.

Say Yes funds tuition at public colleges—the State University of New York and City University of New York—but as mentioned, one of its major focuses is building a network of participating private colleges. (And, as just noted, Say Yes also makes major demands on the municipality and the community, not least of which is coming up with a lot of money for scholarships and support.) The Say Yes compact includes over one hundred institutions, including highly selective universities and small liberal-arts colleges with great retention and completion statistics. In addition, through a partnership with Southwest Airlines, Say Yes flies scholars and their parents to visit, interview at, or travel to schools that are part of the Say Yes compact.

Given the difficulty that first-generation college-goers tend to have at very competitive colleges, the emphasis on making these colleges accessible, in itself, may not be the best way to increase completion among such students. (Tangelo Park, conversely, emphasizes access to community colleges and vocational or technical schools, which are often better acquainted with the life realities of low-income students.) At the same time, Bartik and his colleagues attribute some of the increase in Kalamazoo students' increased college persistence to the ability of students who would otherwise have enrolled in less selective colleges to choose more-selective schools that offered them higher odds of success. Several factors probably contribute to the students' success at the more competitive schools: the selective schools' higher levels of resources to provide needed supports, the quality of the faculty, and greater expectations among peers, among other factors. And Say Yes has focused on ensuring that the smaller colleges it solicits to join the compact will be good fits for its students.

In the design of Promise scholarship programs, there is a natural tension between the desire to make scholarships as accessible as possible (first-dollar scholarships) and the need to make the most efficient and effective use of scarce scholarship funds and endowments (last-dollar scholarships). Promise leaders must grapple with this tension and, ultimately, in their design, decide which kinds of scholarships will accomplish the greatest long-term good in their communities. Similarly, the decision to include or exclude various kinds of colleges—for example, public or private—can make a huge difference in the implications of a scholarship design.

Issues of affordability and the colleges' capacity to support low-income and first-generation students also point to a different kind of Promise, that offered by Berea College to provide tuition-free education to promising students who face a host of barriers—financial, social, and other—to becoming the first in their families to attend college. As previously described, the college enrolls only at-risk students, most of them from Appalachia and many the first in their families to go to college, and it charges no tuition. With its commitment to supporting these students' social and other needs and to helping them graduate debt-free, Berea offers another model for postsecondary support and success. Like the Tangelo Park and Kalamazoo programs, the approach offered by Berea—the only college that currently offers such support—could be adapted to various contexts.

Whether it is through the creation of new Bereas or additional Promise communities or the scaling up and enhancement of existing Promise programs, grounding ISS in a commitment to make a college degree accessible and affordable for many more students is a powerful strategy. We are encouraged by the number of communities that have been inspired by Kalamazoo, Tangelo Park, Syracuse, and Buffalo, and we urge further research to explore which aspects of Promise commitments are the most effective and how to best use the Promise strategy to increase college enrollment and completion.

8

Empowering Mayors to Create Citywide Supports

The By All Means Consortium

The Education Redesign Lab at the Harvard Graduate School of Education was founded by one of us (Paul Reville) in 2013 to address the problem of persistent achievement gaps so readily evident across the country after twenty years of arduous, expensive school reform. Reville postulated that education reform in particular and the nation's school system in general, even in high-performing states like Massachusetts, had been unable to close achievement gaps at scale. As former chair of the Massachusetts Board of Elementary and Secondary Education and former secretary of education under Governor Deval Patrick, Reville echoed the conclusions that Richard Rothstein outlined years earlier in the book *Class and Schools*.[1] While Massachusetts had substantially boosted average test scores—the state's students were now on par with the top-performing countries on international tests of skills and ability—low-income students, students of color, immigrant children, and kids with disabilities continued to lag far behind their better-off peers. Reville and Rothstein argued that schools alone, as currently constituted, could not address these disadvantages. Consequently, the schools could not be expected to educate all students to the high levels necessary to achieve the nation's explicit policy goal: preparing all children for success.

Through movement-building, field work, and research, the lab posed a design question: if we could build a system of child development and education from scratch (instead of retooling an education system built for other purposes in the distant past), what would it look like? The lab's By All Means (BAM) initiative aimed to set up a nationwide cohort of laboratories in six communities that are committed to building the new integrated architecture—systems of support and opportunity—needed to fortify a twenty-first-century system of child development and education. Like the other communities featured in this book, these six cities understood that poverty and related factors were at the center of challenges facing their children, families, and schools. These communities developed comprehensive strategies to diminish the negative impact of poverty on students' educational achievement.

BAM's work began with mayoral leadership, since the redesign lab sees the imperative of preparing all children for success as a community-wide challenge, not just a school department one. In 2018, BAM completed its first two-plus-year cycle with six cities that committed to trying to build systems to meet every child where he or she is in early childhood and to give these children the supports they need, inside and outside school, to succeed at each stage of the education system. And with this support, the students would emerge with some postsecondary education and be ready for high-skill/high-knowledge employment, citizenship, and lifelong learning.

BAM's theory of action and point of entry into this system change intentionally begins with mayors because, as noted, BAM believes that schools alone haven't gotten the equity job done and that it takes an entire community to achieve the goal of preparing all children for success. Mayors are not just school leaders; they're community leaders. BAM operates on the underlying premise that the changes needed to make schools effective in closing achievement gaps and preparing all children for success go far beyond schools and must engage the entire community. Therefore, the lab sought mayors who shared these beliefs and were willing to commit their political and financial capital to this collaborative work. The mayors chosen for the first cohort all expressed a conviction that their community's prosperity depends on the success of the city's children and that achieving success at scale will require much more than simply providing an adequate school system.

To participate in BAM, the mayors had to commit to convening children's cabinets composed of the community's leading children's servers and advocates, both inside government and out. These cabinets typically include the superintendent of schools and people like health commissioners, parks and recreation or arts and culture leaders, community-based and parent organizations, philanthropic leaders, and some union and elected officials. These collaborative bodies are then charged with setting goals for providing better support and opportunities to children, devising strategies, gathering data, conducting evaluations, and holding parties accountable for progress.

BAM's belief in the centrality of mayors to this kind of collaboration is based not only on the recognition that schools alone are insufficient to prepare children for success, but also on the power of mayors to convene key leaders from multiple sectors to focus on developing interagency strategies for meeting children's needs. The initiative challenged the mayors and their cabinets to personalize education for all children, to attack impediments to children's attendance at school and readiness to learn, and to create system-wide opportunities that level the playing field with respect to out-of-school learning and enrichment. BAM believes that mayors are uniquely qualified to bring leaders together, to create a sense of urgency, to cultivate meaningful collaboration, and to hold the various parties accountable for achieving results. BAM's distinctive focus on the primacy of mayors sets this initiative apart from others. We hope that the work BAM is doing, and the observations in this chapter, will help reframe the discussion about the important role of mayors in education and encourage more mayors, and more communities, to expand the scope of their child development and education work while tapping rich community resources.

A MAYOR-DRIVEN SOCIAL COMPACT FOR CHILDREN

The Education Redesign Lab's conviction that mayors are the key to creating a new social compact for children seems prescient in the current political climate, which features a local-control-oriented federal government and highly distracted state governments. For some years, the federal government has been gradually shifting away from its strong involvement in the No Child Left Behind Act and the Race to the Top, both of which had created financial incentives strong enough to drive state education policy for decades. The Every Student Succeeds Act, which replaced No Child and shrinks the federal role in education accountability, became law during the final year of Obama's presidency. The arrival of the Trump administration's antigovernment cabinet, including Betsy DeVos at the helm of the Department of Education, has accelerated this devolution of the federal role to the local level.

Urban policy experts such as Bruce Katz and Jeremy Nowak have argued for a "new localism" in which cities and communities are the drivers of action and policy innovation. As they write in *The New Localism: How Cities Can Thrive in the Age of Populism,* "Cities and counties are solving problems because they can. The knowledge-intensive industries that increasingly dominate the U.S. economy seek the convergence of assets that many U.S. cities already possess: anchor research institutions and collaborative ecosystems."[2] For mayors, though, this new localism is nothing new. Although the federal government has provided, at different times, more or fewer resources along with varying degrees of regulation and account- ability, local communities have always been the direct providers of services to residents. Mayors are already keenly aware of the tight relationship between poverty and life trajectories at every stage and in every dimen- sion of the life span.

The question is not whether mayors understand the problem, but whether they use their political capital to address it. A decade ago, there was no shortage of "education mayors" who made public schooling a core focus of their tenures. In recent years, fewer mayors have taken on this mantle, as school reform has hit a plateau, even where it has been suc- cessful in raising overall student achievement. Contentious debates over charter schools and statewide assessments, along with the intractability of poverty, have left many mayors wary of wading in. A few committed mayors, though, are stepping forward to lead on these issues, and it is with those that the lab is partnering, through BAM, to create locally designed and built webs of support and fields of new opportunity for children. These initiatives go beyond schools to embrace the myriad needs and strengths of children growing up in poverty. As Oakland, California, mayor Elizabeth "Libby" Schaaf has said, "As mayors, we have the opportunity to change how public systems work, as opposed to just starting another program. We also have the opportunity to scale things . . . As the controllers of these giant public systems that affect everybody, we can change culture. We can change the expectations and beliefs of an entire generation of children. There is no nonprofit organization that can deliver that kind of promise, and we should really be aware of that opportunity that only government has."[3]

KEY ELEMENTS OF BY ALL MEANS

BAM was launched in 2016 with a group of six cities: Louisville, Kentucky; Providence, Rhode Island; Oakland, California; and the cities of Salem,

Somerville, and Newton in Massachusetts. In choosing the cities to participate, the lab looked for these attributes:

Mayoral commitment and leadership: Mayoral commitment to the organizing principles of BAM and willingness to lead a collaborative-action approach was the first essential element for a city's participation. Addressing all the factors affecting children's well-being requires a citywide effort, which BAM believes starts with strong leadership from the top. Mayors have the unique political capital and convening power to make BAM a high-visibility, high-impact effort.

City-school district partnership: While mayoral leadership is central to the lab's theory of action, schools are and will continue to be the hub of service provision for children. BAM aims to create a broad coalition that shares the responsibility for children with the schools. For this to happen, the mayor and school superintendent must have both a strong working relationship and a shared commitment to the BAM work.

Existing work: By design, each of the cities chosen for the consortium had already begun to take action toward a more comprehensive approach to serving children. The expectation was that BAM would build on and accelerate these actions. BAM would knit together the various initiatives under a single framework, rather than helping cities build something completely new. In some cases, when BAM came on board, cities already had a substantial number of initiatives under way.

Stability: Although there is no way to guarantee this—as illustrated by the unexpected leadership departures in several BAM cities—the lab looked for cities that appeared to have some degree of stability in their key leadership positions. It also looked for sites that were relatively stable financially, while recognizing that cities and school districts, especially high-poverty ones, face constant financial pressures.

Size: The lab intentionally targeted small and midsize cities for BAM, since these offered the greatest chance of success and learning in the early stages of the work. Smaller cities tend to be less organizationally complex, making it easier for them to enact policy and programmatic changes relatively quickly.

CORE COMMITMENTS AND SUPPORTS

Because BAM is designed to be experimental (the lab sought to learn from the fieldwork of its "laboratory" cities), with variation across cities, the lab initially took a light-touch approach to core city commitments and supports it offered. This method fits with the approaches taken by the other communities featured in this book; that is, with a broad range of assets and needs, each community adapted its ISS strategy to draw on its specific assets and meet its unique needs. The result is a diverse set of strategies. Each city agreed to participate in the following required elements of BAM's model, and the lab provided resources on best practices rather than prescriptive requirements on how to best implement or take advantage of them:

Children's cabinet: Children's cabinets provide the governance structure for each city's BAM work. These cabinets create a high-level mechanism to coordinate services for children across municipal and nongovernmental organizations. Each city in the consortium has formed a cabinet that is chaired by the mayor and is cochaired by the school district superintendent or another city leader. The cabinet includes representation from health and social services and other government and community organizations.

Facilitator: To ensure that the work of the cabinet moves forward expeditiously between cabinet meetings, the lab supports a part-time consultant facilitator in each city. The lab and the cities worked together to identify candidates for these positions. In some cases, the consultants already had deep local experience, while in others, they were newcomers to the city. The role is envisioned as a process facilitator rather than a content expert, since the consultant's ability to manage the change process is key to making and sustaining progress.

Twice-yearly meetings: To further support the cities' work, the lab sponsors a series of semiannual conferences at the Harvard Graduate School of Education. Starting with the first gathering in May 2016, city teams have come together five times with lab staff and outside experts to deepen and accelerate the work and to build opportunities for cross-city sharing of information and resources. Each meeting includes panels of top education and policy experts, "team time" for each city's members to work together within their own team, and opportunities for cross-city sharing of progress and challenges. The lab also arranges for individual meetings between cities and experts in particular areas of interest, such as financing, equity, or early-childhood education, to enable one-on-one coaching.

Documentation and evaluation: Cities agreed to participate in ongoing documentation and evaluation—research that serves several purposes. It shares lessons with a broader audience; helps cities track their progress on a range of process, opportunity, and outcome measures; and informs the lab's iterative approach to supporting the cities in this work. This research has included multiple interviews with the mayors, superintendents, and other cabinet members as well as observations of cabinet meetings.

Additional support: The lab offers additional support, which is tailored to the needs of each city. It includes Reville's and others' participation in key city events, helping cities identify and connect with program partners and potential funders, and assistance with data use and outcome measures.

MAYORS AT THE CENTER

Starting with the first BAM gathering in the spring of 2016, mayors literally took center stage. That initial event consisted of a day-long symposium that made the case for citywide approaches to improving children's opportunities and a second day for the city teams to work together to develop their plans for action. The highlight of the event was a public forum in which the mayors discussed the challenges facing children in their communities and the need to do better. The mayors committed themselves, and their cities, to taking on this challenge.

Several of the mayors, including Jorge Elorza of Providence, had personal reasons for joining BAM. Elorza's experience as the son of immigrants whose schooling ended before high school, and his own circuitous path to academic and professional success, fueled his commitment to Providence's children: "There are a lot of kids in our schools that have a great deal of potential, but have for some reason or another veered in the wrong direction. I want to make sure that we build systems so that every single one of them can stay on course as a matter of course, and not against all odds."[4]

Recognizing the leadership challenges of this work, the redesign lab built into BAM a number of supports for mayors. Ron Heifetz, professor at Harvard's John F. Kennedy School of Government, developed the idea of adaptive leadership and led sessions for mayors and superintendents at several of the conferences. In these and other sessions just for mayors, participants could frankly discuss the complex challenges of leading collaborative work and potential ways to tackle these challenges. The relationships that mayors formed with one another also proved meaningful, giving the civic leaders opportunities to learn from one another over time and to share their own accomplishments at the conferences.

BUILDING CITYWIDE MOVEMENTS

During the early stages of BAM, the cities in the consortium created children's cabinets if they did not already have one, identified specific areas of focus for their work, and usually began implementing initiatives directly benefiting children. Among the initiatives the cabinets have undertaken are increasing access to preschool, improving behavioral health services, expanding access to personalized learning and summer programming, and implementing individualized supports and enrichment plans. Several cities have also focused on creating data-sharing agreements between different agencies. In each case, the goal is to move toward creating systems of ISS to enable every child to come to school ready to learn every day. In addition, each city has identified an initial set of measures by which it will track its progress, and most cities have either secured funding or developed a funding strategy.

Community understanding of, and demand for, a comprehensive agenda to support children is important for long-term sustainability, especially as the work begins to involve changing practices and new funding. As Somerville mayor Joseph Curtatone said at the first BAM conference, "To do the necessary work, you need the engagement of every ally and stakeholder in the community . . . We all have to own it, and we all have to do the work."[5]

Initially, community engagement efforts focused on ensuring that the cabinets included representation of community-based organizations. As the work has progressed, most cities have begun developing strategies for engaging their communities more directly and linking the elements of BAM to create a citywide movement. Providence held a community-based education summit in the spring of 2017, with grant support facilitated by the lab, to solicit input on a cohesive local vision for education. The All In: Providence Education Summit, facilitated by a local community organizer, included over four hundred students, teachers, and other community members. That summit resulted in a report with recommendations that are being incorporated into the BAM work.

Several other cities are giving the work a name, such as Our Salem, Our Kids, or Louisville Promise, as a way of framing and messaging a complex set of undertakings. Other efforts to engage the community include the cocreation of a short elevator speech that Louisville cabinet members can use to describe goals and actions using common language, and Salem's development of a website that describes the comprehensive work and includes links to a broad set of community resources. Although these efforts are still in the early stages, cities are finding that engaging with their communities more actively—particularly the high-poverty communities they are hoping to improve—is an important component of the work and is likely to be an effective strategy for sustaining momentum through leadership changes.

This timeline for community input and engagement contrasts with that of most of the other communities highlighted in this book. In the other communities, the initial impetus for adopting ISS came from school or community leaders, or both. In a city-led initiative, of course, the engagement of involved parties will be slightly different. Community engagement becomes a bigger challenge for ISS initiatives in cities than it is in towns or clusters of schools within cities. This is one reason, for example, that scaling up ISS work in Austin, Texas, and Montgomery County, Maryland, has been more complicated than in a city the size of Vancouver, Washington, or the tiny town of Pea Ridge, Arkansas.

FINDING FUNDING FOR CITYWIDE INITIATIVES

Obtaining funding for new efforts is a perennial challenge, but it is one that mayors are uniquely positioned to address, both by identifying priorities for new public investment and by finding the means to fund them. Several mayors have used their leverage to help raise money for their cities' BAM and other child-focused efforts.

In Salem, Mayor Kimberley Driscoll expended significant political capital in 2017 on behalf of an effort to bring ISS to schools by pushing through a funding mechanism that the city council did not initially support. Her persistence resulted in substantial benefits for K–8 students that fall. In Oakland, Mayor Schaaf has used her prominent position to raise millions of dollars in scholarships for students. One such effort, an annual birthday celebration, raises money for the cause. Major donors include Kaiser Permanente, the Benioffs (of Salesforce), and Pacific Gas and Electric Company.

SUSTAINING INITIATIVES DURING LEADERSHIP TURNOVER

A key challenge for any mayor-led initiative is how to sustain it beyond the tenure of a given mayor. Of the six mayors who began BAM, five remained in 2018. Mayors Greg Fischer of Louisville, Elorza of Somerville, and Schaaf of Oakland successfully secured reelection in November 2018, and Mayor Curtatone of Somerville and Mayor Driscoll of Salem won reelection in 2017. Setti Warren of Newton opted to run for governor in 2018 and consequently did not run for reelection in 2017. The work in Newton did suffer somewhat because of the transition.

Two of the six original BAM superintendents also left. Antwan Wilson opted to leave Oakland to become the chancellor of District of Columbia Public Schools, and Jefferson County (Louisville) superintendent Donna Hargens resigned under pressure from the local school board. In both these cases, the BAM work persisted. In Oakland, the mayor's office and advocates on the children's cabinet kept the initiative moving while the new superintendent, Kyla Johnson-Trammel, was being chosen. In Louisville, Marty Pollio, a strong BAM supporter, was appointed relatively quickly to succeed Hargens. Louisville navigated this transition smoothly because the cabinet had already identified and articulated a shared vision for children before the superintendent's departure. When encountering this obstacle and others, the cabinet members agreed that the work was too far along to stop or slow.

Although it is too early to assess the long-term persistence of BAM in any city, the participants have identified several factors as most central to the initiative's continuation during changes in school district leadership. These factors include the continued support of the mayor, the continuity of key staff, the cross-agency relationships developed among staff, the existence of tangible plans to carry out the work, and the strength of broad-based support in the cabinet and the community.

MINI CASE STUDIES

We conclude this chapter with short descriptions of what the work looks like in two of the BAM cities, Oakland and Salem. We hope these examples will give readers a more real-time, in-depth understanding of what it takes to build a mayor-led campaign for ISS, including challenges and how communities face them.

Oakland

Oakland is an ethnically diverse, midsize city just east of San Francisco. The Bay Area tech boom has brought an influx of workers, new restaurants, and a youthful energy to the city. It has also brought the challenges of gentrification, including stark income inequality and an acute housing crisis. In just a five-year period between 2011 and 2016, the median home price nearly doubled, and homelessness has become such a widespread problem that the city has put up storage sheds for temporary housing as a stopgap measure.[6] More than a quarter of Oakland's children live in poverty, with stark geographical differences in the poverty rate across the city. Crime continues to be a challenge, although violent crime has declined steadily in recent years.[7]

Libby Schaaf, who was born and raised in Oakland, was elected mayor in 2014 on a platform of addressing economic and racial inequality citywide. Schaaf signaled her focus on Oakland's children early in her tenure, filling a new director of education position in the summer of 2015. In the announcement, Schaaf said the director's job would be "to transform my vision of a cradle to career pipeline into reality, creating a true continuum of excellence from pre-K through K–12 and beyond. Oakland will only succeed if our kids do."[8] The mayor's initiative was certainly not the first one aimed at improving conditions for children—Oakland has been part of the full-service community schools and restorative justice movements, among others—but it reflected a new citywide approach.

In 2016, Mayor Schaaf partnered with the Oakland Unified School District, the East Bay College Fund, and the Oakland Public Education Fund to launch Oakland Promise, a cradle-to-career initiative aimed at tripling the number of college graduates from Oakland. At the time of the announcement, only about 10 percent of Oakland public school students who started ninth grade went on to complete college within five years of graduating from high school.[9] The city, schools, and hundreds of partners joined forces to create four interrelated Oakland Promise initiatives:

> *Brilliant Baby:* This initiative creates college savings accounts seeded with $500 for babies in the highest-need families. It also offers incentives of up to $300 for parents to work with a financial coach and up to a $200 match for contributions to a savings account.
>
> *Kindergarten to College:* This effort opens early college savings accounts seeded with $100 for all Oakland public school kindergarteners. It encourages families to open their own college savings accounts, offering up to $100 in savings incentives, and aims to instill a college-bound mindset through school-based activities.
>
> *Future Centers:* These college-and-career hubs in middle schools and high schools help students navigate the college application process and find scholarships.
>
> *College Scholarship and Completion:* Through this initiative, students receive multiyear scholarships paired with persistence support (one-to-one mentors, peer support, retreats, college partnerships) that gives them the holistic supports they need to graduate and succeed in a career.

Mayor Schaaf led an ambitious fund-raising effort that generated approximately $25 million of support for Oakland Promise's first four years of operation. As mentioned, she celebrates her birthday every year by holding a fund-raiser for the program.

Even before Oakland joined BAM, the city had an official group to coordinate services across agencies. The Youth Ventures Joint Powers

Authority (JPA), a legal entity in California, brings together the county, city, and school district to work together to eliminate health, wealth, and education disparities in Oakland. The JPA established the Oakland Thrives Leadership Council in July 2016. Composed of civic and business leaders, the council aims to involve the broader civic community in raising young adults who graduate from high school with the potential to go to college, have a career, and be successful. The leadership council is chaired by Schaaf and an executive vice president of Kaiser Permanente and—together with the JPA and consulting firm FSG—was instrumental in developing the JPA's data dashboard and *impact tables*, which are working groups setting goals and outlining strategies to address challenges in education, health, wealth, housing, and safety.

Knowing that Oakland's landscape in this area was already crowded, the Oakland team—a group chosen by the mayor's office to attend BAM conferences—decided that the JPA would act as Oakland's children's cabinet. The team reasoned that the JPA, which meets every six to eight weeks, included many of the same leaders suggested by BAM. Besides the typical BAM cabinet members such as the mayor, superintendent, director of human services, city council president, and the school board president, the cabinet also included executive representation from the county government and the Oakland police department. It became evident, though, that the JPA was too broad a governance structure and was dealing with policy questions at too high a level to be an effective governance body for the BAM effort. Recognizing this, the Oakland team instituted smaller, monthly steering committee meetings along with the larger quarterly meetings attended by the mayor and superintendent.

Oakland's superintendent, Wilson, caught many in the city by surprise when he left for Washington, DC, soon after the start of BAM. Because the superintendent-mayor relationship is central to BAM, Wilson's departure posed a challenge to the pace and direction of the BAM work. In this case, Wilson was the primary champion of the Future Centers, so his departure slowed their expansion. However, the team used the transition as an opportunity to step back and evaluate options for creating a broader college-going culture in Oakland.

As an outcomes-oriented city, Oakland believes in using data to guide decision-making. In March 2017, Oakland collaborated with Bloomberg Associates, Policy Link, and My Brother's Keeper Alliance to create the Equity Intelligence Platform, a cross-agency data dashboard that will be the first of its kind in the nation. The platform aims to make local data come alive, specifically to improve outcomes for boys and young men of color, by presenting the data in a way that makes clear the shocking differences in achievement and experiences for this group relative to others on measures ranging from kindergarten readiness to incarceration rates. City managers, community-based organizations, and provider agencies will use the Equity Intelligence Platform to measure and track their progress in improving outcomes for boys and young men of color. This platform will align with the goals of the JPA's five impact tables, which identify discrete short- and long-term goals for the city in the areas of education, health, wealth, housing, and safety. These impact tables are supported by working groups that meet regularly to identify and track goals and outcomes in each of the areas.

As it moves forward, Oakland is continuing its efforts to align its supports for children into a more unified governance structure that incorporates the measures identified by the impact tables as benchmarks. The mayor's leadership in both public and private resource development will clearly have a long-lasting impact, enabling more of Oakland's youth to make college a reality.

Salem

Salem is a small coastal city an hour north of Boston. Its motto, "Still Making History," acknowledges its significance as one of the country's oldest cities and as the infamous site of the Salem witch trials. Kim Driscoll, who has been the mayor since 2006, often likes to say that "Salem is a city that punches above its weight." Despite having a population of less than forty-three thousand, Salem is home to a world-class museum, a university, and a major medical center. The downtown area has seen a resurgence of restaurants and commerce. In 2016, the city began planning to develop a community vision, Imagine Salem, to "develop a set of shared values and a shared vision" ahead of its 400th anniversary.

Both the city and its schools are becoming increasingly diverse, largely because of immigration, although there is a notable difference between the diversity of the city's population overall and that of its schools. In the 2010 census, over 80 percent of city residents were white, whereas just under 50 percent of students in Salem Public Schools were white during the 2016–2017 school year. More than a quarter of students speak a language other than English at home, and close to half are low-income.

In 2011, Salem learned that the Massachusetts Department of Elementary and Secondary Education had designated its public school system an underperforming district because of low scores in one of its schools. (In Massachusetts, the entire district is classified by its lowest-performing school.) The designation, which came as a surprise, ignited a new focus on the city's schools and the challenges its children face. As the district entered turnaround status, city and school leadership began mobilizing to address the underlying causes of this designation and improve outcomes for children.

Mayor Driscoll's decision to join BAM cemented the strong relationship between the city and the school system and had the added benefit of formally bringing other stakeholders into the conversation. Driscoll spoke of the turnaround work: "The superintendent, myself, and some of the school officials were used to being in each other's company and thinking about this. But it's not often that we would have the director of the community health center or the teachers' union president or other stakeholders directly engaged."[10]

Salem's cabinet includes senior representatives from North Shore Medical Center, Salem State University, the United Way, LEAP for Education, the local YMCA, the Peabody Essex Museum, city government, Salem

Public Schools, and the teachers union. The mayor and school superintendent attend every cabinet meeting; these clear signals of support and commitment from both the city government and the school district have enabled the work to move forward quickly.

When the cabinet identified social-emotional well-being as an initial focus, the mayor and superintendent agreed that this was an area in which coordinated effort could make a meaningful difference. In recent years, Salem had seen an uptick in trauma-related issues for students, and the city was eager to more systematically address their needs.

The team formed a partnership with City Connects, a Boston College–based initiative, to create a solution for their social-emotional support, data, and framework needs. City Connects had pioneered a systematic approach to addressing the out-of-school factors that limit learning.[11] The approach, which is described in detail in chapter 3, pairs a sophisticated data system that tracks the holistic needs of each student with a staffing model that embeds a specially trained City Connects coordinator in every partner school, with the purpose of matching every child with the resources he or she needs to thrive.

Mayor Driscoll negotiated funding for the first and most expensive year of City Connects implementation in Salem through the city's community benefits agreement with North Shore Medical Center—making the funding a unique private-public combination. This negotiation required a great deal of persistence on the mayor's part, and its successful conclusion is a testament to her commitment to the effort. Salem also undertook two other initiatives: a new website to connect the community to available resources, and a series of training sessions aimed at improving adult-youth relationships in the city. To build a clearer overarching frame for the different elements of its work and community buy-in, the cabinet created a framework called Our Salem, Our Kids.[12]

As with all other BAM cities, Salem's cabinet has been working to improve its capacity to use data to decide on priorities and track progress.

Because of its small size, Salem has a limited staff capacity to analyze its data; both the mayor and the superintendent have identified analytics as a key need for the city. The Education Redesign Lab has supported the development of a strategy for improving data-driven decision-making for the Salem team through phone calls and in-person meetings. The Salem team also hopes that the partnership with City Connects will help it develop a robust data system from which to draw and expand capacity to use this data.

Salem has successfully secured funding from some of its cabinet members, including North Shore Medical Center's funding for City Connects' first year of implementation. The team is currently seeking longer-term funding to ensure that City Connects can continue to operate in Salem's schools. Other cabinet members—United Way and Salem State University—provided resources to implement the cabinet's citywide training sessions. The cabinet has also received a grant from the Nellie Mae Foundation to support its Our Salem, Our Kids messaging work.

Salem has moved rapidly from planning to implementation to create new citywide supports for its children and youth. Driscoll describes the city's collaboration with BAM: "This initiative has been what jump-started us, and it has served as a catalyst both for programs like City Connects and for helping us think more cohesively about the system. The strategic plan effort that we have for the district is being implemented now, very much informed by the work we did with By All Means."[13]

Building on the momentum of the schools' strategic planning process and the imperative to improve its designation as underperforming—which the school district exited in September 2016—Salem has put in place tangible interventions to ensure that no child falls through the cracks. It introduced the City Connects model into all its K–8 schools to ensure that each child will have a personalized support plan and a coordinator tasked with ensuring its implementation. The new community resources website provides centralized, comprehensive information on programs and services available within the community. And the new community training program broadens Salem's view of its collective responsibility for the well-being of its children.

ESTABLISHING CITYWIDE SYSTEMS

The Education Redesign Lab is continuing its partnership with cities and communities through a second phase of By All Means, called BAM 2.0. In 2018, five of the original BAM cities—all except Newton—along with two additional communities in Illinois, plus the city of Chattanooga, Tennessee, have signed on for two more years of the BAM initiative, thereby committing to continue and extend the work already begun. The BAM cities have committed to strengthening their cabinets and other backbone structures that provide organizational support and staffing while creating financial sustainability. The cities plan to continue using a measures-of-success framework the lab has developed to track their progress across a range of indicators. The BAM communities will also continue piloting individual student success plans that will facilitate the personalization of supports and services for each child. The success plans are an important symbol and tool of BAM's central principle of personalization. They directly counter one of ERL's central critiques of the current "factory model" of schooling. They are the educational equivalent of a running medical record designed to meet children where they are and give them what they need to succeed both inside and outside school. BAM communities have begun experimenting with the ways and means of developing systems of personalized planning.

The lab is also creating a new network of communities that already have children's cabinets or are interested in creating them, to engage more cities and counties in its work. This new network will provide a forum for disseminating the lessons the lab has learned as well as connecting communities that are working on similar efforts. The lab and the Forum for Youth Investment, the nation's leading advocacy organization for youth development, cosponsored an initial meeting of this network in July 2018.

The lab plans to continue to support this network through periodic meetings, webinars, newsletters and virtual consultation.

The first phase of BAM has demonstrated the importance of mayoral leadership for collaborative citywide efforts. In interviews, other cabinet members repeatedly pointed to the mayors as the most crucial factor signaling BAM's high priority and keeping cabinet members engaged. Mayors also have a unique platform to shine a spotlight on the imperatives—moral and economic—of ensuring the success of their cities' children. Still, other factors also contribute to progress. Cabinet members must have the decision-making authority to enact change. The cabinets also need dedicated staffing and funding to support their work as well as the broader system-change effort. Strong working relationships between the mayor and superintendent and their staffs are important as well. The cabinets and the broader effort need a facilitator who is independent of both the mayor and the superintendent and who can serve as a trusted and politically neutral honest broker. Finally, the initiatives must be part of a network that provides external support and opportunities for the teams to convene and work together.

The Education Redesign Lab's experience with the BAM consortium confirmed our original choice of developing community-based, local solutions to the pressing challenge of rethinking and strengthening our systems of education and child development. The BAM cities have time and again demonstrated the initiative, resourcefulness, and perseverance to press forward in constructing the architecture of new integrated systems of support and opportunity for their children and young people. Because of the strength of local, face-to-face relationships in communities where people know how to overcome superficial differences and get things done, BAM facilitated substantial progress on very complicated, challenging work. As the lab moves forward in its collaboration with cities, it will continue to seek out and support mayors willing to assume strong, activist leadership positions in prioritizing children's needs and in inventing new ways of working across agencies and communities to meet these needs.

9

Advancing College and Career Readiness Through Integrated Student Supports

While students' readiness for college and careers is widely embraced as a goal for school districts, major challenges remain to clearly define readiness, develop valid metrics to determine whether students are truly ready, and, perhaps most critically, design new programs to help them get them ready. Many communities are also increasingly interested in understanding how schools can better model and nurture a third C, besides college readiness and career preparation. Civic readiness is increasingly seen as an important skill, given signs that our democracy is not as strong as needed, and that many students are poorly equipped to be active participants.

Many ISS communities do cutting-edge work to prepare all students for college, careers, and civic engagement. This work builds on the strengths of ISS communities and illustrates two major advantages these communities confer. First, by focusing on a broad range of developmental domains from children's earliest years, ISS communities help more students develop the "soft skills"—such as problem-solving skills and persistence—that employers report are the most important but often lacking among young adults applying for jobs. Second, these communities have developed partnerships with a diverse set of public agencies, businesses, and nonprofit service providers, all of which enable districts to expose students to extensive work opportunities and to prepare them to succeed in both postsecondary education institutions and jobs. This chapter explores three kinds of whole-child ISS strategies that communities have successfully employed to advance college and career readiness and to cultivate the next generation of civically engaged Americans.

EARLY-CHILDHOOD EDUCATION AND EMPLOYABILITY SKILLS

Traits like the ability to focus on the lesson being taught, to work well with classmates, and to stick with a project through completion—sometimes called *soft* or *noncognitive skills*—are widely recognized by educators as going hand-in-hand with traditional academic skills like reading comprehension and computation. Research shows, and teachers know, that noncognitive skills can be just as critical as academic skills in preparing youth for success. And parents understand how closely their children's capacity to listen to instructions, to get along with others, and to deal with adversity are linked to their performance in many areas of life, school in particular. In recent years, these commonsense observations have been documented by education researchers and increasingly acknowledged in education policy and practice.[1] Scholars also link the rapid and extensive brain development that takes place in children's first years to the development of these skills, making the birth-to-kindergarten period critical in a child's development.[2]

Community-school partnerships that invest in early-childhood education as part of their whole-child approach lay a strong foundation for the
skills that employers demand and that are key to sustaining a functioning
democratic society. While these early-childhood programs tend to focus
heavily on early literacy in response to large gaps in that area, evidence
is clear that stimulating early experiences and interactions with nurturing,
skilled adults also help establish critical noncognitive, social and emotional
skills.

In Joplin, Bright Futures delivers new-baby literacy kits with information
on why reading is so important, board books, and bibs printed with the
message "Read to Me: 30 minutes, Every Child, Every Day" to two area
hospitals. The organization also created public service announcements
that air on local radio stations and has supported the Little Blue Bookshelf
project. As described earlier, the group placed bookshelves stocked with
children's books in high-traffic locations throughout Joplin to enable low-
income families to bring home children's books and create their own little
libraries at home.

On the Pacific Northwest coast, Vancouver Public Schools is engaged
in similar strategies. It distributes early-childhood literacy packets with
fun activities and lessons that families can do at home to support their
children's development. More than six thousand children, from birth to
age five, receive the packets each year. The district's 1-2-3 Grow and
Learn initiative is a weekly, ninety-minute literacy-rich program for young
children and their parents or other caregivers.

The isolated, rural settings in which Berea College's Partners for Education (PfE) supports students and families across four counties through
its Promise Neighborhoods grant require unique approaches to enriching
young children's experiences. PfE has funded early-childhood specialists
to enhance the quality of classrooms in the state's preK program and to
improve teachers' relationships with their young students. It built community storywalks in several area parks and outside an elementary school
to give parents and other caregivers opportunities to learn together with

young children while getting much-needed exercise. And early-childhood specialists travel around Clay County in two Readiness Buses to some of the most isolated and vulnerable households to provide dual-generation early literacy support for children and financial and parenting skills for their parents.

Communities that incorporate support and education for parents and other caregivers through these kinds of initiatives promote the nurturing relationships that build early social and emotional skills. The data show that early investments are building life skills in these districts' improved kindergarten readiness among at-risk children. Disadvantaged children in Vancouver—students who are low-income, Hispanic, black, and/or non-English-speaking—are substantially more prepared for kindergarten than are their peers across the district and the state.[3] In Berea, social workers who visit some of Clay County's most vulnerable families on the Readiness Bus every week describe the important "baby steps" that the parents and children have made. Children who had not even known the alphabet when they first began were now starting to read and were waiting eagerly for the bus to arrive, their little faces pressed against the front windows of their homes. And parents who had initially been reluctant to even take part in the weekly one-hour, dual-generation sessions are now asking how they can sign their kids up for regular preK. Two of the bus staff explain: "They see how much progress their children have made from just our one hour a week with them, and they understand why they need to be playing and learning with other kids every day."[4]

MAKING TIME FOR OTHER TYPES OF LEARNING

An intentional focus on nurturing all the students' skills—not only traditional academic ones but also employability and social skills—is a hallmark of whole-child K–12 education systems that are supported by ISS strategies. It is also an approach that sustains early gains and supports students' college, career, and life readiness.

Social and emotional learning—the cultivation of traits like tolerance and patience and skills like collaboration and perseverance—is woven into the curriculum and classroom activities in Vancouver Public Schools as part of the district's strong commitment to whole-child education. Every Vancouver student learns, starting in kindergarten, how key brain functions affect their ability to learn and to operate effectively outside school. Posters illustrating the location and functions of the prefrontal cortex, the hippocampus, and the amygdala are prominently displayed on classroom walls.[5] And teachers conducting "mindful minutes" use that time to have students discuss with classmates how relaxing calms their amygdalae and enables their prefrontal cortex (or PFC, as a group of adorable second graders at Eisenhower Elementary School call it) to help them make smart choices, like stepping away from a fight on the playground. One principal grins as she tells the story of a student who recently translated that knowledge into helpful life advice for her mom. When the two were at the supermarket trying to pick up food for dinner, the mother, who had had a very stressful day at work, was struggling to keep her cool while figuring out an affordable and acceptable option. The daughter explained how deep breathing helped her and her friends calm down in class during such moments. After the mother found the technique effective, she suggested that they spend ten minutes on joint mindfulness activities every night before bedtime as a way to spend quality time together and ensure good sleep.

The Bright Futures strategy advances both social and emotional learning and the kinds of real-world skills that help students make a smoother, more successful transition to postsecondary education and jobs and do well there. In addition to building a system to meet every student's basic needs within twenty-four hours and cultivating community ownership of schools so that longer-term needs can be anticipated and addressed, Bright Futures embeds service learning in daily classroom activities. This means hands-on activities that help all the students build life skills like persistence, the ability to collaborate with peers, and creativity.

Simple projects like organizing shoe and sock drives help younger students better understand the needs among their friends and other community members and cultivate empathy, while secondary students take on more-challenging service projects. For example, technical school students worked with local contractors to design and install an HVAC system to heat and cool a local homeless shelter. One principal describes how engaging in these hands-on projects can also nurture students' sense of civic engagement: "The Royal Heights [Elementary School service learning] council is testing out a new concept—students as leaders and decision makers! . . . This group also identified the need for curbside recycling in our community. They researched the issue, marketed their ideas, and are now encouraging everyone to get registered, and then get out and vote on Proposition A at the April 8, 2014, election. The proposition missed passing by a small margin but we couldn't be more proud of their efforts."[6]

Enhancing the students' social and emotional well-being is also critical to addressing severe challenges schools face because of the children's difficult home and community situations. *Toxic stress* refers to the impacts of persistent poverty and its associated aftereffects, such as parental depression, hunger, and homelessness, on children's brains. Schools in eastern Kentucky, where a growing share of students are touched by opioid addiction, are all too familiar with the consequences of toxic stress. Grant funds from PfE Promise Neighborhoods grants are being used to cushion children from toxic stress through various activities. For example, the community brings counselors into elementary schools during Red Ribbon Week (a week dedicated to the prevention of alcohol, tobacco, and drug use and violence) to encourage children to open up to adults and one another about their traumas. The counselors also show the children how to acquire coping skills to replace acting out by fighting, disrupting school, or internalizing their anger through cutting or other types of self-harm.

Just as important, PfE builds on Berea College's strong grounding in the region's arts traditions by establishing artist residencies in schools in Clay,

Jackson, and Owsley Counties. Appalachian artists work with students to create colorful murals that illustrate positive aspects of their communities, and their aspirations for their academic and life futures. These artists also lead classes in drawing, painting, music, and theater. Teachers describe the transformative effect that they have seen from incorporating art into their daily activities and curricula. At one elementary school, a Native American basket maker doing basket-weaving instruction found that a student who was known to be a "problem" got so engaged in the project that he was the first to finish and was even able to help other students with their baskets. And, a principal who had initially been reluctant to devote time to arts instruction became one of the initiative's most enthusiastic advocates after the school's first arts night drew so many parents he could not find a parking spot. He had worried that the arts might distract from efforts to raise his school's low test scores and to engage disconnected parents, but his view changed as the new program helped disengaged students connect with their teachers and test scores started to rise.[7]

USING PARTNERSHIPS TO DEVELOP A COLLEGE-GOING CULTURE

One major challenge schools face in cultivating college and career readiness is making higher education and future jobs closer and more realistic for students who may view these goals as geographically, logistically, or financially out of reach. To address this issue, ISS communities are bringing colleges and careers into high schools. These strategies take advantage of the partnerships that schools have developed with city agencies, local businesses, and faith institutions and help develop the college-going culture that may be lacking in many students' homes.

CULTURE AND OPPORTUNITIES MATTER

With a large share of Joplin's students unaware of college possibilities, and conversations about going to college missing in many of their homes, district leaders knew that getting more students to graduate and enroll in college had to start early. After a group of teachers at Columbia Elementary School were inspired by the Operation College Bound program they observed at a Model Schools Conference, superintendent C. J. Huff encouraged the adoption of this program districtwide. Operation College Bound aims to expose K–5 students to six college campuses during their time in elementary school. Through these visits, students start to learn about careers that might be of interest to them and how higher education can help them fulfill those goals. Another component of the program, career day, brings representatives from local businesses to school to meet with students face-to-face to discuss future career paths and how a college education accelerates progress on those paths.[8]

When Joplin began rebuilding a high school after the devastating May 2011 tornado, the district had the opportunity to build a high school that would advance its vision of a college- and career-ready culture. The new Joplin High School, which opened its doors in September 2014, houses five career-path academies that are designed to ensure that students are academically ready for postsecondary learning or jobs *and* that they have the broader set of abilities needed in these environments. The centers range from the STEM-focused Franklin Technology Center to a performing arts academy. These investments were among the factors that led the U.S. Department of Education to include Joplin on its fall 2015 list of just nine districts deemed to be "future ready."[9] And as noted before, Bright Futures advances social, emotional, and practical or life learning through service projects it embeds in the curriculum. Recently, for example, high school students have been working with the city's water treatment facility to assess and ensure the health of the community's drinking water. Students go out and collect samples from area water sources and bring them back to the school for analysis in their chemistry labs. Subsequently, students write up the results and present them to city officials.

The partnerships that Bright Futures has cultivated with city agencies and businesses have also evolved to provide new career-readiness opportunities. When the initiative was first launched in 2008, Huff sought out these partners to provide lunch buddies, volunteer tutors, and outside participants on school-site councils. As the relationships matured from the courtship to the marriage stage, however, businesses began to come forward with suggestions to deepen their engagement. Several companies offered students the chance to intern at their places of business, and more recently, Joplin School District initiated apprenticeships in health care and manufacturing. As Huff notes, there has long been a gap between the education and workforce worlds, and he finds this gap illogical and frustrating.[10] After all, he points out, no one has a greater stake in ensuring that students graduate from high school ready for the next step in their lives than do the potential employers with whom the youth will take that step. ISS initiatives use partnerships to create career opportunities that bridge those two worlds. These partnerships advance collaboration among key stakeholders so that they begin to speak the same language and work together toward their common goals.

Schools in Appalachian Kentucky face some of the highest barriers in the country to graduating students who are college and career ready. Historically most jobs in Appalachia did not require a college degree, so there is a distinct lack of a college-going culture among the area's families and schools. Only 22 percent of adults in the region have a college degree, and many children in the counties served by PfE through its Promise Neighborhoods grants do not personally know any colleges graduate other than their teachers, principals, and other school staff. Most students are severely limited in their understanding of how college works, how they might access college, and even why going to college is so important.

With coal and manufacturing jobs dwindling, a college education is quickly becoming a necessity for students who want to avoid a life of poverty. Consequently, schools are prioritizing the creation of a college-going culture. Many schools, including elementary schools, create bulletin boards to display pennants from area colleges—four-year, two-year, and voc-tech schools—so that the idea of college is present from students' first years in school. School leaders also understand that getting parents to support their children in making a different life decision from their own is going to be key if the effort is to succeed. So PfE's family engagement task force in Owsley County sponsors annual college nights at Owsley County High School. There, parents can get information from people they trust about the application process, college options, financial aid, and more. They can also get help on the spot with filling out financial aid forms, which can be a daunting process even for more savvy parents.

Nurturing a college-going culture is important, but in an area with very few job prospects, schools also must help students understand what going to college can do for them. The best options for good local jobs are those of public-school teachers, counselors, and principals, along with librarians, nurses, and social workers. The larger Lexington area offers many other skilled jobs, from high-tech manufacturing to medicine, but they are too far away to be on the radar of area families. Educators recognize the difficulty of helping students understand career possibilities and linking those options to the required higher education.

Owsley County High School principal Charlie Davidson wants his students to know about the broad range of job prospects, so he reached out to the Toyota plant in Georgetown, Kentucky, near the Ohio border, to create a job shadowing program for seniors. It has been a difficult endeavor, but one that he believes is worth the effort. "It takes about two hours by bus to get the kids there, so if [my wife] Stacey and I have to be at the school at five a.m. to get the kids on the road, we're here. If we need to be here at eleven p.m. when they return, we're here. Ideally, we'd love our kids to get a college education and come back to Clay County and help build up the community. But if there aren't jobs here for them, we need to get them to places where they can have a real future."[11]

UNIQUE MODELS AND PROGRAMS

Berea College itself provides both a model and an inspiration for area students. Founded in 1855 by "radical abolitionists," Berea enrolls only academically promising students from low-income families. Most of these students are the first in their families to go to college, and many of them are from Appalachia. Because Berea charges no tuition, this barrier is removed. And because it has a student body of only about sixteen hundred at any given time and all of them come from similarly disadvantaged backgrounds, Berea is equipped to provide the social and other supports that are critical to keeping such students in school so that they can earn their degrees.

Berea College's commitment to preserving and elevating the region's rich cultural history also includes showcasing its traditional crafts. Expert craftspeople teach courses on traditional Appalachian weaving, basket making, glassblowing, and a range of woodworking and carving activities. The college describes its embrace of this cultural heritage: "Over 100 students work 10 to 15 hours per week in the various departments of student crafts . . . [O]ur students produce and market works that maintain strong ties to the elemental nature of the Appalachian region—design excellence, a respect for materials, and the honor that comes from hard work."[12] (Students can sell their masterpieces to Berea visitors and tourists at the Log House Craft Gallery in the center of town.) The craft program also advances the college's commitment to experiential learning and helps prepare students for relevant area careers. For example, it established the Deep Green Furniture Team, a group of fifteen students who worked under the guidance of a master craftsman to design and build the furniture for Berea's new Deep Green residence hall, so named because of its high LEED (Leadership in Energy and Environmental Design certification) rating.

Vancouver students' challenges to college and career readiness may appear less pressing than those of their peers in Joplin and Berea, but district leaders point to real and growing problems. The transition over the past few decades from blue-collar jobs in fishing, logging, and traditional manufacturing to higher-tech electronics manufacturing, along with the proliferation of low-paying service-sector jobs in health care, retail, and hospitality, poses barriers for students in this medium-sized city, and these barriers are familiar in communities across the country.[13] And as Portland, Oregon, right across the Columbia River, expanded and became an increasingly expensive place to live, Vancouver has absorbed both residents looking for affordable housing and a growing number of lower-skilled immigrants. The school district has responded with robust initiatives for college, career, and civic readiness.

Most Vancouver elementary schools and all the district's middle and high schools offer AVID (Advancement Via Individual Determination), a national college-readiness program that equips students with the skills and tools they need to successfully progress through a four-year university program. In elementary schools, AVID is reflected as enrichment embedded in a rigorous curriculum. In middle and high schools, a key aspect is tutors who work in AVID classes twice per week to help students in study groups and individually to ensure their progress across all academic areas. Like other aspects of whole-child education, Vancouver schools customize AVID to their unique needs. McLoughlin Middle School, for example, which has a large Spanish-speaking student population, has developed a bilingual AVID program to improve vocabulary and processing skills among ESOL (English for speakers of other languages) students.[14]

Career and technical education (CTE) is embedded in all middle and high schools, and 120 CTE staff across the district support 7,890 participating students. Superintendent Steve Webb proudly notes the district's 300-to-1 student-to-counselor ratio, which is close to the 250-to-1 ratio recommended by the American School Counselor Association and compares favorably with the national average of 491 to 1. (The dearth of counselors is especially pressing in two states: the ratio is 822 to 1 in California and 941 to 1 in Arizona).[15] These investments in counselors offer more opportunities for the one-on-one support that is critical for disadvantaged students, in particular, to navigate the complex and often intimidating processes of choosing college preparatory courses, exploring college options, filling out postsecondary applications, and applying for financial aid. For example, they enable high schools to track students' completion of the Free Application for Federal Student Aid and intervene with every student who has not yet done so.

At Hudson's Bay High School, two full-time career guidance counselors and an assistant staff the Career Center. Students can come in at any time to use Career Cruising, an online system that helps them explore teen internship and employment opportunities, course options, community and four-year colleges, and much more. The specialists help students access local volunteer and internship opportunities—from planting neighborhood trees or serving on the library's Teen Council to a design internship with a Vancouver architecture firm—as well as researching test preparation and scholarships and other financial aid options. The center also hosts admissions officers from colleges across the country and representatives from the armed services, and students can be excused from class to come meet with them and ask questions.

Similar supports are available to juniors and seniors districtwide.[16] Every high school has career specialists who work with these students to complete so-called High School and Beyond plans, which set out required and recommended activities to ensure that the students navigate these critical academic years productively and successfully.[17] Mark Wreath, director of CTE at Vancouver Public Schools, notes that "students also have multiple opportunities to participate in college and career fairs, field trips, company tours, and other Career Connected Learning Opportunities as part of the career guidance they receive from the Career Center resources."[18]

The enriching opportunities available through CTE programs at Hudson's Bay High School would be the envy of many prestigious private schools. One of Vancouver's many schools of choice, Hudson's Bay serves as both a general high school for students graduating from Discovery Middle School and a CTE magnet for students seeking the specialized options. Hudson Bay's ACES program—architecture, construction, and environmental services—enrolls both students who are just looking to gain real-world skills that will serve them as adults, along with others looking to enter a solid career path. Tenth graders in the introductory construction class, for example, work in pairs in a lab where they will learn, over a semester, to build many of the key pieces of a house. One team may be using a video to learn how to use a jigsaw to cut wood planks to the correct lengths and angles to build a scaled model of a roof, while another pair of students is weather-stripping a miniature home, complete with doors and doorknobs. A third pair is analyzing the relative strengths of four types of insulation to determine which they should use. As one observer commented admiringly, "This is not your father's woodworking shop."[19]

In his introductory horticulture class, Steve Lorenz, who teaches classes at Hudson's Bay and also owns a local landscaping and construction company, is helping students price out a corsage for the upcoming wedding of one of their teachers. Not only will they learn to use the flowers they have grown in a new way, but they are also engaging in technical writing (and computing), skills that will translate to many future jobs. Lorenz notes that, thanks to the state's flexible laws, students in his class can get dual credit. For example, in addition to the science credit needed for high school graduation, horticulture students can earn up to twenty-one college credits toward an associate's degree at Clackamas Community College. Thanks to the state's support for dual-credit programs, students in the district have several options to earn early college credits: completing and passing college courses through Running Start (a program in the states of Washington, Hawaii, and Illinois for obtaining college credit in high school); obtaining a score of 3 or higher on AP, International Baccalaureate, or Cambridge International exams; or completing a CTE dual-credit course.

In 2017, the school decided to put its resources—most prominently its student talent—to use solving a pressing community problem. The Vancouver City Council had declared the region's lack of affordable housing an official crisis, and the district estimates that more than one thousand students experienced homelessness in the 2016–2017 school year. City shelters could not keep up with demand, and churches that wanted to assist reported that they were struggling to address area residents' concerns that homeless families were sleeping in their cars in church parking lots.

Hudson's Bay's CTE director decided to try an innovative approach. He brought together two groups of students—those studying construction and those studying AP physics—to come up with pop-up housing that could enable churches to serve families in a more dignified and socially acceptable manner. The result is impressive, to say the least.

In January 2018, two physics students proudly showed off their prototype. Designed to house two people, the structure had walls that would be held together at the corners by a combination of pins and straps with brackets that attached to the walls. The pop-up would be both quick and easy to assemble (and disassemble) and totally weather-proof. Because it had to be small enough to fit in a parking space, the house could be heated to a comfortable temperature by a tiny space heater that could be connected, along with others in the parking lot, to a single extension cord that would be run from inside the church.

Asked where the roof was, one student sheepishly admitted that he was still tweaking that piece. He had realized that the roof needed to be a bit longer so that it would create small eaves to ensure that rain wouldn't drip down the sides of the house and disturb its residents. He had also been working to figure out how he and his partner could use empty water bottles from the Vancouver district schools as part of the insulation—heavier materials were impracticable on such a small, light frame, and the team was convinced that they could make the home environmentally friendly. In warmer months, or when there was no demand for the homes, they could be disassembled into flat bundles of walls and stored in the church basement.

INNOVATING FOR COLLEGE AND CAREER READINESS

Communities that employ ISS in service of whole-child education have particular advantages in helping students get ready for college, career, and civic engagement. These advantages stem from the communities' nurturing academic, life, and employability skills in their students early on, as well as their many partnerships with business, faith, and other organizations to better enable students to explore a range of postsecondary options.

While many of the strategies described here are cutting-edge, most are inexpensive to implement and many can be easily and quickly initiated. Others take more time and require a gradual building of relationships. But all these strategies are proving effective in getting more students, especially at-risk and vulnerable students, to the high school finish line and into college or jobs. School and community leaders give these strategies high marks for their positive impact. And given the very different contexts—geographic, demographic, political—in which they are being employed, it is clear that such creative strategies for advancing college, career, and civic readiness could work in virtually any district. We just need to commit the resources and make the investments necessary to fully support our young people to become the kind of successful, thriving adults who will contribute to prospering communities all across the country.

PART III

The Path Forward

10

Community Schools

A Promising Model for Building a Movement

Part 1 of this book established the societal need for ISS strategies. It then provided snapshots of a dozen community-level ISS initiatives that are making real progress toward closing opportunity and enrichment gaps and, ultimately, achievement gaps. Part 2 described in detail various aspects of those strategies, including laying the foundations for a strong, early life start; engaging faith institutions in the work; and leveraging whole-child ISS approaches to better prepare students for college, career, and civic involvement. From these examples, we know both that ISS has to happen and that it is happening in a diverse set of communities.

Part 3 examines what needs to change to transform whole-child ISS initiatives from isolated efforts to broad application across the national landscape, in other words, to make ISS a norm in our systems of education. In these three final chapters, we explore several key themes that, taken together, chart a path forward for our actions, individually and collectively, to scale the successes described in this book.

One promising vehicle for scaling ISS is *community schools*—a popular strategy for providing ISS, traditionally at the school level. In this chapter, we explore the history and creation of the community-school movement, its current status and impact, the progress it can claim, and the challenges its leaders have encountered. Finally, we assess where community schools need to go if they are to lead a movement for ISS to scale up to a much more expansive and systemic level.

A focus on community schools is timely, as several big-city districts have included the expansion of this particular strategy in their school improvement plans. In Chicago; Los Angeles; Newark, New Jersey; New York City; Philadelphia; and other large cities, community schools have become the preferred alternative to the market-oriented reforms that dominated those cities' efforts over the past decade plus. New York City mayor Bill de Blasio made community schools a core component of his 2014 campaign platform and has since expanded the number of new community schools opened, from an initial goal of one hundred to more than two hundred. In Philadelphia, the 2016 passage of a soda tax dedicated to funding community schools helped boost their prominence in improving the city's infamously resource-starved schools.

These initiatives' potential, if they gain real traction, to serve millions of children would massively expand existing ISS efforts. They also offer the possibility of validating the capacity of community schools to turn around some of the nation's hardest-to-improve schools.

UNDERSTANDING COMMUNITY SCHOOLS

Community schools (sometimes referred to as full-service schools) as a concept have existed for roughly a century. They evolved from the settlement houses established in the early twentieth century to help low-income immigrant families and children adapt to American life and succeed in school. In the past few decades, the strategy of developing schools to be community hubs not just for students but for their families and neighborhoods more broadly has gained substantial momentum. As part of that growth, advocates are intensifying efforts to better define community schools and develop a research base that addresses implementation and best practices as well as outcomes. At the same time, proponents are working to unify the community school/ISS field and improve advocacy and expansion efforts.

Organizations, practitioners, and advocates employ various definitions of community schools. According to Joy Dryfoos and Sue Maguire, two founders of the movement, the modern concept of full-service schools has its origins in innovative legislation enacted by the state of Florida in 1991. That law promoted meeting student and family needs more effectively and accessibly by integrating educational, medical, and social or human services. Community schools thus include certain elements: they are "open all the time, run by a partnership, providing access to an array of services, responsive to the family and the community, and focused on overcoming barriers to learning."[1] The Coalition for Community Schools, which, as described below, has played an important role in advancing community schools and advocating for policies that support them, provides this aspirational definition:

> A community school is both a place and a set of partnerships between the school and other community resources. Its integrated focus on academics, health and social services, youth and community development and community engagement leads to improved student learning, stronger families and healthier communities. Community schools offer a personalized curriculum that emphasizes real-world learning and community problem-solving. Schools become centers of the community and are open to everyone—all day, every day, evenings and weekends.
>
> Using public schools as hubs, community schools bring together many partners to offer a range of supports and opportunities to children, youth, families and communities. Partners work to achieve these results: Children

are ready to enter school; students attend school consistently; students are actively involved in learning and their community; families are increasingly involved with their children's education; schools are engaged with families and communities; students succeed academically; students are healthy—physically, socially, and emotionally; students live and learn in a safe, supportive, and stable environment, and communities are desirable places to live.[2]

Few schools that identify as community schools, however, have attained anything close to this depth of support and community transformation to benefit students. Rather, most community schools embody some aspects of this definition, for example, after-school programs embedded within the school, a health clinic, or active parent engagement. There are also a smaller number of comprehensive, full-service models that are in two cases—Cincinnati and, as described in earlier chapters, Vancouver—close to or fully citywide. Even in those cases, however, the surrounding communities, while indisputably bolstered by effective community schools that serve them, have a long way to go to become the thriving cities envisioned by the coalition. The level and quality of the implementation of the community-school strategy depends on multiple, contextual factors and results in a wide range of variable outcomes.

BUILDING A MOVEMENT

As just noted, community schools have been around as a concept for roughly a century, and while they are much greater in number today—an estimated five thousand—they still serve only a small fraction of the children and communities that might benefit from the strategy. Understanding how they and the movement that supports them have evolved is critical to identifying effective strategies to expand whole-child ISS on a much greater scale.

With origins in the early 1900s, community schools have gained steam since, especially in the past two decades. A brief history of the movement describes the forces that prompted the first steps toward creating community schools; the details feel just as relevant today:

> The concept of schools centered in community life can first be traced to the reform era of the early twentieth century in America. Leaders of that time, among them John Dewey, Jane Addams, and urban planner Clarence Perry, first sketched the outlines of model schools that serve as the center of neighborhood social life and the agent of neighborhood-based social services, while also educating children. Facing the daunting social disruption in American cities of the Industrial Age, social reformers sought ways to improve the lives of newly arrived urban residents and immigrants through community-based education and development.[3]

In the 1930s, at the height of the Great Depression, another step toward creating the community-school strategy took place in Flint, Michigan, with the development of "lighted schoolhouses" to serve working parents and their children in vacant school buildings during the evenings. First Lady Eleanor Roosevelt learned of the effort by Charles Stewart Mott (who later founded the Mott Foundation) and helped spread the word across the country. Many of the precepts employed in those evening schoolhouses, like the use of community assets in the curriculum, putting volunteers to good use, and parents' involvement in their children's education, became foundations of today's community schools.

Mott supported and expanded the community education movement through training in Flint and across the country from the 1950s to the 1970s. By the late 1950s, as many as ten thousand people had attended Mott-sponsored workshops. In the two subsequent decades, he also supported year-long graduate fellowships that provided intensive training for nearly seven hundred educators to become superintendents, directors of community schools and other community organizations, and public policy consultants.[4] The Mott Foundation also devoted large sums to community-school development, nearly $180 million over a sixty-year period.

In 1962, Mott's foundation produced a movie about the work in Flint. The film opens by showing why leaving school buildings empty in the evening and over the summer wastes precious public resources.[5] As the film illustrates, the benefits of keeping schools open and using them as centers for their communities are varied. Not only do the schools provide space for recreational and instructional activities for both children and adults, but the centers' use beyond the school day helps all the community's residents feel a personal stake and ownership in their schools. The initial success of the concept in Flint led to demand so high that five community schools opened in the first year, and fifteen the next. Eventually, every school was open to the community in Flint, and all sorts of benefits ensued. For example, the availability of the school's swimming pools enabled every child to learn to swim. And adults had access to a wide variety of courses and could gain a range of new skills. Many who came to take one class went on to earn their diplomas.

With many schools segregated either by law or by practice during this time, community schools also emerged across the South as a way for African American students to gain a good education while the schools also empowered their parents and neighbors through gatherings, classes, and other activities that took place in the evenings.[6]

At the same time, the movement also began to grow through intentional new advocacy strategies. In the 1970s, a time of increased civic and education activism nationwide, two new organizations, the National Association for Community Education and the National Center for Community Education, became foci of community-school advancement. Advocates successfully passed federal legislation in 1974 that provided support to build a national community-school infrastructure as well as legislation coordinating their expansion in some states. Federal funding for the program ended in 1981, but it had lasting impacts: the law introduced a number of federal legislators to the concept of community schools, and there are still residual state-level programs.[7]

In 1994, the movement gained further steam when the Children's Aid Society created the National Center for Community Schools to respond to requests for information about community schools and guidance on implementation. The center provides a range of supports and services. In addition to offering opportunities to learn from the society's community schools work in New York City and elsewhere and conducting advocacy at the local, state, and national levels, the center also provides international support. It reports having hosted visitors from more than seventy countries and having consulted extensively with community-school colleagues in England, Wales, Scotland, Ireland, and the Netherlands, among others.[8]

LAUNCHING THE COMMUNITIES IN SCHOOLS ORGANIZATION

The 1970s also produced another key actor in the community-school movement. In 1977, inspired by his ecumenical work to start "street academies" for at-risk youth in the 1960s, Bill Milliken founded the nonprofit organization Communities In Schools. His goal was designing a large-scale comprehensive program to prevent students from dropping out of school. The resulting program (originally named Cities In Schools until the 1996 change of title), which Milliken led through May 2004, "repositioned existing community resources into schools."[9]

In addition to the Christian principles that led him to launch CIS, Milliken was influenced by the importance of systems sustainability and sound management, two guiding pillars of the expansion of CIS over the past forty years. From its inception, CIS has relied on a combination of public and private funding, believing that private support adds not only financial stability, but also credibility with schools and communities. The program has also maintained a bipartisan bent; in Texas, for example, return-on-investment data has been key to strong support from very conservative policy makers.

Over those decades, however, CIS has evolved from what Milliken describes as a "pioneer" approach to growth under his leadership. Following this approach in its early decades, CIS sought to identify and stake a claim in as many districts and schools as possible in states across the country. In 2004, the shift of leadership to Dan Cardinali, who had been working as CIS vice president for field operations, represented a shift in attitude, Milliken says, from a pioneer to a "settler" mentality. Milliken credits Cardinali with injecting rigor and the use of evidence to drive CIS practice and to improve the quality of its work. In 2016, Dale Erquiaga, who had led the major expansion of CIS in Nevada through his role as state superintendent of public instruction and adviser to Governor Brian Sandoval, took the helm of CIS as a "craftsman," a leader who would pay close attention to the nuts and bolts of implementation and how the initiative is shaped in each school it supports, representing another step in the organization's evolution.[10]

CIS operates at three levels: national, state, and local or "grassroots." Its national office, just outside Washington, DC, serves as the advocacy, organizing, and fund-raising hub. It also supports state capacity-building efforts and leads the organization's research and evaluation work. The thirteen state CIS affiliates work closely with the national office, serving much the same role at the state level—spearheading fund-raising for locals and providing technical assistance, training, and capacity-building. At the local level, each of the more than 150 CIS affiliates are independent nonprofit organizations. The affiliates come to schools at the invitation of the district superintendent and, like community-school initiatives, collaborate with volunteers and various community partners to meet the range of identified student needs.

In 2017, CIS was serving students in 2,300 schools across twenty-five states and the District of Columbia. As described next, the evolution and expansion of CIS over the past four decades is also related to the nascent community-school movement that gained steam starting in the late 1990s. This movement has been fueled by key ISS advocates and actors, including CIS, the National Center for Community Schools, and others that have increasingly come together under a joint banner.

BUILDING THE COALITION FOR COMMUNITY SCHOOLS

In 1997, a small group of advocates convened in a hotel to explore how to best advance full-service community schools, namely, schools in which a broad range of services are delivered to children on-site. This group, which included founding members of the National Center for Community Schools, Joy Dryfoos and Ira Harkavy, officially became the Coalition for Community Schools.

The coalition brings together dozens of organizations, including traditional education associations, advocacy organizations, and national civil rights and other groups whose missions overlap with those of community schools.[11] In the two decades since its inception, the Coalition for Community Schools has become a powerful motivating force for advocacy in favor of community schools at the local, state, and federal levels; technical assistance to support the creation of community schools in dozens of other districts; and dissemination of the community-school strategy on the ground.[12] (Sometimes that advocacy has been led by the coalition and at other times has been spearheaded by one or more partners, such as CIS, working to take the lead in their own right.) The coalition has begun to grow as a brand and a movement, while experiencing both the advantages and disadvantages of that growth. Housed at the Institute for Education Leadership in Washington, DC, the Coalition for Community Schools describes itself as "an alliance of national, state and local organizations in education K-16, youth development, community planning and development, family support, health and human services, government and philanthropy as well as national, state and local community school networks."[13]

CHARTING PROGRESS

In the two decades since the inception of the coalition, a movement has begun to take shape, with visible progress in several respects. Community schools have gained in numbers, resources to guide their expansion are increasingly available and sophisticated, and advocates have notched policy successes at both the federal and the state levels, including the cultivation of legislator champions. Still, progress on each of those fronts is smaller than the need.

Increasing the Number of Community Schools

As of 2018, as many as five thousand schools called themselves community schools.[14] While they have much in common, these schools, which also describe themselves as Beacon schools, Elev8 schools, and other names, also look very different from one another. In many of these schools, CIS delivers ISS. However, few meet the full range of characteristics that the coalition describes as model community schools. Partly for that reason, in 2002 Dryfoos and Maguire described a disagreement on the number of full-service community schools; some schools have instituted one key component while others have multiple components. Some schools are long-standing, stable efforts, while others are newly opened.[15]

This emphasis on increasing the number of community schools highlights a unique characteristic of community-school advocates' efforts to advance ISS: unlike other ISS initiatives, such as Promise Neighborhoods, Bright Futures, Say Yes to Education, By All Means, and the Campaign for Grade-Level Reading, the coalition and CIS have focused mostly on the individual school, rather than district, community, or system level. While this approach has clear advantages—advocates can initiate an effort in a specific school with a committed principal, for example—it also has some substantial downsides. A school-by-school strategy is inefficient and potentially poses communication and coordination problems when partners are simultaneously engaged by multiple schools. For these reasons, and in an effort to substantially expand their impact, both CIS and the coalition have recently increased their emphasis on advancing whole-district or community ISS and addressing issues on a systems level.[16]

While the Coalition for Community Schools has given much of its assistance to individual schools or small clusters of them, a major goal (though not necessarily the priorities of some or all partners) is encouraging district leaders to make many, or even every, school a community school. If all schools were community schools, they would serve every student in this whole-child setting, ensuring a seamless set of supports for children and their families. One of the coalition's flagship publications is a scaling-up guide, which targets districts seeking to systemically expand the number of community schools.[17]

Several cities, including Albuquerque, New Mexico; Cincinnati; Evansville-Vanderburgh, Indiana; Grand Rapids, Michigan; and Lancaster, Pennsylvania, have made substantial progress toward the goal. Perhaps the largest community moving toward the goal is Multnomah County, Oregon, which counted eighty-five community schools across six school districts, including Portland, as of 2015. As described earlier, Vancouver, Washington, which is across the river from Portland, has grown in one decade from a single community school established in 2008 (Fruit Valley), to eighteen Family-Community Resource Centers, along with two mobile FCRCs that serve the district's other seventeen schools, as of the 2017–2018 school year. With consistent leadership that has led the community-school effort almost from the start—Superintendent Webb and chief of staff Tom Hagley have both been on board since 2008, a rarity in any district, let alone a high-poverty one—Vancouver has utilized its ISS systems not just to ensure that basic needs are met for many more students, but to advance whole-child education. When Vancouver Public Schools, which serves roughly twenty-four thousand students, updated its strategic plan in 2014, it set a goal of providing FCRC services in every one of its thirty-five elementary, middle, and high schools by 2020.

Probably the best known of these district-level community-school efforts is Cincinnati, whose full-service community schools are called community learning centers. The CLCs have been explored in case studies and news stories, including a National Public Radio feature about Oyler Elementary School, the school where the initiative began.[18] Oyler was also the focus of an American Public Media documentary film tracking a year in the efforts of then principal Craig Hockenberry to put the community-school strategy to use to turn around one of the highest-poverty schools in a struggling district.[19] Since the inception of CLCs in 2000, and supported by a ten-year, $1 billion taxpayer levy to build or update Cincinnati Public Schools starting in 2002, the district had resource coordinators in thirty-five schools in 2012 and has committed to ultimately expanding the community school strategy to all schools.[20]

In 2008, the district created the Community Learning Center Institute to further advance the development and sustainability of CLCs, and in 2010, the Ohio Department of Education deemed the district "effective" for the first of two consecutive school years. Cincinnati's success has also helped spur the creation of community-school efforts in several other Ohio cities. These include Akron; Dayton, which operates university-assisted neighborhood school centers in five Dayton public elementary schools; and the Schools as Community Hubs effort in Toledo.[21] The United Way is playing a key role in Akron and Toledo, as well as in Cleveland, where the strategy has more recently emerged.

Outcomes in some of these districts are impressive. Cincinnati Public Schools, which serves both urban and rural Appalachian areas and had been the lowest-ranked urban school district in Ohio, gradually rose to become the top-ranked urban district in the state. Vancouver has also made significant progress in closing income- and race-based achievement gaps in test scores, enrollment and success in advanced high school coursework, and graduation rates. It now sends large shares of disadvantaged students to college.

In spite of these notable successes, however, the majority of districts that aim to convert schools to community schools have made only moderate progress. In Oakland, which established that goal under the leadership of then superintendent Tony Smith in 2011, thirty-five of the district's eighty-seven schools—40 percent—were community schools in 2017–2018. Austin Independent School District, which got its first community school in

2010 and has plans to expand districtwide, had just thirteen community schools by 2018 (of dozens of district schools). And the only district to achieve the universal goal is relatively modest in size: Vancouver and its twenty-four thousand students.

However, as we have seen, community schools have also begun to gain momentum in some of the biggest cities targeting schools long considered among the hardest to improve. Some of these efforts by the coalition overlap with those of CIS, which serves many of the community schools and has affiliates in several of the nation's largest urban districts, including Atlanta; Dallas, El Paso, and Houston (Texas); Los Angeles; Miami; and Philadelphia.[22] And, as discussed below, collaborative work led by the Coalition for Community Schools and CIS promises to greatly expand district- and city-level efforts.

It is also important to note that in many communities—some of those explored in this book and others—multiple players are bringing varying perspectives to ensure that children are well supported. In Cincinnati for example, StriveTogether, which approaches ISS through a broader, system-building approach, was founded in 2006 through a convergence of efforts in the city. In the years since, StriveTogether has become one of the nation's leading ISS providers. Working in twenty-nine states and Washington, DC, the StriveTogether network now touches more than 13.7 million students. StriveTogether's vision is clear: "the success of every child, cradle to career," and the organization is highly disciplined about measuring results in terms of student achievement and success at transitioning through major life milestones like kindergarten readiness and high school graduation. StriveTogether, like Harvard's By All Means initiative and Say Yes to Education, works at the community level, in partnership with local leaders, inside the government and out, to build sustainable systems to guarantee student success.

Also worth noting is that StriveTogether counts impressive progress in Cincinnati as one of its "proof points," as does the Coalition for Community Schools, though neither organization tends to note the contributions of the other in driving that progress. As discussed in the final section of this book, this combination of collaboration and tension/turf battle that has been common in the ISS world is one of the factors we believe must be addressed to substantially move the field forward.

Developing a Research Base

As the numbers of both individual and district-level community-school initiatives have grown, a body of research has evolved. Researchers have explored various issues, including the best ways to implement community schools and whether and how these efforts improve outcomes for students, schools, and even the community. However, more than two decades into the coalition's existence, and despite an increasing number of studies examining these issues, the evidence remains thin. We still lack the definitive data establishing the effectiveness of community schools—data that advocates and practitioners alike rightly consider necessary. This insufficient evidence is a daunting concern for advocates, analysts and policy makers.

Recent publications and conferences speak to both the importance of developing such a research base and the challenges of doing so. For example, Child Trends found that none of the evaluations of community schools were sufficiently rigorous to include in its 2014 assessment of the effectiveness of ISS.[23] A 2017 update to the report finds stronger overall and empirical evidence, including that from City Connects and CIS in Chicago. In Chicago, both elementary and middle school students in CIS programs had higher English language arts test scores, as did students in City Connects schools. (Results from CIS in Austin; Jacksonville, Florida; and Wichita, Kansas, showed no difference between CIS schools and other schools.) The 2017 update also draws on findings from studies of other initiatives, including Diplomas Now and Harlem Children's Zone, and asserts that the evidence for the efficacy of ISS is increasingly strong, but it does not include any evidence from a community school that describes itself as such.[24]

The importance of demonstrating the efficacy of community schools was also the motivation for a major 2017 paper coauthored by scholars at two leading education research think tanks, the Learning Policy Institute and the National Education Policy Center.[25] Gearing their analysis to the level of evidentiary rigor required to meet the standards in the Every Student Succeeds Act, Jeannie Oakes and her colleagues report plenty of evidence to justify federal investments in community schools. The 2017 study affirms Child Trends' conclusion that the evidence base for ISS is promising and increasingly solid. For its strongest evidence, however, the Oakes study, which explicitly explores the community-school strategy, relies heavily on initiatives that don't describe themselves as community schools. In addition to citing studies of community-school initiatives in Tulsa (Oklahoma), Baltimore, and other cities, Oakes and coauthors draw on the same evaluations Child Trends employed for CIS, City Connects, and the Harlem Children's Zone charter schools. Many of the other studies cited are of assessments of initiatives at individual schools, and a number of the researchers who conducted these assessments accessed data from only a few students. Also, although the report covers all the key components of community schools, most of the studies on which it relies address only one component, often after-school programs.[26]

The lack of solid, large-scale, and longitudinal data prevents researchers from studying initiatives that identify as community schools. Other problems include researchers' disagreement on how many schools are actually full-service community schools—versus those that have instituted one or more components—as well as how long the schools have been employing the community school strategy, and the broad variation in the quality of existing assessments of these programs.

The lack of available resources to devote to rigorous evaluation also contributes to the problem, as does the ongoing fragmentation of the ISS field. and resulting lack of a coherent body of scholars and research institutions to take on the task. In response to the latter, in October 2017, the Center for Optimized Student Support, which houses City Connects, convened an international group of researchers, practitioners, and other experts to establish a research agenda for the ISS field. The conference report produced by the center in 2018 builds on the growing foundation established by Child Trends. It sets forth a bold and comprehensive research agenda—spanning the issues of context, implementation, outcomes, and methodology—that provides guidance for researchers working in a broad range of areas related to ISS.[27]

Ramping Up Policy Advocacy

Despite the relative weakness of the research base, the Coalition for Community Schools, the National Center for Community Schools, CIS, and the various groups that partner with all these organizations to advocate for community schools have notched significant federal policy victories. These legislative advances both reflect the current strength of the community-school movement and help support the expansion of community schools across dozens of states and hundreds of districts.

Since the 1974 passage and 1982 expiration of the first federal legislation supporting community schools, several federal laws that have been enacted support the strategy in various ways. In 2011, Congress passed the Full-Service Community Schools Act, which has since been merged with the Keeping PACE (Parents and Communities Engaged) Act in the DIPLOMA (Developing Innovative Partnerships and Learning Opportunities that Motivate Achievement) Act. The combined law advances a collaborative approach to education by authorizing grants to promote partnerships between schools, parents, business leaders, higher education institutions, and community-based organizations. And in response to frustration at the narrowly prescriptive nature of the four strategies mandated for federal school "turnaround" dollars and school improvement grants under Title I of the Elementary and Secondary Education Act (ESEA), advocates successfully promoted a fifth alternative that allows community-school-type strategies to be used.[28]

The Every Student Succeeds Act, the newest iteration of ESEA, supports community-school efforts in a variety of ways. In addition to reallocating decision-making to states and local districts and emphasizing broader definitions of student success, Title I's 7 percent set-aside for school improvement in the lowest-performing schools provides a potentially large source of funds for community schools. Aside from Title I funds, the most important federal program supporting the community-school movement is the 21st Century Community Learning Centers. Part of ESEA Title IV, the program supports the creation of centers that provide out-of-school enrichment for disadvantaged students. Since its first major expansion in 1997, this program has grown to over $1.5 billion annually. The majority of the communities we highlight in this book rely to some degree on these funds, as do hundreds of community-school and other ISS initiatives across the country.

Since the 1991 passage of the Florida law that helped define full-service community schools, other states have also enacted legislation that supports community schools and ISS more broadly in a variety of ways. CIS affiliates work at the state level to advance three general types of legislation: (1) direct appropriations, where CIS is the designee for pass-through funds from the governor's budget, an agency, or a corporation (in other words, it is the immediate recipient, providing subgrants to districts or schools, technical assistance to help implement the grants, or both); (2) advancing the field of ISS by helping its providers access state funds for critical ISS activities; and (3) positioning CIS as a leading provider and thought leader in this space, often by changing existing legislation to unlock additional funds for ISS and CIS.

In Nevada, for example, the second strategy led to an overhaul of the state's education system and in particular its funding formula in 2015. The allocation of substantial new money to high-poverty schools provided them with the resources to fund programs promoting ISS, and it doubled CIS's presence in the state. Nevada is also among several states, including Massachusetts and Washington, that have introduced ISS protocols into their legislation.[29]

The *Community Schools Playbook*, published in 2018, offers models of four types of state policies that support community schools: grant programs, other state budget support, technical and other assistance, and state board of education regulations that advance community schools.[30] In the past few years, a number of states, including California, New York, Minnesota, and Kentucky, have passed laws that fall into one of these four types of state support, helping to expand funding and capacity for these community-school initiatives.[31]

Along the way, the community-school movement has also gained some prominent champions on Capitol Hill. Coalition staff, CIS, and many of their partners worked closely with Senators Lamar Alexander and Patty Murray, who collaborated on the Every Student Succeeds Act, to ensure the explicit inclusion of ISS, a major victory for the field.

Adopting a Community-School Strategy

The advocacy efforts of the Coalition for Community Schools are also reflected in the emergence of several other organizations—both within the education policy space and more broadly—that have adopted the community-school strategy as their favored approach to education improvement. In the past few years, for example, the Center for Popular Democracy has organized low-income communities of color around school improvement as a central part of its popular-democracy work. Using the term *community wraparound schools*, the center frames its work as a response to reforms that rely on student test scores and emphasize firing teachers, opening new charter schools, and school closures. It works closely with the coalition to produce advocacy materials to engage community members, with the stated goal of ultimately establishing new community schools in twenty-five states.[32]

Social-justice-oriented education coalitions that connect the national teachers unions—the National Education Association (NEA) and the American Federation of Teachers (AFT)—with grassroots organizers likewise have evolved to advance community schools. One of these is AROS, the Alliance to Reclaim our Schools. The first of AROS's five policy priorities demands "full funding and support for neighborhood-based community schools: don't close or privatize them."[33] Another is the Journey for Justice Alliance (www.j4jalliance.com), which grew out of Chicago education organizer Jitu Brown's decades-long efforts to effect grassroots school improvement in that city. Sustainable community schools are one of the alliance's three official campaigns, with two other complementary goals—local control over neighborhood schools and education as a human right.[34]

The Center for Popular Democracy and Journey for Justice Alliance, along with AFT and NEA, are among AROS's ten core partners, illustrating the groups' closely intertwined relationships.[35] These cross-organization links are also reflected in the list of resources AROS offers to advocates who seek to create or scale up community schools in their communities.[36]

Convening for Growth

The rise of the community-school movement can also be seen in the expansion of both the number and the size of conferences devoted to the community-school strategy. In addition to plenary sessions and panel discussions, the coalition's national conferences offer dozens of workshops where participants can learn everything, including basic information about community schools for those new to the concept to guidance for educators and principals on implementation at the school and classroom levels. Other workshops focus on messaging and advocacy and send their participants home with information to take to their local policy makers.

The first conference, a planning conference in 1998, was attended by 150 people. By 2001, conference participation had grown to over 500 people. More-recent meetings have showcased the growth in community schools and hotspots of that growth, offering opportunities for site and school visits. The 2010 conference was held in Philadelphia, which was then both on the front lines of "market-oriented" school reform and at the start of a community-school movement in that city. In 2012, the forum in

San Francisco "was [the Coalition for Community Schools'] biggest forum to date with more than 1,400 participants from around the United States and Canada."[37] In 2018, in Baltimore, another large city where community schools have gained momentum as a school improvement strategy, 2,000 people participated.

ADDRESSING THE CHALLENGES OF SCALING

Like all coalition-building efforts, however, the community-school movement has also encountered challenges with respect to building the ISS field, messaging, and amassing sufficient resources to support its work, among others. Understanding these challenges can help explain why, despite substantial growth in recent decades, the number and quality of community schools still fall far short of the need for them. Education and community leaders must identify strategies to overcome these challenges to scaling up programs if they are to meet the need.[38]

Conflict Between a Movement and Its Various Messages

From early on, the Coalition for Community Schools has encountered an impediment common to building up a movement: bringing on board a diverse set of signatories and "partners" makes it increasingly hard to get those allies on the same page for messaging and advocacy. As the Democratic Party, among other big-tent efforts, has learned, the flip side of having a large and powerful body of advocates to promote your cause is having to deal with a loose coalition that is difficult to corral and often fractious.

These challenges have led to competition for resources, funding, and policy attention and some fairly public divisions between members. For example, the coalition has had a sometimes-tense relationship with one of its most prominent partners, CIS. With similar names and the potential to mistake one for the other, both organizations have struggled to secure their unique space in the ISS field. One reason for this tension may be that by citing ISS as just one of several criteria for a community school, the coalition set up an inherent conflict with CIS, which bills itself explicitly as a replicable, reliable deliverer of ISS. Adding to this tension are independent evaluations that enable CIS to call itself an evidence-based strategy in ways that community schools cannot claim to the same extent, and CIS's strengths in fund-raising, branding, and messaging—strengths that further elevate its status.[39] As described below, however, these tensions seem to be waning and more meaningful collaboration is taking root. The more these and other ISS players see themselves as able to complement one another, and the less stress on each for resources, the better it will be for building the field and the movement.

Another prime example of these tensions can be seen in the trajectory of a federal law that has been vital to supporting community schools: the 21st Century Community Learning Centers initiative.[40] In the late 1990s, the Mott Foundation had a close relationship with the US Department of Education partly because of a public-private partnership created under Bill Clinton's administration. Several of the foundation's grantees worked to generate support for a bill, introduced under President Clinton, that would increase funding for the then-nascent community learning centers program from less than $1 million to $40 million and provide training and technical assistance.

The Mott Foundation was eager to scale up the work it had been doing in Flint, Michigan, for several decades. In advocating ISS, Mott focused on after-school enrichment as the hook, because polling research showed that after-school programs resonated better than the concept of community schools did. (The research suggested that the idea of community schools was then too broad to garner widespread support and effective advocacy.) But the legislative goal was to provide a growing pot of money that could be used for various ISS purposes and activities, and Clinton's 1999 proposal for an $800 million increase over the next five years promised to do just that. However, the provision's placement in education law and, thus, its emphasis on academic success rather than on community engagement, childcare, or youth development engendered some opposition within the field. Leadership at the coalition, for example, wanted to carve out dedicated funds for community schools specifically, even though the law's flexibility already allowed for their support. The Forum for Youth Investment opposed the bill because of its lack of an explicit youth development focus.

The George W. Bush administration's proposal to cut funding by 30 percent, however, helped these disparate camps rally together to protect the legislation in 2003. Arnold Schwarzenegger, who was about to announce his candidacy as a Republican for governor of California, became the public face of the campaign. And the Coalition for Community Schools joined the Mott Foundation, the Afterschool Alliance (which Mott had recently established in partnership with the US Department of Education and other backers), and other key after-school and ISS stakeholders to protect full funding.

This story provides lessons for the field as it continues to grow. While broadly defining community schools enables a desirable big tent, it also creates the potential for destructive internal division over support of various components. Figuring out how to better reconcile inclusiveness with strategic focus will be key to developing a stronger advocacy campaign. The goal should be to come up with ways of defining ISS and community schools so that that all coalition members feel that their work is accurately described and represented. Only then will collaborative advocacy be truly effective.

Limited and Inconsistent Resources

Another challenge has been the mismatch between the need for resources to scale up the community-school movement and the availability of such resources. This disparity is evident in the coalition's website (www.communityschools.org), which serves as a resource clearinghouse for community-school advocates, practitioners, and other potential supporters. The website bears telltales of inadequate support. The scaling-up guide, for example, a flagship publication and prominent website feature, was published in 2011, has not been updated since, and is missing content.[41] Several links no longer function. In general, the site is difficult to navigate, resources can be hard to find, and many publications are outdated in their reference to policy makers no longer in office or legislation that no longer applies.

In other respects, too, gaps between the coalition's claims of work it is doing and the reality of work on the ground illustrate how insufficient the resources are to support this work and how thin they have been stretched. The coalition leads seven networks, but it is unclear which and how many are active and productive, or even how a staff of five or six could support half, let alone all, of these networks.[42] (The networks include the Community Schools Leadership Network, the Community Schools Superintendents Leadership Council, the Community Schools Coordinators Network, the United Way Community Schools Learning Community, the Community Schools State Coalitions Network, University-Assisted Community Schools, and a research consortium.)

Longtime community-school leaders in California report struggling to set aside time for Leadership Network calls, which are often sparsely attended and poorly organized. A prominent district superintendent who was listed on the Superintendents Leadership Council in 2015 was surprised to find his name on the list, given that he had never joined. A Drexel University professor who was conducting community-school research in Pennsylvania and who was directed by a national partner to the coalition's research group noted that the partner herself admitted that the research group's work was more aspirational than solid. And during a research webinar he later attended, the speakers devoted as much time to asking about other research that might be available and requesting that the participants conduct additional research as they did to presenting their own work.

After sitting in on several network calls with few participants, and recognizing that staff are stretched thin and may not always be the right experts to drive learning, José Muñoz, who came on board as director in 2017, says the coalition is scaling back its leadership of several networks. With the goal of modeling democracy-building to spur democratic engagement among partners, he is guiding his staff to focus on encouraging coalition partner advocates and practitioners in the field to take the lead on much of this work.[43]

Gap Between Goals and Realities of Community Schools

Perhaps most central to these disparities is the gap between the ideal of a community school and the reality among the vast majority of programs across thousands of schools. As just described, few individual schools meet the lofty description set forth by the coalition, and only a handful of the community-level efforts match up. The leaders of Bay Area community schools, whose work the coalition website and staff describe as cutting-edge, depict a much more mixed reality in which leadership is inconsistent and resources are vastly uneven across districts. These leaders are much more in the know; they say that attention to within-school enrichment and opportunity are more often the exception than the norm and that thirty years after San Francisco established its first community school, only a fraction of students in that city are well supported. A major concern for advocates, practitioners, and policy makers, then, is the degree to which the high standards set for individual community schools and districts are realistic, and if so, what it would take to attain these standards with far more frequency than at present.

GOING FORWARD

One of the biggest opportunities to expand community schools as a way to scale ISS lies in the prominent, big-city efforts noted above. New York City, in particular, demonstrates the strong promise as well as the pitfalls of such high-profile community-school efforts. On the heels of a decade of school reforms that focused narrowly on standardized student testing—to evaluate teachers, identify schools for improvement, transform some schools to charters, and even close some schools—the city saw little improvement but substantial protest. In this environment, the community-school strategy, in addition to a focus on early childhood education, represents a refreshing change. This new direction is designed to engage parents and the community in addressing core poverty-related issues with which schools and their students struggle. The mayor put in place a team to scale up community schools and provide ongoing support and technical assistance. Led by the former Children's Aid CEO, the team can draw on years of experience with what works in the city.

At the same time, funding the huge expansion encountered obstacles from the start, with Mayor de Blasio's call for a tax on the wealthiest New Yorkers engendering pushback from the business community and exacerbating his already-fraught relationship with that key constituency. And even if the state funding that Governor Andrew Cuomo and the legislature have allocated is sufficient, building up other critical resources, especially the human capital capacity, will pose a major challenge to transforming more than two hundred of the city's highest-poverty, lowest-performing schools.

Expectations are high, elevated in part by the mayor's and community-school advocates' own messages. As a result, if these expectations are not met, the community-school effort may risk being considered the latest failing reform fad or, worse, may "prove" that big cities like New York simply cannot turn around their struggling schools and that people should stop trying. And even if the effort is relatively successful, the divisive nature of school reform in recent years, especially in New York, makes this effort a prime opportunity for skeptics of community schools and opponents of the mayor to claim failure. Proponents of ISS, whether or not they consider themselves within the community-school aegis, have a lot of skin in this game.

The stakes may be slightly lower in Philadelphia, but the odds of success are also to some extent more stacked against that city's community-school effort. For over a decade, severely insufficient state funding for the high-poverty, heavily minority district has made it increasingly difficult for Philadelphia public schools to function. Class sizes have grown substantially, older buildings are crumbling, basic materials are in short supply, and nonteaching staff like nurses and librarians, who are critical to student well-being, have been stripped from many schools. Proponents who helped advance a soda tax to fund the city's community schools notched an important win when the Pennsylvania Supreme Court affirmed the tax's legality in July 2018, but they still have many uphill battles ahead.

The community-school movement will clearly play a major role in both of these high-profile efforts, as well as in hundreds of smaller ones across the country. Questions we have raised on scaling, capacity, and research should be front and center if this movement is to thrive. How will the coalition's new director, Muñoz, who replaced founder Marty Blank in September 2017, position it? What is Muñoz's strategy for amassing the financial and other resources needed to sustain and scale up the coalition's many ambitious projects? How will key players, in particular CIS, which also recently got a new executive director, work with the coalition? Will the school-by-school approach continue to dominate and drive the growth of community schools, or will a different approach surface?

The initial signs after a changing of the guard in both organizations are promising. In December 2016, the Coalition for Community Schools and CIS collaborated with StriveTogether, a third key ISS leader, on a joint statement of principles.[44] The statement calls for more aggressive, united, and effective action: "In hundreds of communities all across the country, our three nonprofit networks—The Coalition for Community Schools, Communities In Schools and StriveTogether—have been making measurable progress toward educational equity. *Now we come together to say explicitly that we can achieve our shared goals more effectively if we align our assets and expertise across networks, across school districts and across communities.*"[45]

The three organizations have since joined forces to administer a grant funded by the Ford Foundation and the Chan Zuckerberg Initiative that supports community-school work in ten communities. Through the Students at the Center Challenge, ten communities will receive planning grants of up to $150,000 each to "move toward a student-centered learning system . . . [It combines] quality educational opportunities with health and wellness services, mentoring, college readiness activities and work-based learning experiences."[46] After the initial six-month planning period, communities may receive implementation grants and technical assistance or capacity-building grants and support. While a promising step in the right direction, like many other philanthropic efforts supporting ISS, it provides only a fraction of what communities will need to do this work well and to make it sustainable.

Tiffany Miller, who came on board at CIS as vice president of government relations soon before Dale Erquiaga took the lead, says that her organization is developing a stronger and more collaborative relationship with the Coalition for Community Schools, with both CIS and the coalition recognizing that they need each other to achieve their respective, and joint, missions. This sentiment is echoed by Shital Shah, who managed policy and partnerships at the coalition, led community-school fieldwork for the AFT for six years, and still oversees that strategy: "Over time, [coalition and CIS] efforts have become much closer. CIS's role has been significant in that they are helping coordinate services. Traditionally, those coordinated services have been mostly targeted (and case management style), but they are evolving, where they can, into a more whole-school approach for their coordinated services/opportunities."[47]

In August 2018, Muñoz and Erquiaga took the stage with community-school researchers and policy advocates at the Center for American Progress to announce the publication of two new products: the center's study exploring several district-level community-school initiatives, and the *Community Schools Playbook*. As described earlier in this chapter, the playbook, produced by the Partnership for the Future of Learning, gives comprehensive guidance for practitioners, advocates, and policy makers seeking to support district-level community-school work. More detailed than any existing technical assistance resources, the book emphasizes the comprehensive framework and high standards that the coalition has established in the past few years. It also offers concrete information on supportive policies (state and local) and talking points that draw on polling and other data on what is effective.

In sum, the community-school movement and the coalition that has helped to drive it forward offer real potential to scale ISS to levels that, to paraphrase our president, have never been seen. CIS wants to expand from its current footprint of twenty-three hundred schools to five thousand in the next few years. And the coalition has set the ambitious goal of having twenty-five thousand community schools across the country by 2025. This goal, says Muñoz, would mean being in one-quarter of the nation's schools and half of its high-poverty schools. It would enable the community-school strategy to attain the critical mass that can sustain momentum and growth.

The next few years will therefore be critical in determining how well community-school partners who have historically squabbled can come together to collaborate meaningfully. We will also see how seriously researchers take the need to address hard questions in ways that provide key answers, not only for those who make policy but also for those doing the hard work on the ground. As the next chapter illustrates, the next few years will also be important predictors of how growing success in the field translates to more, and more stable, sources of funding for ISS, both public and private, and how those resources in turn translate into better work in the field and at the national level.

11

Financing
Integrated Student
Supports at Scale

I n this book, we have described a variety of approaches to building
community-level ISS initiatives that form the kind of cradle-to-career
pipeline that would channel all our children to success. Although pieces
of this pipeline are currently operating successfully in many communities
or sometimes even at the state level, we do not yet have any examples of
fully developed, fully functioning, effective cradle-to-career pipelines.
As discussed, such systems will be critical to closing the opportunity and
enrichment gaps that perpetuate our achievement gaps.

We know and have shown that some of the pipeline architecture can
be built by repurposing existing resources, but there will be unavoidable,
additional costs if we are to build such a system at scale, making it available to all children. This chapter explores two questions: What will such
a scaled pipeline cost? And how will we pay for it?

A CRADLE-TO-CAREER PIPELINE

To determine systems for, and sources of, funding, organizations must first define the pipeline itself. Many organizations have developed their own descriptions of cradle-to-career pipelines. For example, the Harlem Children's Zone; StriveTogether; Promise Neighborhoods; and the cities of Louisville, Kentucky, and Hayward, California, have developed their own descriptions of these pipelines. Two descriptions that we find particularly compelling and useful are those created by the Forum for Youth Investment, which describes the pipeline as the Ready by 21 Insulated Education Pipeline, and the Brookings Institution's Social Genome Project.

The Forum for Youth Investment's pipeline schematic is based on the premise that traditional academic systems sit at the center of child development and should be buttressed by a variety of enrichment opportunities and social supports provided by families, peers, and community members. Childcare providers and after-school programs provide key developmental support in children's earlier years, while work opportunities and placement and coaching supports are critical to getting teens to the twenty-one-year finish line in good shape. Surrounding all this support are public systems

FIGURE 11.1

The Ready by 21 Insulated Education Pipeline

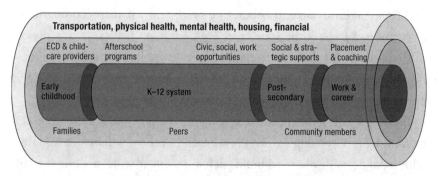

Source: Forum for Youth Investment, "Getting Communities Ready," 2009, www.readyby21.org /what-ready-21/getting-communities-ready. Used with permission.

of transportation, physical health, mental health, housing, and others, such as financial institutions. Figure 11.1 reflects the approaches taken by many of the communities described in the preceding chapters. It also makes clear the complex web of policy and funding mechanisms that are needed to make a functioning pipeline a reality.

The Social Genome Project takes a slightly different perspective. Basing its work on the concern that social mobility in the United States has stalled, the project's leaders assert that "achieving the American Dream depends on being born to adults who are ready to be parents, and then succeeding at each subsequent stage in life."[1] The five life stages it identifies include being raised by two nonpoor parents, kindergarten readiness, academic and social skill proficiency at the transition to middle school, avoidance of risky teen behavior on the road to high school graduation, and a solid career path, preferably based on a college degree, by young adulthood. The project is designed to evaluate programs that can help students succeed at each point in that trajectory, with the goal of identifying the programs that merit substantial private and public investment.

Various components of the pipeline have been illustrated through the work of the communities described in this book. Several of these communities can rely on high-quality state preK systems that serve most or all of their district's children. Others have created their own systems to ensure that children enjoy strong early-educational experiences that prepare them for kindergarten. Schools in all these districts partner with local organizations to provide a range of after-school enrichment and support opportunities, and most extend these over the summer as well, so that disadvantaged children do not lose ground to their better-off peers. Some communities support school-based health clinics, while others collaborate with community doctors, dentists, and mental health providers to meet students' needs in these areas. And several have begun to use the community partnerships they have cultivated to create internship, apprenticeship, and other work opportunities for middle and high school students.

All of the communities, of course, draw on families, peers, and community partners to enable these pipeline components. All also demonstrate that although schools are central to the building of such a pipeline, many other components and partners are critical. Schools may not always be at the center of the cradle-to-career pipeline. Indeed, we have argued that ultimately, the provision of this pipeline is a community obligation and ought to be part of a new social compact between families and communities. The theory of action embodied in this approach harkens back to the proverb, possibly African, made popular in the United States by the Children's Defense Fund and Hillary Clinton: "It takes a village to raise a child."

THE LIMITATIONS OF TODAY'S SCHOOLS' FINANCIAL SYSTEMS

We never intended for our schools to do many of the things that we are now asking them to do. Over the past fifty years, however, as society has recognized the influence of issues such as segregation, poverty, social and emotional health, and parent engagement on children's ability to learn effectively, schools have taken on a range of new responsibilities. Simultaneously, the economy and culture have changed, bringing about phenomena like single-parent families or families in which both parents work. These changes have meant families have less time for functions that schools are often now expected to handle like nutrition, health care, behavior, and recreation.

Over this same period, we have evolved from a public school system originally designed to sort students into groups and to educate only a few of them to very high levels. We now expect our schools to educate every student (or at least the vast majority of them) to a level higher than what used to be expected of just a few children. This expectation that the school system will educate all students to high levels, leaving "no child behind" and ensuring that "every student succeeds" is unprecedented and audacious. In most cases, government leaders have exponentially raised the bar for school performance while doing little or nothing to provide the resources or additional capacity (time, personnel, training) to achieve policy makers' aspirational goals. (In fact, over this period, funding for education has fallen in many places, sometimes dramatically.)

U.S. schools have never been funded or structured to achieve at such a high level, let alone provide all the extra support that educators have increasingly been expected to undertake in recent decades. If schools are to achieve these ambitious policy goals and educate children properly, we'll need to not only strengthen existing school finance mechanisms but also look beyond the schools to communities, states, the federal government, philanthropists, and nongovernmental organizations for additional support to meet students' wide-ranging needs. Schools will often be curators and coordinators of ISS, though other organizations in the community will sometimes be expected to be the backbone of an ISS system. Either way, responsibilities will generally need to be distributed much more broadly.

Not only do most schools currently lack the capacity to provide all the needed ISS and opportunities, but schools are also typically not even funded at levels that enable them to fulfill their narrower, traditional, academic mission.

Even if we were to systematically fund all schools at the levels required to deliver a solid basic education, high-poverty schools would still face a substantial barrier to effective teaching and learning. To deliver a sound education, these schools must first tackle a wide range of student needs driven by outside social challenges that are disproportionately prevalent in low-income communities. Thus, communities and schools must routinely ensure that the students have everything they need to come to school ready to learn. These needs include preschool services, physical and mental health services, social workers, summer activities, and after-school enrichment. Let's now explore what both a basic education and a full cradle-to-career ISS system would require.

CHALLENGES TO PROVIDING THE BASICS FOR ALL STUDENTS

To provide adequate education for every student, schools must, at the very least, hire and retain well trained, qualified teachers and other staff; maintain the building in good shape; and purchase key resources such as textbooks, desks, paper and pencils, and computers. Other costs include school nurses, librarians, and up-to-date books, counseling offices and staff, and athletic facilities and equipment.

At no time in U.S. history, however, have schools consistently provided these basics to most, let alone all, students. For much of that history, the country did not even intend for schools to do so. In recent years, as poverty and the associated needs of American students have risen, federal and state budget cuts have often reduced the resources available for public education. Consequently, the number of schools that can provide interventions to compensate for students' unmet nonacademic needs, or can even attend to their basic necessities, is shrinking.

Reliance on Local Funding

A major culprit in the failing traditional academic formula is our system for funding schools. A review of the extensive literature on this critical issue lies outside the scope of this book, so we will limit this discussion to a few cogent points. The United States is alone among its peers in compelling schools to rely heavily on local funding. Across Europe and Asia, schools are a national responsibility, and central governments provide the majority of funding. State funding of public education varies widely, from 90 percent in Vermont to 25 percent in Illinois, while on average, 47 percent of U.S. school district revenue comes from these local taxes.[2] Although many states have increased their support of public education over recent decades, the school financing system is still too heavily reliant on inherently inequitable local property taxes.

This unique system virtually guarantees that children who arrive at kindergarten already far behind because of a range of familial and community disadvantages are consigned to the least-resourced schools. These schools are typically staffed by the least prepared and least experienced teachers. Students in these schools are often isolated by race or are concentrated in classes with very high proportions of similarly low-income students or are segregated in both these ways.[3]

As many European countries recognize, schools serving disadvantaged students require more, not less, funding; these countries tend to allocate resources in this way at the national level.[4] Mental and emotional health needs, for example, tend to be greater in schools with disadvantaged children, because of the added stress children experience from living in high-poverty and violent neighborhoods. Schools consequently need more counselors and social workers, as well as smaller classrooms to enable more one-on-one attention.

All the extra services necessary in some U.S. schools require that state and federal funding schemes distribute monies not only to equalize funding across districts but also to ensure that higher-poverty schools have greater resources. Neither financial scheme, however, has happened. Rather, our country's school finance systems tend to further advantage the advantaged.

Inequitable State Funding Schemes

As the communities explored in this book illustrate, few states spend anything close to the $17,000 per pupil that Massachusetts spends or the nearly $20,000 per pupil that New Jersey spends. Not remarkably, then, Massachusetts and New Jersey are two of the highest-performing states.[5] In fact, they are two of only four states that fund schools at high levels and do so equitably.[6] Maryland, home to Montgomery County Public Schools, is close, at around $15,000, but Washington (Vancouver Public Schools) and Michigan (Kalamazoo) both spend under $12,000. Missouri (Joplin), Arkansas (Pea Ridge), and Kentucky (Berea) spend less than $11,000; and Texas (Austin) and Florida (Tangelo Park) spend less than $10,000 per pupil. North Carolina (East Durham Children's Initiative) is near the bottom of the pack (forty-fifth out of fifty states), at just over $9,000 per pupil in 2014.

Most of these states also fail to compensate for inadequate local funding of low-income schools in their state systems. Instead, they provide roughly the same dollars per pupil for those schools that they do for wealthier ones.[7] Massachusetts received an A on equitable distribution, but two other case study states—New York and Missouri—received D and F grades, for funding their low-income schools at just 93 percent and 88 percent, respectively, of the levels they provide higher-income schools. Moreover, Florida, North Carolina, Texas, and Washington received Fs for effort—failing to raise revenue for their public schools commensurate with their capacity to do so.

Inadequate and Poorly Distributed Federal Funds

Understanding that the needs of disadvantaged students in high-poverty communities typically exceeded the capacity of their local communities to amass resources to meet these needs, Congress passed the Elementary and Secondary Education Act (ESEA) in 1965 as part of President Johnson's War on Poverty. This legislation was a major step for the federal government, which had heretofore been reluctant to take a significant role in K–12 education. The cornerstone of this flagship federal education legislation, which is designed to level the playing field for historically disadvantaged youth, is Title I.[8]

From its inception fifty years ago, Title I has never been funded at a level that would enable it to completely address the impacts of poverty. Moreover, over its past five decades and multiple reauthorizations and iterations, changes in the legislation have made federal funding both less equitable and less sufficient in meeting its original stated goal of equity. Compounding these problems, schools in small rural towns like Pea Ridge and isolated, deeply impoverished communities like Clay, Jackson, and Owsley Counties in Appalachian Kentucky face particular disadvantages because of quirks in how Title I funds are distributed.[9]

The major recession of 2007–2010 exacerbated these multilevel challenges to school funding. Most states cut education funding in response to budget crises, and by 2015, five years after the official end of the recession, twenty-nine states had still failed to restore funding even to prerecession levels.[10] The three states that enacted the biggest cuts—Arizona, Florida, and Alabama—were already among the country's lowest-spending, so schools with bare-bones budgets had few options other than to make further cuts. Several of the hardest-hit states, Arizona, Idaho, Kansas, Michigan, Mississippi, North Carolina, and Oklahoma, also cut state personal or corporate income tax rates, thus limiting resources to restore funding in the coming decades.

To ensure adequate funding for basic education services, advocates have pursued various strategies, most targeted at the state level. Some have successfully pursued lawsuits designed to attack states' failures to achieve equity (basic fairness in the distribution of state education resources) or adequacy (to ensure that schools receive sufficient funding to educate all students to a level of proficiency), or both. Equity-friendly decisions in states like Kentucky, Massachusetts, and New York have forced legislatures to develop more equitable and adequate funding formulas.

The success of plaintiffs' claims in such lawsuits often depends on the respective state's constitutional language relative to education. This language varies widely from state to state, ranging from weak and vague to explicit language situating responsibility for education squarely on the state. Sometimes, however, these cases rest on the particular court's interpretation of pivotal concepts such as equity and adequacy. One court may assume that schools should only be expected to provide their graduates with a minimum of an eighth-grade level of proficiency, while other jurisdictions strive for levels of proficiency aligned with the high skills and knowledge demanded in a twenty-first-century economy. For plaintiffs, the verdicts in this state-by-state quest for equitable finance can be elusive, erratic, and frustrating. This inequitable nonsystem demonstrates that the United States is unable to guarantee that all children have access to schools that are fairly and adequately funded.

Other advocates have pursued political strategies designed to persuade legislatures to "do the right thing" on education funding. More often than not—as in a recent hard-fought ballot initiative in Colorado—these campaigns have failed, leaving proponents with no recourse but the courts, assuming they could afford to mount a lawsuit.

ESTIMATING THE COST OF A BETTER SYSTEM

Above and beyond sufficient funding for traditional academic school systems, then, we must ask, what will it cost to build (at the local, state, or national level) an ISS system, an insulated cradle-to-career pipeline that will fully prepare all children for success? We know that the first steps are to take better advantage of existing resources by improving coordination and making them more accessible, but beyond those steps, additional costs remain. While there is no single estimate available for a full-wraparound, equitable child development and education system, some efforts have been made to develop credible estimates of the cost for constructing a system strong enough to deliver on our policy aspirations of educating all for success.

Michael Rebell is a well-known school equity and adequacy litigator and a professor of education at Teachers College, Columbia University. He and his colleagues have developed a constitutional cost methodology—a rubric based on state constitutional provisions regarding equitable and adequate education. Their work builds on the four established methods for estimating the cost of adequate education: professional judgment of experts; evidence-based assessments; successful-school models; and cost function (a calculation of costs using past statistical data).[11] The authors ultimately promote an enhanced professional-judgment approach that minimizes the potential for bias and political manipulation, uses real-world data and scenarios, and embeds specific requirements into state law so that costs cannot be negotiated or cut back in any given year.

While Rebell and colleagues' approach is technically targeted to the needs of schools only, their framework pays close attention to the unique needs of students who are disadvantaged by poverty, disability, and other factors. It also assumes that outcomes for all students include not just the traditional academic ones (the three Rs), but also preparation for civic engagement and a meaningful career. In other words, the group's approach to cost estimating goes much of the way toward producing a reasonable cost model for ISS. The authors suggest, for example, widespread adoption of the broad range of student outcomes set forth by the Kentucky Supreme Court in the *Rose* case. The Education Law Center describes the case as follows: "In 1989, in *Rose v. Council for Better Education*, the Kentucky Supreme Court held that the General Assembly did not satisfy the constitutional requirement to provide an efficient system of common schools throughout the State. To meet the constitutional requirement, the Court explained, the education system must be adequately funded, ensure equality, and be designed to provide every child with seven delineated capacities," including "oral and written communication skills," "knowledge of economic, social and political systems," and self-knowledge of physical and mental wellness.[12]

According to Rebell and his coauthors, the decision in the *Rose* case assumes the need for meaningful extracurricular activities, internships, and a wide range of health and human service supports. These authors also argue that the minimum inputs set forth by the New York courts could also be adapted to support other aspects of student support, like essential counseling services. Finally, the framework's cost-effectiveness requirement would mean exploring other options, like community-school partnerships, that have been found to be most effective in efficiently achieving desired academic outcomes.

The Brookings Institution's Social Genome Project offers a different way to obtain a cost estimate for a successful ISS system. Building on its five-stage rubric for appropriate student progress leading to long-term success, the team of experts from Brookings is collaborating with Child Trends and the Urban Institute. Using a life cycle model, they draw on longitudinal data from multiple sources to compare the impacts of various interventions, noting that they can also estimate indirect and longer-term effects as well as the impacts of multiple interventions.[13] A series of papers also provides estimates of various aspects of the project's program agenda, both the costs of current noninvestment and the benefits of investing. For example, one Brookings paper uses estimates from the Social Genome Project to predict how to improve a child's chances of a successful life.[14]

Perhaps the most directly relevant study on this subject is a 2011 white paper jointly authored by Richard Rothstein of the Economic Policy Institute and two fellow researchers for the Campaign for Educational Equity. The second in a five-part series, the paper offers an estimate of the cost of "providing comprehensive educational opportunity to low-income students."[15] Their model, which goes beyond schooling expenses (the cost of school is not included), comprises the full range of opportunities and supports needed to raise "success-ready" children. Their approach begins with prenatal support for expectant mothers and includes age-appropriate family support, academic instruction and enrichment, physical and mental health care, and after-school and summer programs for children from birth through age eighteen. Assuming that children eligible for subsidized school meals would use the program, the authors estimate the cost for a New York City family that took advantage of all the recommended services in the full model would be $290,000 (cumulative over the lifetime), or $15,700 per child per year.[16]

That might seem like a lot at first glance, but it is actually much less than what taxpayers must spend to support the food, health, housing, and criminal-justice costs of young people unprepared to succeed in the twenty-first century. It also compares to a U.S. Department of Agriculture estimate of around $230,000 (national average, not adjusted to New York City) to raise a child.

As members of a field that is growing toward a movement, ISS proponents must bear down on developing more-precise cost estimates for providing holistic support and opportunity to every child. Despite being initially daunting, these figures will provide a long-term goal and a realistic answer to those who ask, How much will this cost? From a political standpoint, it would be unwise to lead with discussions of the full price of the fully realized model of child development and education. At the same time, the movement would be remiss if we didn't outline the components of a system—the actual education, supports, and opportunities needed—and then accurately project the costs of such a model. We must make better use of existing resources. And we must collaborate better and make better financial estimates to build public support and demand for a full opportunity system for all children.

HOW WILL WE PAY FOR IT?

One approach to tackling the financing challenge is for community leaders to follow the steps set out by the Forum for Youth Investment's Children's Funding Project:

1. *Find:* Leaders map community assets to assess the local resources that already exist.
2. *Align:* Leaders must seek to better align the use of these resources with their goals for children and youth. Then analysts should conduct a gap analysis to calibrate the difference between available and needed funding and other resources.
3. *Generate:* This step sets the financing challenge and provides targets. The community then will need to develop strategies to achieve the established funding goals.
4. *Evaluate:* Finally, the programs and services that the assets enable must be rigorously evaluated for their effectiveness in achieving the desired goals for children and youth.

Just as we must explore a range of options for costing out a scaled-up ISS system, we should explore, and utilize, the broad range of sources to pay for it. These include public funding at all three levels (local, state, and federal); public-private options (such as housing preK centers in empty business spaces); and wholly private ones (although it can play only a limited role, philanthropy will certainly continue to be important).

Public Funding: Critical and Multilayered

Like other societal goods—roads, national defense, the environment—public education has been funded largely by taxpayer dollars. And given that ISS is a necessary complement to public education, tax revenues would logically constitute the largest share of support for this effort. One consideration is in finding the optimal balance between federal, state, and local dollars to support both education and ISS. Ideally, a twenty-first-century finance system for children and youth would be less reliant on local revenues, which inherently compound and perpetuate existing economic inequities. Deriving larger shares from both state and federal sources would reduce sharp disparities across districts and states that continue to make zip code a key predictor of a child's school success. These sources should include both general and special-purpose revenue streams.

Moreover, since a solid education requires children to be healthy, well-nourished, and emotionally well, we should look more closely at other, non-education-related pots of money, such as social security disability funds, Medicaid, public housing support, and Temporary Assistance for Needy Families funds. Leaders should strive to make better use of these funds and to better align various other sources of government funding to support students and their families.

To build up to the necessary large-scale funding, however, we will need to first establish a stronger compilation of local success stories enabled by local funders. These examples can inspire local action and build local demand for ISS interventions; such demand is the best driver of political will at the state and federal levels.

Social impact bonds (SIBs) are another avenue that more communities—and states—should explore. This increasingly popular strategy secures near-term financing from both public and private sources to underwrite the cost of services that have quantifiable long-term financial benefits in the form of savings for government entities. (The first SIB ever created was used to fund a prisoner rehabilitation program in Britain.[17]) For example, early-childhood education is expensive up front, but the long-term benefits enable a much higher percentage of graduates to pay taxes, contribute to society, stay out of prison, and avoid reliance on costly government programs for housing, health, and other services. An SIB for early-childhood education would find outside investors to share the costs of high-quality, universal early-childhood education. Twenty years later, when more students have graduated from high school and college and, consequently, are paying more taxes and costing less in public services and criminal-justice expenditures, governments can use those savings to repay investors.

In Utah, for example, a successful SIB helped persuade the state's conservative legislature to finally join virtually every other state in funding a preK program. More recently, Northern Virginia hedge fund manager and early-childhood advocate Robert Dugger is exploring the creation of SIBs that would use savings from reduced costs for elementary school special education to fund preK programs.[18] A handful of SIB-backed success stories could go a long way toward persuading conservative legislators, in particular, that extensive public investment in ISS is worthwhile and politically viable.

Private Funding: Necessary but Risky

Leaders of communities employing ISS have responded to limited public funds by turning to private philanthropists. In all twelve communities featured in this book, foundations or wealthy individuals, or both, have played important parts. And in Tangelo Park and the East Durham Children's Initiative, integrated student supports are funded entirely from private sources—in Tangelo Park, by a single individual.

Having failed to obtain the federal Promise Neighborhoods grant for which they had applied, leaders of the EDCI decided to pursue only private donations, at least for the initial phase. They believe that this strategy affords them more flexibility in how to allocate funds and entails less of the red tape that recipients of government grants describe.

In Tangelo Park, the advantages of a private system are obvious. Having a single sponsor has transformed the neighborhood over the past two decades from a drug-ridden and violent place with very high rates of mobility to a desirable, stable one with high levels of student achievement and virtually no crime. That overwhelming success led the sponsor, Harris Rosen, to take on a larger and more challenging Orlando neighborhood, Parramore, starting in 2016. But even if the second endeavor is as successful as Tangelo Park has been, and even if Rosen's model were to persuade a dozen other billionaires to make similar investments across the country, private funding is obviously not a feasible way to meet the country's ISS needs. This approach is more like the lottery. A few will win, but a systemic, scalable approach is needed.

Other communities that implement ISS to enable students to take advantage of their Promise scholarships illustrate the limitations of this model when applied to an entire city. Kalamazoo, Syracuse, and Buffalo are still far from ensuring that all students graduate from high school, let alone succeed in college. In Kalamazoo, advocates are still working toward transforming the Promise into sufficiently consistent support for all the district's students. Because of multiple problems in Syracuse, the large private donations could not generate the desired success. The Say Yes work in Buffalo looks more promising, but the long-term outcomes are far from clear.

Like federal and state government grants supporting ISS initiatives, private grants have their downsides, some of them similar to the shortcomings of government grants. Most are either onetime pools of funds or time-limited awards, thus requiring time and effort for multiple proposals and the need to replace funds when the grant expires. Like public grants, their size rarely meets the needs for which they are targeted. Private funders often have high expectations—after all, it is their own money that is being spent—and they may make demands that districts cannot fulfill. Or the demands may not match community needs. And as is true of public funds, it is much harder for small or rural districts like Pea Ridge or those in Appalachian Kentucky to obtain private grants, as philanthropists are fewer in these regions, donor dollars scarce, and the personnel needed to apply for them very limited.

Perhaps most critical, large foundations that invest in education policy and practice have leaned heavily toward narrower strategies that not only bypassed the implementation of ISS but also distracted other philanthropists from investing in strategies to advance whole-child education systems. (These follow decades of other philanthropic efforts that have failed to address core poverty-related obstacles to effective teaching and learning.) For this reason, private funding has sometimes proved to be a poor strategic choice. Most prominently, the Bill and Melinda Gates Foundation, a generous contributor to a variety of antipoverty endeavors, has struggled to achieve its goals in several prominent K–12 education reform strategies despite success in some areas such as early-childhood education, teacher development, and postsecondary opportunities.

In the past few years, as public opinion has shifted to acknowledge the impacts of poverty and to view education policy more broadly, the reform conversation has been evolving in the philanthropic world as well. In June 2016, the *Los Angeles Times*, which a few years earlier had defended the public release of so-called value-added scores advanced by the Gates Foundation, scolded Gates and fellow philanthropies for trying to dictate what public school agendas should be.[19] And in their 2018 annual open letter, Bill and Melinda Gates acknowledge that their ($700 million) focus on improving teaching had made little progress, as was true of their prior effort to create smaller high schools.[20] Similarly, Mark Zuckerberg, Facebook founder and CEO, recognizes the limitations of his philanthropic ventures into education. Responding to criticisms of the largely ineffective uses of his $100 million investment in charter schools and other efforts in Newark, Zuckerberg argues that some successes had been achieved. But he also admits that effective, sustainable school improvement strategies must address poverty-related impediments to learning and that communities must be engaged from the outset in the process.[21] Consequently, the Chan Zuckerberg Initiative, a foundation that he established with his wife, Priscilla Chan, is now dedicated to advancing a "whole child approach to personalized learning" and focusing on local efforts that engage schools and draw on input from educators.[22]

One of the foundation's first projects, for example, is a partnership with the nonprofit organization Vision to Learn to provide low-income students in California with vision exams and eyeglasses. The decision was made in response to extensive evidence that low-income students are often misdiagnosed with learning disabilities and unnecessarily placed in special education classrooms because they do not see well. Another is the foundation's decision to support the holistic work of Harvard's Education Redesign Lab. The Chan Zuckerberg Initiative also decided to team up with the Ford Foundation, a longtime ISS proponent, to support a new joint initiative led by CIS, the Coalition for Community Schools, and StriveTogether. Finally, the Gates and Chan Zuckerberg foundations have recently come together to fund high-quality research on topics as wide-ranging as writing, math, and executive function. Such redirection of philanthropic resources represents a potentially promising new phase that could have significant implications for ISS.

Major philanthropic commitments will be key to building the local successes needed as a bedrock to scaling ISS up to become a standard feature of education, especially in disadvantaged communities. Private funding was critical to launching and expanding many of the strongest ISS communities, to enabling many others to explore individual components of ISS and whole-child education, and to piloting innovative ISS strategies. And philanthropic support will surely continue to play this role. But as this chapter makes clear, even if it were much better structured and more generous, private funding, while necessary, will always be insufficient to completely meet the support and enrichment needs of the nation's most challenged students.

Philanthropic Successes

Other philanthropists, however, have long understood the need to expand ISS. Indeed, philanthropy has played a central role in creating this field.

As previously described, Charles Stewart Mott's firsthand experience of the transformative power of community schools in his hometown of Flint made him a lifelong advocate of ISS. His foundation paved the way for philanthropic support of ISS through a range of avenues. Among these efforts, the foundation helped develop new community schools, train community-school leaders, and document Flint's success story. Over the past two decades, the foundation has helped build a network of after-school alliances that advance ISS in states across the country. Advocacy efforts of Mott grantees were critical to growing the 21st Century Community Learning Centers initiative, to sustaining it in the face of threatened budget cuts, and to supporting a private-public partnership to enable the evaluation of its impacts.

Former Mott education program officer An-Me Chung points to the foundation's smart avoidance of "funding the next shiny penny," as other foundations have, but rather focusing on effective, evidence-based solutions directed at systems change and sticking with them over many decades. If the ISS field is to better leverage opportunities to expand this strategy within the Every Student Succeeds Act and secure new funding, she also believes, then key actors will need to do much better at compromising and finding ways to join forces than they historically have: "The challenge is that there's only X amount of resources available. People in general need to find ways to join forces and to make smart use of existing efforts without fracturing the field. This will lead to more resources."[23]

The Ford Foundation approached ISS through a broader social and racial justice lens that looked to close racial disparities in youth-serving systems. The ISS approach, for Ford, was about changing the conditions that build inequality into the system structure and not simply about providing social services. The foundation funded field-building around the idea of community schools through the Coalition for Community Schools and through StriveTogether's cradle-to-career community work. It also helped launch and sustain the Broader, Bolder Approach to Education and other efforts. Though the foundation is no longer funding education systems work directly, some of its final energies in this area involved efforts to unify the field by supporting increased coordination among key ISS organizations and by partnering with the Chan Zuckerberg Initiative to fund a collaborative effort that draws on the joint expertise of the Coalition for Community Schools, Communities In Schools, and StriveTogether. The Ford Foundation's senior program officer Sanjiv Rao outlines these recent efforts:

> We realized that one role of philanthropy could be to catalyze conversations to support a healthy ecosystem that is both diverse and interdependent. To their credit, the national networks did the real work: they came together to build relationships, identify comparative advantages, strategize around a field—rather than organizational—agenda, and align nationally in ways that facilitated better and more coordinated implementation by their local partners. That effort represents real progress, and it is my hope that the next horizon of work in the field, and in government, moves along three key dimensions that elevate structural change:
>
> - One is recognizing that the ongoing provision of programs and services will never be enough on their own to overcome structural inequality; we also need community- and youth-led solutions. And philanthropy should play a greater role in supporting efforts to change structures so that programs and services are public responsibilities rather than sustained or significantly subsidized by private philanthropic dollars.
> - Second is that the cornerstones of ISS work should expand to include the conditions for learning, from restorative practices to school climate to youth civic engagement—these are conditions for young people to thrive, not just to mitigate the harms of poverty and racism.
> - Third is that an ISS agenda must be paired with a school improvement strategy; student supports in schools that don't serve young people well will only get you so far; an insufficient solution matched by at-

tempts at school reform that ignore the lived experiences of young people.

If civil society and government make progress on these three areas in a coordinated way, I think we might see real progress in closing what are now highly racialized, structural inequalities.[24]

John Jackson, Schott Foundation for Public Education's president and CEO, came to the foundation from the NAACP and brings to his current role a social- and racial-justice orientation for ISS work. Schott's 2011 launch of the Opportunity to Learn campaign reframed achievement gaps as opportunity gaps and armed grassroots organizers in target states with research and advocacy tools to advance comprehensive, support-based education policy. Advocates have also drawn on numerous policy briefs and playbooks Schott has produced on a range of ISS-related topics such as early-childhood care and education, and restorative justice as an alternative to harsh and disproportionate school discipline practices.

More recently, Schott launched the Loving Cities Initiative, which calls attention to the historical policies and practices rooted in racism and hate that it believes create inequitable living environments, where students miss the opportunity to learn and thrive. Jackson believes that "philanthropic and public dollars must be invested in replacing damaging, punitive policies and practices with those that provide love and support in order to create local systems that ensure care, stability, and capacity-rich learning environments to all students, regardless of race and socioeconomic background."[25]

Other foundations have also played key roles in promoting ISS. The Annie E. Casey Foundation supports intensive work in its home city of Baltimore and enables ISS initiatives across the country to quantify the impediments poor children face through the Kids Count data initiative it launched and supports. In 2011, former foundation senior vice president Ralph Smith launched the Campaign for Grade-Level Reading in response to evidence that students who did not read well by third grade were at high risk of school failure. The campaign builds on the belief that communities needed to come together to tackle the obstacles to poor students' early literacy and, subsequently, school and life success.

Harris Rosen is heartened by the transformation of Tangelo Park, the Orlando community he has supported for over twenty-five years. The progress he has witnessed in greatly reduced crime and mobility and consistently high rates of high school graduation and postsecondary success led him to replicate the program in a second, five-times larger urban Orlando community. While Rosen knows that public investment in support of disadvantaged children must play more of a role than it does now, he also believes strongly that dozens more wealthy individuals who sponsored communities in need could have a huge impact on poverty in cities across the country and change the lives of thousands, even millions, of children: "Children who don't have the opportunity to receive a good education are at a disadvantage in developing lucrative careers and subsequent lifestyles. Those of us who were lucky enough to get that education, job, and life can pay our communities back and reap the benefits for generations to come."[26]

These forward-looking philanthropists' perspectives bring to mind the work of Geoffrey Canada. Having grown up in a low-income community and married a woman who was raised by parents with white-collar jobs, Canada recognized the many poverty-related barriers to learning posed to children in his Harlem neighborhood. He wanted to help those children attain some of the advantages that he was now conferring on his own kids. He went about fashioning an ambitious experiment: creating, across a large swath of Harlem, a cradle-to-career pipeline of supports and opportunities to give children in that neighborhood many of the advantages typically available in more-affluent areas. To realize this dream, Canada recruited some of New York City's wealthiest individuals. By 2013, the Harlem Children's Zone (HCZ) had built up an annual budget of over $100 million to serve more than twelve thousand children and the same number of adults in a ninety-seven-block area of central Harlem.[27]

Canada's efforts have helped advance ISS in several ways. By cultivating support among a powerful group of hedge fund managers and other millionaires, he expanded the reach of philanthropic knowledge about, and support for, ISS. As HCZ grew in prominence and attracted widespread, national media attention, the concept of a cradle-to-career pipeline inspired other community leaders, like those in East Durham, to visit and adapt the concept in their communities. President Obama and his secretary of education, Arne Duncan, were so taken by the concept that they created a federal grant program, Promise Neighborhoods, to enable distressed communities across the country to replicate HCZ's strategy. Albeit at a fraction of the funding enjoyed by HCZ, Promise Neighborhoods planning and implementation grants support the work of Partners for Education in eastern Kentucky, the Northside Achievement Zone in Minneapolis, and dozens of others. They also spurred the creation of a learning network under the auspices of the nonprofit organization Policy Link. In addition to offering a range of technical assistance and other guidance, Policy Links' Promise Neighborhoods Institute helps disseminate the cradle-to-career model and advocate for policies that advance it, strengthen the practice in the field, and sharpen the focus on results and accountability.

While its recipients face the same kinds of challenges posed by other government and private grants—such as goals that are often unrealistic and insufficient funding to achieve their stated goals—the Promise Neighborhoods initiative bridges the philanthropic and public funding worlds. It demonstrates the power of private ISS funding to generate new public funding and to expand a place-based effort to dozens of diverse communities in the process. It also shows how government funding can be used to drive the measurement of broader metrics of student, family, and community well-being. Finally, Promise Neighborhoods grants, and the Promise Neighborhoods Institute, illustrate the potential power of a learning community to inform and improve the work of like-minded ISS efforts and, accordingly, to contribute in a critical way to the movement building the field seeks and needs.

MAKING THE CASE FOR ISS

There is no chance of building a twenty-first-century system of education coupled with the necessary opportunities and supports for all children to succeed until the public demands it. The number one financing challenge is therefore making the case that such a system is in our collective interest and addresses an urgent national problem—our failure to educate large numbers of youth to participate successfully in our economy and society. Until we persuasively make this case, ISS funding will continue to be a piecemeal quest yielding much frustration and notable islands of success but no real system. In the words of education historian David Tyack, we will continue to "tinker toward utopia."

On the other hand, it would be foolish to become preoccupied with finances and fail to continue to build more models of game-changing ISS work. That work will become the basis of a more potent value proposition enabling us to make a compelling case for much greater public support. As James Fallows, Bruce Katz, and Jeremy Nowak have recently argued, the most promising places to envision a hopeful future for America will be found in the diverse communities that make up America. Local leaders in these places will be the problem solvers that Katz and Nowak envision:

> The ability to get things done has shifted from command-and-control systems to the collective efforts of civil society, government and private institutions. It is vested in and affected by leaders and institutions that convert market and civic power into fiscal, financial, and political power. In sum, power increasingly belongs to the problem solvers. And these problem solvers now congregate disproportionately at the local level.[28]

It is leaders in communities like those described in this book who will forge the new social compact between our communities and our families. These compacts will revolve around the creation of comprehensive systems of opportunity and support that enable all children to thrive in school and beyond.

Financing these integrated systems will be the greatest challenge for leaders in the field of ISS. We will need to build on existing models of success and to pilot nascent initiatives, as well as develop accurate cost models for taking them to scale, resourcefully tap and redirect existing resources, use philanthropic dollars strategically, and persuasively build public demand for the commitment of more public dollars for building genuine success systems that guarantee every child a real chance to succeed.

12

Bringing It Together

*Moving Integrated Student Supports
into the Mainstream*

Effective and sustained school improvement efforts have largely evaded US policy makers and practitioners for decades. In 1954, the US Supreme Court affirmed the severe consequences of racial segregation in *Brown v. Board*. Just over a decade later, sociologist James Coleman identified segregation and poverty as the main culprits driving achievement gaps in a well-known report that was the first of several reports assessing the state of US public education. In the decade and a half that followed, policies enacted in response, including school desegregation measures, President Johnson's War on Poverty, and the enactment of the federal Elementary and Secondary Education Act sharply reduced poverty rates and helped cut race-based achievement gaps in half. More than fifty years after the release of the Coleman Report, however, poverty rates are again high and rising, and segregation is near or above the levels that existed when the *Brown* decision was handed down.

Over the past quarter century, the states and the federal government have engaged in a massive array of expensive school reforms ranging from school-based management to standards and accountability to enhanced school choice. Yet student performance, as measured by instruments like the National Assessment of Educational Progress, has seen only modest improvements in some areas and stagnation in others. Likewise, progress toward closing achievement gaps, whether they are based on race, income, or ethnicity, has been modest to nonexistent.

Growing economic inequality and shifting demographic trends—including the fact that our public schools are educating more low-income children, more children of color, and more non-English-speaking and immigrant children than ever before—create an imperative for national, state, and local leaders: do a better job of preparing our young people for success, or the nation's future is imperiled. This imperative impels us to find and implement more-effective strategies for educating all our children to high levels.

As we argue in this book, brain science research points toward a new strategic direction by emphasizing the importance of meeting children's basic needs so that they can learn—and so that teachers can teach—effectively. Recent US school reform efforts have been too narrow and heavily focused on optimizing the current model of schooling. If, as many reformers have argued, the key business of education lies in the transactions—and the relationships—between teacher, student, and curriculum, then school reform efforts have overemphasized strategies targeted at improving teachers (and teaching) and content (standards, curriculum) at the expense of any concerted focus on students or their readiness to engage with and absorb optimized curriculum and instruction.

Students were treated as an immutable given, and education systems would have to work with them as they presented (or didn't present) themselves. We are proposing a strategy that prioritizes student well-being and insists that we put into place the opportunities and support, beginning in early childhood, to guarantee that each student can show up to school every day healthy, ready to learn, and motivated to put forth his or her best effort—critical ingredients in any successful education recipe.

Building the systems of opportunity and support required to meet this goal of every student's being ready to learn every day is the job of community and education leaders all across this country. Yes, we do need to improve the quality of teaching and learning in many of our schools, and that need continues unabated. Society invests a great deal in its school system, and that investment should be optimized, but at the same time, we can no longer neglect the needs of students, particularly those challenged by poverty and other disadvantages. This broader focus is especially urgent when we consider that 80 percent of K–12 students' waking hours are spent outside school. What does or doesn't happen in their lives outside of school matters profoundly to how much they learn in and benefit from school.

Strong, practical examples of ISS work abound, and we have described in this book some of the most promising components of the systems we need. The problem is that these pieces have not been linked into systems. Why? There is no broad public mandate to enact such systems, let alone publicly support them. The value proposition for this work has not been sold to the American public. Consequently, we lack both the will and the resources to scale up the fine ISS examples illustrated in this book.

Sharing effective examples of the work is one step in a communication strategy to persuade the public and its leaders that this work isn't just "nice to do" but is essential to achieving our policy goals of preparing all children for success. Failing to achieve those ambitious policy goals for all students jeopardizes our nation's well-being, because it means we fail to produce the innovators and workers needed to drive a prosperous twenty-first-century high-skills, high-knowledge economy. It leaves us without robust consumers, with a dwindling middle class, and with a growing underclass that can't pay taxes and that requires expensive public services and support. Just as importantly, our democracy is increasingly destabilized, as a substantial and growing proportion of our population cannot attain the American middle-class dream or make meaningful civic contributions. Leaders must find more persuasive ways to communicate the message that preparing all students for success is vital to the future of our economy and our democracy. Doing so would shift our national norms and concepts not only about education but also about what we must do, more broadly, to ensure that all children are ready for full participation in society. Leaders can use evidence and examples in making the case that ISS works, but this is just the first step in changing minds and hearts.

STATE OF THE ISS FIELD

The good news is that the ISS field has evolved substantially over the past few decades. Community schools, which embody the ISS ideals, have gained momentum as a school improvement and equity strategy, and the constituency supporting such work has grown in members, resources, and visibility, thereby calling increased attention to approaches that wrap supports and opportunities around students, families, and schools while making community voice and engagement central to these efforts. The expansion of Communities In Schools to serve tens of thousands of students has also made ISS a much more visible strategy, and CIS evaluations have contributed to the growing evidence base supporting ISS. Strive-Together has likewise gained strength and is collaborating actively with the Coalition for Community Schools and CIS to advance ISS as part of a whole-child education improvement strategy.[1]

The establishment of the Harlem Children's Zone was a landmark event in the field not only because of the promise of Geoffrey Canada's vision and work, but also because of all the national attention he drew to the concept of a more holistic approach to student success. More recently, the

HCZ-inspired enactment of federal Promise Neighborhoods grants, the resulting Promise Neighborhood Initiative (supported by Policy Links), the Campaign for Grade-Level Reading, and Bright Futures USA have helped bring ISS strategies to new states and communities. Considering that many of these initiatives have spread to some of the country's more ideologically conservative regions, this dispersion offers important political promise in today's polarized climate.

Meanwhile, in Massachusetts, City Connects and the Center for Optimized Student Support that houses it at Boston College are working to build up state-level systems to advance ISS and to share best practices and lessons learned from their successful, two-decade-long ISS initiative. And the Kalamazoo Promise has sparked Promise scholarship initiatives in dozens of communities across the country, anchoring ISS in long-term strategies that culminate in full college scholarships.

Still, we write cautiously about our field. The degree to which these various networks speak with and learn from one another is still quite limited. Recent conversations among some of the groups about how they can compete less and collaborate more have borne fruit but so far only to a limited extent. The field is still not the kind of unified body suggested by that term.

NEED FOR UNITY

Several factors stand out as impediments to enabling an effective movement to advance ISS. First, the internal politics of the field has created a lack of unity with respect to advocacy and messaging. There are also external factors that inhibit the growth of the field. The scarcity of resources spawns fierce competition, and policies at the federal, state, and local levels impede ISS. At the same time, the entire environment is constrained by societal conceptions of education that limit schools to an extraordinarily narrow mission. The aforementioned insufficient resources, private and especially public, have also long made it difficult to expand existing initiatives and to scale them to meet greater needs. The scarcity of resources also limits the efficacy of even the strongest programs currently operating. Simultaneously, the lack of a sufficient research base compounds many of the above factors, feeding a vicious cycle that makes building the ISS field and movement difficult.

At the same time, efforts already being undertaken by various leaders—practitioners, advocates, researchers, policy makers, parents, and others, including students themselves—highlight the potential for field and movement building and, thus, substantial expansion of ISS at this key point in time. Likewise, policy and politics have shifted sharply in the ISS direction in recent years. Widespread acknowledgment of the serious impacts of poverty and the need to take a whole-child approach have replaced both the dismissal of poverty as an excuse and the heavy emphasis on test scores as a catalyst for education improvement.

One of us (Elaine) describes the changes she has perceived over the past few years as being like sailing on the ocean. When she started doing the ISS work in 2010, she felt as if she were sitting on a life raft watching a tidal wave—a tsunami of criticism of BBA's emphasis on poverty's impacts—come toward her and looking for any other life rafts to grab on to so that she and her colleagues could survive together. By early 2016, she felt as if she were part of a growing flotilla of organizations advocating for ISS and other poverty mitigation strategies. And while she and others still faced some definite headwinds, Elaine and her colleagues were more and more frequently catching and riding friendly waves, making headway toward comprehensive, equitable education.

As Ralph Smith, founder of the Campaign for Grade-Level Reading, asserts, perhaps the most critical work is "muscle-building" by leaders and advocates.[2] Across the ISS field, efforts to build trust; to share resources, lessons, and questions; and to identify small projects on which to collaborate are important ways to make working together comfortable and effective. In September 2016, ISS leaders at a BBA-led conference agreed on the need to develop unified language and messaging as an important muscle-building step that could also enhance future fund-raising efforts. In June 2017, Paul Reville and Harvard's Education Redesign Lab convened another group of ISS leaders from the practice, research, and advocacy areas to discuss which steps they might take together to build more muscle. He and his team highlighted several ways the Education Redesign Lab might help build the ISS field. Two practical projects have resulted directly from that meeting: a leadership training institute, successfully conducted at Harvard in the fall of 2018 and sponsored by many of the nation's leading ISS partners, as well as a developing joint policy advocacy effort focused on the state of Michigan.

Expanding the existing evidence base and responding both to urgent research needs identified by ISS advocates and practitioners and to other demands could further build critical muscle to advance the field. The research agenda that was developed by the Center for Optimized Student Support and that evolved from its October 2017 meeting offers much promise on that front, including the potential for new collaboration among researchers working on the qualitative and quantitative fronts and across disciplines.

All these efforts also continue to be hampered by a basic challenge that has long made it difficult to call this field a true one. We lack a clear definition of the work, do not agree on what we will call it, and are still working to figure out the other terminology that we will use.

NEXT STEPS

Building a movement is a long and complex process, and building systems of ISS that advance whole-child education will likewise be complicated and difficult. But those realities should not dissuade us from undertaking that work. There has never been a more urgent need for it or, perhaps, a more propitious moment to take it on. We should seize our many current opportunities to build on existing progress, to strengthen our collective muscle, and to move quickly and cohesively toward creating a united research and advocacy field.

Perhaps the most immediate opportunity for advancing the field is better leveraging several new opportunities under ESSA to make policy and practice changes at both the district and the state levels. Indeed, organizations that advocate for ISS strategies point to the differences between ESSA and its predecessor, No Child Left Behind, and urge their supporters to take advantage of ESSA's provisions.[3] In its updated 2017 report, which upgraded its evidence-based assessment of ISS from potentially promising to more solid, Child Trends cited ESSA's explicit support for ISS as one factor driving the push to document and further expand that evidence base. The law's built-in openings for ISS, specifically, and its buckets of potential funds for community schools and for other school-community partnership strategies mean that as states develop their education improvement plans, ISS is more likely to be a core component.

Less direct, but still very significant, is ESSA's emphasis on broadening the accountability metrics that schools and districts will use for measuring student progress and well-being. After decades of complaining about the narrowness of existing testing measures in the field of education, the ISS field was suddenly and surprisingly faced with an ESSA opportunity to define new, broader goals for states' education systems. In the first round, ISS advocates and the states were mostly flat-footed, failing, embarrassingly, to propose innovative approaches to measuring the less tangible but important outcomes of education. Meeting this challenge should be a priority for state and ISS leaders. Defining valid, measurable, and reliable indicators of student well-being, readiness to learn, engagement, motivation, and social-emotional health is urgent for the successful scaling of ISS. Families, teachers, and communities should have a strong voice in defining these measures.

In order for ISS organizations and networks to effectively share with and learn from one another, they must first have a basic understanding of available resources. While you might expect that organizations working toward similar goals (or the same ones) and interacting frequently are already aware of their peers' research, advocacy, and technical tools, this is often not the case. Indeed, a surprising but common comment among participants at the September 2016 meeting of national ISS leaders was that they would like to be better apprised of such resources, especially with respect to timely issues like guidance on leveraging ESSA-related opportunities. As a result, BBA and Drexel University co-led a small independent asset-mapping effort to create a database and basic review of available reports, briefs, tool kits, and other resources, including an assessment of their quality, relevance across the ISS field, and timeliness.[4]

THE IMPORTANCE OF STATE-LEVEL WORK

Notwithstanding public attention to federal policy and investments in education and children, the state is (and will be, at least in the short term) the level at which the most critical policies affecting ISS will be made. It is at the state level that much local policy and practice is shaped. And the 2018 midterm elections produced several new governors and dozens of state legislators committed to more investments in public education and in child development broadly. Consequently, ISS advocates are wise to concentrate their advocacy time and resources in state capitals. Scaling up community-level ISS initiatives and transforming them from exceptions to the norm will rely on effective state-level advocacy and big changes in state education and children's policies. Recognizing this reality, several leaders have already begun to build state "teams" to advance this effort.

Probably the most advanced team is in Massachusetts, where the strong foundations laid by a twenty-five-year-old commitment to education investments and reform strategies are strengthened by an enlightened state position. A supportive state department of education is bolstered by comprehensive health care, a growing preK program, and vigilant advocacy efforts that aim to hold the state's feet to the fire on existing commitments while broadening its vision for the future.

There are promising signs in many other states as well. The Coalition for Community Schools hosts a state network, where state-level teams can build on community and regional efforts. California, New York, Pennsylvania, and Texas are among the states where multiple district-level community-school initiatives are beginning to cohere into regional and state advocacy efforts, showcasing both the strength of the burgeoning movement and the substantial challenges to achieving state policy wins. In Pennsylvania, for example, long-standing community-school initiatives in the Lehigh Valley and Bethlehem could be the link bringing together newer work in Pittsburgh and Philadelphia. And in New York, the massive expansion of community schools in the city could boost efforts in smaller cities and rural areas. The size of these states and thus the levels of organizing and resources needed, however, necessarily render these efforts uneven and investments in ISS patchwork at best.

CIS has also made progress on the state front, with Nevada the most prominent example. When Brian Sandoval was elected governor in 2010, he hired his childhood friend Dale Erquiaga for state superintendent. Although Erquiaga's last-minute push to have Nevada submit an application for federal Race to the Top funding did not produce a grant, it did enable the application team to successfully push through several comprehensive legislative reforms in 2013 that opened the door for CIS to expand substantially. At the time, Nevada had virtually the lowest and least equitable per-pupil K–12 funding of any state. So the twenty-six reforms in the package, twenty-five of which passed, included a range of investments designed to "prepare the new Nevada family—minority, living in poverty—for the new economy."[5] The law added funding for low-income students, English language learners, immigrants, and special education students, along with flexibility for the state's powerful teachers' unions. It also funds teacher pipelines and leadership training, with a total cost of around $1 billion. Punam Mathur, executive director of the Elaine P. Wynn & Family Foundation, describes the law as having "something for everyone to love and something for everyone to hate."[6]

Perhaps most importantly, these reforms were not just big investments into distributive school accounts but were targeted to the identified highest-poverty schools. Each school received a specific amount of extra money and guidelines as to how the money could be spent. A stipulation of a third-party evaluation of what worked would determine which programs would get future investments and which would not. With demand for ISS on the rise and money available, CIS has more than doubled its footprint in Nevada since 2012. It now serves fifty-seven schools in Clark County, the largest district, which includes Las Vegas, and sixty-five to sixty-seven schools statewide. These numbers also grew to the point where CIS needed new local affiliates to support the expansion, so it added three, including one in Washoe, the state's second-largest district. As part of this effort, Mathur has convened nonprofits that the Wynn foundation supports, like eye care and dental providers, to help them better align their efforts to serve children (often the same children served by the ISS schools) and gear up to collectively apply for federal grants.

Nevada's example also points to the potential for comprehensive state education reform initiatives to advance ISS. Indeed, the work in Massachusetts has evolved out of education reform laws and their failure to do enough to close historic achievement gaps. Also driving the work was the recognition that although various education reforms boosted academic achievement averages, they failed to sufficiently advance equity or to prepare anywhere near all students for success. State courts, too, can provide avenues for progress. Court decisions mandating more equitable state funding and policies, like those in New York, New Jersey, and Washington, can drive major reforms.[7] In Kentucky, the aforementioned *Rose* case revolutionized education in that state while serving as a model for states throughout the country on how to reform schools and achieve greater school finance equity. Importantly, the Kentucky reforms included the statewide establishment of Family Resource and Youth Services Centers, which deliver ISS targeted to the unique needs of the particular high-needs area. (Family Resource and Youth Services Centers bolster the Promise Neighborhoods work of Partners for Education across Appalachian eastern Kentucky.)

Other states highlight the potential for multiple ISS organizations to join forces to increase the impact of their advocacy efforts. In Virginia, for example, long-standing work by CIS in several key regions, including the capital, Richmond, could join forces with the Bright Futures Winchester regional initiative to capitalize on new opportunities in ESSA, a strong preK program, and a governor who is focused on education improvement.

Other state networks that advance components of ISS—like early-childhood education and after-school programs—could also be leveraged to form strong state ISS advocacy shops. In Michigan, for example, discussions are under way to utilize the state's strong state after-school network to enhance the work of community-school advocates. And in Nebraska and Arkansas, early-childhood advocacy efforts supported by the Sherwood Foundation and the Schott Foundation, respectively, could lead efforts to advance ISS. Taken together, these various examples illustrate the potential of states to provide strong policy support for ISS, including new funding for its expansion.

ADVANCING RESEARCH AND ADVOCACY EFFORTS

The 2018 report that the Center for Optimized Student Support produced after its 2017 conference lays the foundations for a cohesive research agenda that will address critical holes in the current body of evidence for ISS. The center calls for researchers to investigate various questions, including how resource levels and other contextual factors influence implementation and program or initiative quality; the steps and stakeholders required for implementation to work well and lay a strong foundation for effective programs; and which nonacademic outcomes should be explored and prioritized. Well-developed case studies are recognized as a core component of that work.

The lack of the solid, reliable data needed to feed this research is another impediment to building the evidence base that researchers, advocates, and practitioners alike cite as a top priority. And here, too, efforts have sprung up to meet that need. The Coalition for Community Schools has begun a partnership with the University of Wisconsin to document the benefits of ISS.[8] Bright Futures USA has similarly paired up with a team at Drexel University focused on ISS initiatives to launch a parallel data collection effort with a grassroots angle. Starting with a pilot cohort of six Bright Futures affiliate districts in Arkansas, Missouri, and Virginia, a leadership team is working with the communities to set goals for student, school, and community well-being that reflect the joint priorities of educators, parents, students, businesses, social service agencies, and city leaders. The team will also design and implement systems to collect and assess data that helps those districts understand where they are making good progress toward those goals and where they are falling short and need to adjust their efforts to improve.

As described above, there is also a nascent effort to bring together national-level ISS advocates and practitioners to begin to build effective state-level advocacy campaigns that can leverage strong regional efforts to begin to advance state policy.

CALL TO ACTION

We hope that the work described in this book, coupled with promising new initiatives, such as the fieldwork funded by the Ford and Chan Zuckerberg foundations, invigorated state advocacy, and the community-school playbook, will lead to a stronger, more visible, and more effective ISS field. Bringing the state efforts just described together under a single umbrella could further strengthen the work and increase its impact. There are also relevant models for creating such a network. The PreK Now campaign of the Pew Charitable Trusts built up diverse state-based efforts to advance early-childhood education into a coherent, national voice for the issue through the creation of a learning network, grants to staff up state early-childhood organizations, and support for an aligned research institution, the National Institute for Early Education Research.

By 2018, key leaders had begun to build such a network to advance ISS, but thus far, these efforts have lacked a single central hub institution or a major source of committed policy financial support, critical elements in making organizations like PreK Now (and the Afterschool Alliance) such successes.

For this reason, we urge, too, that several of the nation's major education philanthropies, which have so far been reluctant to commit to this ambitious and critical work, step forward and prioritize growing the ISS movement. In doing so, they should legitimize and invest in the work and lead substantive, norm-changing national discussions on equity, poverty, and the ingredients required for children's success in twenty-first-century America. Ultimately, the conversation must shift from a narrow focus on school reform to a focus on children's well-being and success. Poverty matters, and its causes and effects must be addressed if all children are to succeed, if "all means all" is to be more than a hollow, rhetorical promise. In the end, it will take major new public investments—at the local, state, *and* federal levels—to transform systems and broadly incorporate the ISS practices needed to move whole-child education from margins to mainstream. But such a transformation needs champions and will require that private funders, who believe in this broader path for US public education, step forward to put their stamp of approval on this child-centered strategy and commit their substantial financial support to it.

As in other areas of education policy and practice, the evidence is finally spurring long-needed movement. Over the past few decades, evolving brain science and economic research has prompted more states to invest in larger, and higher-quality, preK and other early-childhood care and education programs. States and districts are likewise following the evidence in expanding after-school and summer enrichment opportunities, and philanthropic foundations are funding data-based evaluations that demonstrate their effectiveness, creating a virtuous cycle. School-based health clinics are growing in number, as are policies that help them open and stay viable. Guided by evidence that all children learn better when their physical, dental, and mental health needs are met, these clinics reduce absenteeism, improve students' ability to focus in school, and thus boost achievement. And ESSA's attention to a fuller range of metrics of child development and student skills has begun to move some states toward the enrichment needed for all students.

Each of these strands of progress helps build the momentum and infrastructure for ISS. But, like the full-fledged ISS initiatives we explore in this book, all this action, taken together, still falls far short of what's needed. So, we take this moment to send up a rallying cry to build on the energy coming from these various critical strands and the mounting effort to bring them together to meet every child's needs, to provide quality enrichment opportunities, and to maximize her or his talents, skills, and dreams.

We hope that the examples in this book of excellent community-level work currently taking place inspire readers to identify how you can participate in and contribute to improving education. We hope these cases spur philanthropists, boards, and presidents of foundations to make (and keep) advancing ISS as a top priority. We hope they drive policy makers to act on the growing mountain of evidence that ISS is not just an effective strategy, but one that our social, economic, and demographic trends, and the twenty-first-century global workforce, demand. We hope that they do justice to the hard work of those who have laid the foundations for them—from John Dewey, Horace Mann, and Jane Addams to Joyce Dreyfus, Bill Milliken, Marian Wright Edelman, Geoff Canada, Marty Blank, Jeff Edmondson, and Bill Milliken—to carry that work to the next level and next generation.

Finally, the ISS movement should not only be about addressing the impact of poverty and the lack of opportunity afflicting so many of this nation's children. It must also be about transforming systems of racial oppression and economic exploitation that cause the poverty and inequality of opportunity that ISS seeks to address. Those of us privileged to lead this movement must not be content with treating the symptoms of inequity. We must attack the causes that block the next generation's pathway to success.

Speaking of the next generation, we most of all hope that this book and the work it presents lifts up the voices of those at the center of this movement—teachers, students, community leaders and organizers, and families. These voices will be vital to shaping a successful movement. Such a movement, if we build it properly, will finally give us the excellent and equitable systems of child development and education that will enable us, as a nation, to make the most of our human talent, to ensure a prosperous economy and vibrant democracy, and to realize our ultimate objective: providing every child with a viable, accessible pathway to success. There is no more important work in our nation than this. Failure is not an option. The time is now.

Integrated Student Support Communities at a Glance

COMMUNITIES WITH INITIATIVES THAT SERVE SOME OF DISTRICT

Austin, Texas

The whole-child approach was developed in Austin Independent School District (AISD) schools with the highest-poverty, immigrant, and non-English-speaking families through a combination of parent organizing, intensive embedded social and emotional learning, and community-school strategies.[1]

- *Organizing partners:* Industrial Areas Foundation (IAF) / Austin Interfaith, the Collaborative for Academic, Social, and Emotional Learning (CASEL), the American Federation of Teachers (AFT), and National Education Association (NEA).

- *Schools and students reached:* Alliance Schools (created through IAF) reached one-fourth of AISD elementary schools and half of high-poverty district schools; CASEL worked in five high schools plus seven feeder middle and forty-three feeder elementary schools; and community-school work in a middle and high school had expanded to thirteen schools by 2017–2018 and led to the development of a plan to ultimately expand the strategy to all AISD schools.
- *General makeup of the student body:* AISD served 81,400 students in 2017–2018. In the district overall, 53 percent of students are "economically disadvantaged," 28 percent are English language learners, and 11 percent are special education students. In schools targeted for whole-child ISS supports, the students are poorer, more are students of color and immigrants, and more are likely to be living in single-parent households.
- *Key features:* Parents organize with teachers in Alliance Schools, and social and emotional learning is embedded in all aspects of school efforts in three cohorts of schools that worked with CASEL. The ISS approach is practiced in community schools and includes health and other wraparound supports in high-need middle and high schools and is expanding to other schools.
- *Core funding:* CASEL district grant for social and emotional learning plus in-kind support from NoVo Foundation, United Way of Greater Austin funds for wraparound support, and AFT and NEA funding for community-school work and expansion.

Boston

The City Connects program provides every child targeted academic, social, emotional, and health supports in twenty of the city's schools with the highest proportions of poverty, immigrants, and students of color.

- *Organizing partners:* Boston College's Center for Optimized Student Support, Boston Public Schools, and community agencies.

- *Schools and students reached:* Twenty district schools serve more than 8,000 of the city's most disadvantaged students (out of 125 district schools and 56,000 students).
- *General makeup of the student body:* The diverse student body is urban and poor and includes a heavy concentration of Hispanic English language learners. Over 80 percent are eligible for free and reduced-price meals (FARMs eligible), and roughly half do not speak English at home.
- *Key features:* School-site coordinators in each school connect students with a tailored set of services and enrichment opportunities provided by various public and private agencies. Universal state health care supports all students' physical and mental health, and Boston's universal preK program now offers quality preK for all four-year-olds.
- *Core funding:* In addition to school district budget revenue, Race to the Top funds allocated to City Connects help defray costs. Several private foundations support various aspects of City Connects' work and its evaluation.

New York City

Children's Aid Society community schools wrap physical health, nutrition, mental health, and other services around students along with enriching in-school and out-of-school experiences and extensive parental and community engagement through more than twenty community schools in some of the most disadvantaged neighborhoods in four of the city's five boroughs.

- *Organizing partners:* Children's Aid Society, New York City Public Schools, the New York State Education Department, and other local and state agencies.
- *Schools and students reached:* Over twenty community schools in four boroughs serve some of the poorest immigrant students and students of color in a million-student school system.

- *General makeup of the student body:* Children's Aid Society community-school students are disadvantaged relative to the system overall, in which more than three-quarters of students are FARMs eligible, 27 percent are African American, 41 percent are Hispanic, 13 percent are English language learners, and nearly one in five receives special education services.
- *Key features:* Close coordination with local and state education, health, and other agencies, along with community partnerships at each school, enables wraparound physical and mental health services, after-school and summer enrichment, and deep parent and community engagement.
- *Core funding:* A range of public dollars, including federal Title I and 21st Century Community Learning Centers funds, together with state and local funding for after-school and other programs, is supplemented by funds from individuals and foundations.

COMMUNITIES THAT SERVE ALL CHILDREN IN A "ZONE" OF THE CITY OR DISTRICT

Durham, North Carolina

The East Durham Children's Initiative (EDCI) consolidates services and supports for the children and their families living in a 120-block heavily distressed area of concentrated poverty and high crime within the city.

- *Organizing partners:* Community leaders launched EDCI and engaged with the Duke University Center for Child and Family Health to grow the initiative's capacity. EDCI is now a fully staffed nonprofit that runs the initiative.
- *Schools and students reached:* The 120-block area that is Durham's most distressed neighborhood serves students in two neighborhood elementary schools, one middle school, one high school, and two public charter schools.

- *General makeup of the student body:* Urban and poor with a predominantly black but very diverse student body, 66 percent of Durham schools' students are FARMs eligible, nearly half are black and almost one-third Hispanic, and 18 percent white, with EDCI schools more disadvantaged.
- *Key features:* The place-based initiative modeled on the Harlem Children's Zone provides a pipeline of high-quality cradle-to-college-or-career services. These include early-childhood supports that complement state preK, physical and mental health care, and after-school and summer enrichment.
- *Core funding:* EDCI has an annual fund that receives contributions from individuals, corporations, fund-raising events, and private foundations; it neither seeks nor receives public funding.

Minneapolis

The Northside Achievement Zone (NAZ), a designated Promise Neighborhood, channels individualized supports to the children and families who live in a thirteen-by-eighteen-block area of the city. The area is considered among the city's, and the nation's, most distressed. In the past two years, NAZ has expanded to serve children and families across the city's Northside but outside the designated zone.

- *Organizing partners:* NAZ, the Promise Neighborhoods grantee organization, works with a twenty-member board of directors composed of local leaders.
- *Schools and students reached:* The thirteen-by-eighteen-block zone serves 5,500 students in ten public, charter, and parochial K–12 schools, and NAZ now also serves additional students in other Northside schools.
- *General makeup of the student body:* In this racially concentrated area of poverty, almost all residents are African American, and one-third

of children are homeless or highly mobile (moving from home to home).

- *Key features:* Coaches employed by NAZ help develop family achievement plans, and specialists connect families with various community resources to move toward the goals established in those plans. The zone offers access to high-quality preK and parenting supports, as well as mentoring, enrichment, after-school and summer programs, and college preparatory support.
- *Core funding:* Anchored by a federal Promise Neighborhoods grant, NAZ also leverages the Race to the Top Early Learning Challenge Fund to support preK scholarship slots, along with private grants.

Orlando, Florida

The Tangelo Park Program provides "cradle-to-college" support for all children residing in Orlando's high-poverty, heavily African American Tangelo Park neighborhood.

- *Organizing partners:* Harris Rosen and the Tangelo Park Program collaborate closely with the Tangelo Park Civic Association, the Tangelo Baptist Church, the YMCA, and the University of Central Florida.
- *Schools and students reached:* The semirural urban neighborhood serves all students in Tangelo Park Elementary School.
- *General makeup of the student body:* Virtually all residents in the low-income neighborhood are African American or people of color with Caribbean heritage.
- *Key features:* Universal ("promise") college scholarships are supported by quality neighborhood-based early-childhood education, health, counseling, and after-school and summer programs.
- *Core funding:* Harris Rosen, the hotelier who launched the Tangelo Park Program, supports childcare providers and funds all scholarships, as well as addressing other needs, like a lifeguard at the YMCA, as needed.

COMMUNITIES WITH INITIATIVES THAT SERVE (OR WILL SERVE) ALL OF THE DISTRICT

Joplin, Missouri

The Joplin School District, where the Bright Futures USA model was developed and launched in 2010, has evolved since then to meet every child's basic needs within twenty-four hours of that need's being identified, develop strong school-community partnerships that help address students' longer-term needs, and embed meaningful service learning opportunities in every school.

- *Organizing partners:* Joplin School District superintendent and other leadership, in collaboration with parents and community faith, business, and social service leaders.
- *Schools and students reached:* Bright Futures serves all the district's 7,874 students in its seventeen schools.
- *General makeup of the student body:* By 2015, nearly two-thirds of Joplin students (61 percent) were FARMs eligible. In the heavily white community, 16 percent are classified as needing special education, and just 3 percent are English language learners.
- *Key features:* The three-part Bright Futures USA framework involves three elements. First is a triage system to meet every student's basic health, nutrition, and physical needs within twenty-four hours through contributions from local social service agencies and members of businesses, faith institutions, and the general community. Second, school- and community-level councils build community leadership and partnerships with schools to meet longer-term needs and to sustain the systems. And third, the framework embeds service learning in all schools and ensures supportive training for teachers. Joplin also provides preK for at-risk students, tutoring, mentoring, and after-school and college preparatory programs.
- *Core funding:* Federally funded AmeriCorps VISTA volunteers provide in-kind support, Missouri's Department of Elementary and

Secondary Education and Department of Economic Development funds support Bright Futures work and conferences, and the regional Economic Security Corporation and a range of other private funders supplement the core backers.

Kalamazoo, Michigan

The promise by a group of anonymous local philanthropists to provide full college scholarships in perpetuity has spurred Kalamazoo Public Schools, the city, and the community to come together to develop a set of comprehensive supports that enable more students to take advantage of these scholarships.

- *Organizing partners:* Kalamazoo Promise and the Kalamazoo Public Schools district, in collaboration with CIS Kalamazoo and other nonprofit entities.
- *Schools and students reached:* All district students (12,216 in twenty-five schools) who graduate from Kalamazoo High School are eligible for Promise scholarships. CIS works in all schools but to varying degrees and with varied levels of financial support.
- *General makeup of the student body:* In this combination urban-suburban district, a large majority of students (over 70 percent) are FARMs eligible, 12 percent receive special education services, and 7 percent are English language learners. The share of African American students rose from less than one-third in 1987 to over half thirty years later, with a growing number of Hispanic students as well.
- *Key features:* The anchor for ISS is universal (Promise) college scholarships, which have spurred community leadership to provide quality preK programs, wraparound health, mental health, and other supports, and a districtwide effort to create a college-going culture and the resources to enable it.
- *Core funding:* Anonymous donors have committed to funding Promise scholarships in perpetuity. CIS is supported by a combination of

Title I funding, which helps support school coordinators; 21st Century Learning Centers grants for after-school activities; and private individual and philanthropic organization donors.

Montgomery County, Maryland

All students in Montgomery County Public Schools benefit from zoning laws that advance racial and socioeconomic integration and from strong union-district collaboration that promotes enriching, equity-oriented curriculum, bolstered by the channeling of extra school district funding and ISS to high-need schools and communities.

- *Organizing partners:* The district itself, Montgomery County Education Association (the local teachers union), Montgomery County Council, Linkages to Learning (joint initiative of the district and the county council).
- *Schools and students reached:* All schools and students—160,000 students in more than two hundred schools—benefit from integration, social and emotional learning, and select services. Higher-poverty schools and their communities are served through additional funds and a broader range of more-intensive supports.
- *General makeup of student body:* The Montgomery County Public Schools district, as a whole, is racially and socioeconomically diverse: 30 percent of students are Hispanic, 29 percent white, 22 percent African American, and 14 percent Asian; 35 percent of students are FARMs eligible, and over 40 percent have been at some point. On the eastern side of the county, where more-intensive ISS is implemented, 80 percent or more of students were FARMs eligible in the ten highest-poverty schools.
- *Key features:* High-quality early-childhood education is supported by district, state, and federal policies. Other contributing factors are mixed-use housing policies that enable racial and socioeconomic integration, parent and community outreach and support through

Linkages to Learning, reallocation of funds to support high-needs schools and students, nutrition and health supports, and an emphasis on social and emotional learning.

- *Core funding:* The district is heavily locally funded, with almost no federal ESEA Title I dollars. It draws on a combination of school district and county revenues, along with federal funding for Head Start, state preK dollars, and assorted other grants.

Pea Ridge, Arkansas

The small Pea Ridge School District, among the newer Bright Futures USA affiliate districts, is making good progress toward identifying and meeting students' basic needs, engaging the community to meet longer-term needs, and making service learning a core component of school policy and practice.

- *Organizing partners:* The Pea Ridge School District draws on the support of Bright Futures USA.
- *Schools and students reached:* In this district, about two thousand students are served in one primary, one elementary, one middle, and one high school, as well as an alternative high school and a new career-tech charter high school.
- *General makeup of the student body:* The heavily rural district in "Walmart Country" is mostly white with a small but growing Hispanic population; the district is middle-income, with pockets of both higher income and poverty.
- *Key features:* The Bright Futures USA framework has the same three parts that Joplin Public Schools has. First is a triage system to meet every student's basic health, nutrition, and physical needs within twenty-four hours through a combination of social service agency, business, faith, and individual community contributions. Second, school- and community-level councils build community leadership and partnerships with schools to meet longer-term needs and to sustain the systems. And finally, service learning is embedded in all

schools, as is supportive training for teachers. Pea Ridge also provides preK for at-risk students, tutoring, mentoring, and after-school and college preparatory programs.

- *Core funding:* State funds support meals and other needs for high-poverty schools, and Pea Ridge has secured a three-year private grant to support low-income students' access to preK.

Vancouver, Washington

Family-Community Resource Centers (FCRCs) currently serve eighteen of the highest-need Vancouver Public Schools district schools, with two mobile FCRCs providing lighter-touch support in the other seventeen. The FCRC strategy enables a full-service community-school approach in every one of the district's thirty-five schools.

- *Organizing partners:* The school district and its leadership—Superintendent Steve Webb and chief of staff Tom Hagley—are supported by six central-office staff (three who just support FCRCs), and technical and other assistance from the Coalition for Community Schools.
- *Schools and students reached:* FCRCs serve 24,000 students in thirty-five district schools, with on-site FCRCs in seventeen elementary, middle, and high schools and the Fruit Valley Learning Center.
- *General makeup of the student body:* By 2015, over half of students were FARMs eligible, with some of the district's inner-city schools having over 80 percent. More than one in five students speak a language other than English at home; a higher proportion of these students are in site-based FCRCs. And 12.5 percent of students receive special education services, also with higher representation in FCRCs.
- *Key services:* Vancouver Public Schools supports a range of early-childhood education programs (including quality preK); middle and high school in-school enrichment; and after-school and summer programs provided by its partners. The district also offers help for parents and families through workshops, financial and mental health assistance, and referrals to a range of community resources.

- *Core funding:* District and Title I funds support basic FCRC needs, which are supplemented by the VPS foundation and by cash and in-kind donations from faith-based, social service, business, and association partners.

COMMUNITIES WITH AN INITIATIVE THAT SERVES MORE THAN ONE DISTRICT

Eastern (Appalachian) Kentucky

Federal Promise Neighborhoods and Promise Zone grants help Berea College's Partners for Education serve eight counties in the region—Bell, Clay, Harlan, Jackson, Knox, Leslie, Letcher, Madison, Owsley, Perry, and Whitley—more intensively, and provide less intensive supports to students and their families in an additional twenty-one surrounding counties.

- *Organizing partners:* Berea College launched Partners for Education (PfE), which is now a fully staffed nonprofit that runs the initiative.
- *Schools and students reached:* The twenty-two schools in Clay, Jackson, Knox, and Owsley Counties serve over 35,000 students, with tens of thousands more served less intensively in the region's other counties.
- *General makeup of the student body:* The Appalachian region is rural, very poor, and 97 percent white. The regional poverty rate was around 27 percent in 2015 and as high as 40 percent in some counties. About 80 percent of students are FARMs eligible.
- *Key features:* Family engagement specialists meet directly with families and help coordinate services that are offered by various community partners. Other specialists provide basic academic, college preparatory, health, and other ISS to students.
- *Core funding:* Federal grants from Promise Neighborhoods, the Full-Service Community Schools Program, and Investing in Innovation are the most prominent sources of funding, along with a range of other cash and in-kind support.

Notes

Chapter 1

1. This theory was originally published as Abraham Maslow, "A Theory of Human Motivation," *Psychological Review* 50 (1943): 370–396.

2. This theory has been translated to education contexts many times. See, for example, Tony Kline, "Applying Maslow's Hierarchy of Needs in Our Classrooms," *Matthew Knight.uk* (blog), April 7, 2017, www.matthewknight.uk/2017/04/applying-maslows -hierarchy-of-needs-in.html, which advocates for keeping water and snacks in the classroom and letting students take a nap to help them stay focused.

3. Steve Suitts, "A New Majority: Low Income Students Now a Majority in the Nation's Public Schools," Southern Education Foundation, January 2015, www.southerneducation .org/getattachment/4ac62e27-5260-47a5-9d02-14896ec3a531/A-New-Majority-2015 -Update-Low-Income-Students-Now.aspx.

4. American Federation of Teachers, "U.S. Trends of Child Poverty Moving in the Wrong Direction," Reclaiming the Promise report, 2014, www.aft.org/growth-child-poverty -mapped-county-50-states. Since it has no counties, the District of Columbia map is divided into census tracts. Compared with most states and counties, those remained fairly stable, with the only notable difference being the shift in the northeastern sections of the city from medium poverty (10–20 percent) to high poverty (over 20 percent).

5. Leila Morsy and Richard Rothstein, "Mass Incarceration and Children's Outcomes: Criminal Justice Policy Is Education Policy," Economic Policy Institute, December 15, 2016, www.epi.org/publication/mass-incarceration-and-childrens-outcomes.

6. The Harvard University Center on the Developing Child produced *A Guide to Toxic Stress* to explain how it differs from normal, healthy stress, its consequences for healthy development, relationship to Adverse Childhood Experiences, and other drivers and factors, https://developingchild.harvard.edu/guide/a-guide-to-toxic-stress/.

7. For a summary, see Laura Spinney, "Stressed Out? It Could Be in Your Genes," *Independent*, December 2, 2010, https://www.independent.co.uk/news/science/stressed-out-it -could-be-in-your-genes-2148653.html.

8. See, for example, Harvard University Center for the Developing Child, "Tackling Toxic Stress," accessed November 3, 2018, https://developingchild.harvard.edu /science/key-concepts/toxic-stress/tackling-toxic-stress. This series of articles was produced by the Harvard Center for the Developing Child to help researchers, practitioners, and others understand the causes and sources of toxic stress and effective strategies for addressing it.

9. Anthony S. Bryk et al., *Organizing Schools for Improvement: Lessons from Chicago* (University of Chicago Press, 2010), 176.

10. ExpandEd Schools, "The Learning Gap Infographic," March 25, 2014, https:// elearninginfographics.com/the-learning-gap-infographic/.

11. Betty Hart and Todd Risley, *Meaningful Differences in the Everyday Experience of Young American Children* (Baltimore: P. H. Brookes, 1995).

12. Emma Garcia and Elaine Weiss, *Education Inequalities at the School Starting Gate: Gaps, Trends, and Strategies to Address Them* (Washington, DC: Economic Policy Institute, September 27, 2017), www.epi.org/publication/education-inequalities-at-the-school -starting-gate.

13. Malcolm Gladwell, *Outliers: The Story of Success* (New York: Little, Brown, and Co., 2008), 260.

14. Perhaps the clearest evidence of this dramatic shift in public opinion can be seen in the February 2016 relaunch of BBA; widespread acknowledgement of poverty's many impacts on teaching and learning prompted a shift in focus from those impacts to the policies that would mitigate them. See, for example, Helen Ladd, Pedro Noguera, Paul Reville, and Joshua Starr, "Student Poverty Isn't an Excuse; It's a Barrier," *Education Week*, May 10, 2016, www.edweek.org/ew/articles/2016/05/11/student-poverty-isnt -an-excuse-its-a.html.

15. Education Law Center, "A Tale of Two States: Equity Outperforms Inequity," February 11, 2014, www.aqeny.org/wp-content/uploads/2014/02/Tale-of-Two-States-Report _FINAL.pdf, illustrates how, despite the two states' similar levels of funding, more equitable funding distinguishes New Jersey from New York and has enabled New Jersey to shoot ahead of its neighbor among low-income students and on scores on the National Assessment of Educational Progress overall. An education reporter documents how the combination of more resources (especially for high-poverty schools), higher standards, and quality assessments that held schools accountable worked together to help Massachusetts climb to the top of the academic heap, with the state's students on par with their peers in Singapore in science. Kenneth Chang, "Expecting the Best Yields Results in Massachusetts," *New York Times*, September 2, 2013, www.nytimes .com/2013/09/03/science/expecting-the-best-yields-results-in-massachusetts.html.

16. Reville and others point to the stubborn and increasing burdens wrought by poverty and the critical need to lift them if "all is to mean all" as per Massachusetts' education reform policies' intent. Alia Wong, "What are Massachusetts Public Schools Doing Right?," *Atlantic*, May 23, 2016, www.theatlantic.com/education/archive/2016/05 /what-are-massachusetts-public-schools-doing-right/483935.

17. Bruce Katz and Jeremy Nowak, *The New Localism: How Cities Can Thrive in the Age of Populism* (Washington, DC: Brookings Institution Press, 2018).

18. The Coalition for Community Schools offers technical assistance for schools and districts seeking to develop community schools, including a broad range of online

resources (see www.communityschools.org/resources/default.aspx). The National Center for Community Schools provides site visits for both U.S. and international visitors, as well as guidance at the district level, including tailored full-day sessions to help launch community school initiatives (see www.nccs.org/guiding-practice).

19. Communities In Schools, "About Us," accessed November 3, 2018, www.communities inschools.org/about-us.

20. See Campaign for Grade-Level Reading, list of participating communities, accessed November 3, 2018, http://gradelevelreading.net/our-network/participating -communities.

21. Bright Futures USA, "Why Bright Futures?," accessed November 3, 2018, www.bright futuresusa.org/domain/18.

22. Promise Neighborhoods Institute, "About Us," Policy Link, accessed November 3, 2018, www.promiseneighborhoodsinstitute.org/about-the-institute/framework.

23. Nine of the twelve communities highlighted in the book (Berea/Eastern Kentucky, Children's Aid community schools in New York City, City Connects schools in Boston, the East Durham Children's Initiative, Joplin Bright Futures, the Northside Achievement Zone, Pea Ridge Bright Futures, Tangelo Park, and Vancouver) are described in Broader, Bolder Approach to Education, "Case Studies," accessed November 3, 2018, www.boldapproach.org/case-studies. There, readers can explore each community and its ISS approach in depth. Information from unpublished case studies is cited specifically in the endnotes. The appendix in this book also provides details of all twelve communities, including size, demographics, and other key characteristics.

24. The strongest available data are used to demonstrate this progress. In a few cases, the data come from independent evaluations, but most use state or local data to compare district students with their peers in other comparable districts or statewide. The lack of reliable data to enable valid evaluations and comparisons is explored in later chapters, as are the efforts of many ISS communities to develop new and innovative data collection systems.

Chapter 2

1. Various organizations use the term *integrated student supports* and employ different definitions. Child Trends, for example, uses the term to characterize the interventions and initiatives it studied for a report it produced in 2014 and an updated 2017 version. The nonprofit Communities In Schools often uses this phrase to refer to the wraparound supports it delivers to students in schools with which it partners.

2. Coalition for Community Schools, "What is a Community School?," accessed November 3, 2018, www.communityschools.org/aboutschools/what_is_a_community _school.aspx.

3. According to a cost-benefit analysis conducted by Columbia University economists, City Connect's whole-class review not only helps more students succeed academically, but also benefits society. See A. Brooks Bowden et al., "A Benefit-Cost Analysis of City Connects," Center for Benefit-Cost Studies in Education, Teachers College, Columbia University, July 2015, 6, www.cbcse.org/publications/a-benefit-cost -analysis-of-city-connects?rq=benefit-cost%20analysis.

4. U.S. Department of Education, "Programs: Promise Neighborhoods," U.S. Department of Education, last updated March 5, 2018, www2.ed.gov/programs/promise

neighborhoods/index.html, describes the purpose of Promise Neighborhoods: "The purpose of Promise Neighborhoods is to significantly improve the educational and developmental outcomes of children and youth in our most distressed communities, and to transform those communities by ... [b]uilding a complete continuum of cradle-to-career solutions of both educational programs and family and community supports, with great schools at the center."

5. According to Bright Futures USA, the program "operates under the belief that *when communities invest their time, talent, and treasure in their schools*, students are more likely to stay in school through graduation, have a higher degree of self-worth and confidence, and set and reach goals for the future. In turn, these students grow up to be better neighbors, quality employees, and impactful leaders in their communities." Bright Futures, Connections for Success, "The Framework," accessed November 3, 2018, www.brightfuturesusa .org/domain/56 (emphasis added).

6. A discussion about student mental health and other concerns was from Dave Sovine, Frederick County superintendent, and teachers at Orchard View Elementary School, interview with Elaine Weiss, October 2016.

7. The W. E. Upjohn Institute for Employment Research houses a research initiative devoted to documenting and collecting data on Promise communities across the country, as well as studies of the most promising ones, such as Kalamazoo, which inspired many of the others. W. E. Upjohn Institute for Employment Research, "Kalamazoo Promise & Place-Based Scholarships," Upjohn Institute Research, accessed November 4, 2018, "www.upjohn.org/research/education/kalamazoo-promise-place-based -scholarships.

8. Timothy J. Bartik, Brad Hershbein, and Marta Lachowska, "The Effects of the Kalamazoo Promise Scholarship on College Enrollment, Persistence, and Completion," working paper 15-229, Upjohn Institute for Employment Research, June 2015, http:// research.upjohn.org/up_workingpapers/229.

Chapter 3

1. A. Brooks Bowden et al., "A Benefit-Cost Analysis of City Connects," Center for Benefit-Cost Studies in Education, Teachers College, Columbia University, July 2015, 6, www.cbcse.org/publications/a-benefit-cost-analysis-of-city-connects?rq=benefit -cost%20analysis.

2. The Bright Futures framework describes the development of a close-knit relationship between communities and schools that creates a synergy in which they are "working together for change." Bright Futures, Connections for Success, "The Framework," accessed November 3, 2018, www.brightfuturesusa.org/domain/56.

3. C. J. Huff and Kim Vann, conversation with Elaine Weiss, May 2018.

4. See the Beaufort County Bright Futures Facebook page, www.facebook.com/pg/bright futuresbeaufortcounty, for numerous examples of this active community.

5. Foundation for Vancouver Public Schools "What We Do," accessed November 4, 2018, http://foundationforvps.org/what-we-do; Nada Wheelock, email correspondence with Elaine Weiss, July 2018.

6. The Foundation for Vancouver Public Schools achieves this consistent level of support for principals through an annual fund-raising luncheon with a high-end raffle, annual staff campaign, and student drives that draw many school staff, along with individual

donations from community members. See, for example, the invitation to the May 10, 2018, luncheon at http://foundationforvps.org/registration. See also "VPS Staff Campaign and Student Chest Drive Raise over $263,000 for the Foundation for VPS," Foundation for Vancouver Public Schools, December 14, 2017, http://foundationfor vps.org/vps-staff-campaign-student-chest-drive-raise-263000-foundation-vps.

7. In recent years, in response to pressure from the U.S. Department of Education to provide information on progress at the whole-school level, and given that its partners work all over the Northside, NAZ started to enroll kids and families outside the designated zone.

8. Sondra Samuels, CEO of Northside Achievement Zone, conversation with Elaine Weiss, June 12, 2018.

9. NAZ, "Internal Evaluation Report: Family Engagement" (October 2014).

10. In his book documenting Geoffrey Canada's development of the Harlem Children's Zone, Paul Tough describes how Canada encountered similar barriers in his attempts to persuade new teen parents to participate in "Baby College" parenting classes. He found that using young neighborhood parents as recruiters was most effective. He also trained residents from Harlem to lead the sessions; they were uniquely able to persuade their peers that long-standing practices like hitting children were counterproductive. Paul Tough, *Whatever It Takes: Geoffrey Canada's Quest to Change Harlem and America* (New York: Houghton Mifflin Harcourt, 2008).

11. M. E. Walsh and G. DePaul, "The Essential Role of School-Community Partnerships in School Counseling," in *Handbook of School Counseling*, ed. H. L. K. Coleman and C. Yeh (Baltimore: MidAtlantic Books & Journals, 2008), cited in City Connects, 2012 Progress Report, 5.

12. Besides being customized to students and comprehensive in its developmental domains, the City Connects model has four other characteristics. It is coordinated among families, schools, and community agencies; it is cost-effective to schools by utilizing the resources provided by community agencies; it continuously monitors for effectiveness by collecting and analyzing data to evaluate and improve service delivery and student outcomes; and it is implemented in all sites with fidelity and oversight. City Connects, "The Impact of City Connects: Progress Report 2012," Boston College Center for Optimized Student Support, www.bc.edu/content/dam /city-connects/Publications/CityConnects_ProgressReport_2012.pdf, 6.

13. Alyssa Haywood, "The Power of Whole Class Reviews," *City Connects: Optimized Student Support* (blog), December 1, 2016, https://cityconnectsblog.org/2016/12/01/the-power -of-whole-class-reviews.

14. According to Massachusetts Department of Elementary and Secondary Education, "Statewide System of Support (SSoS): About Underperforming Schools," accessed November 4, 2018, www.doe.mass.edu/turnaround/level4/about.html, "Level 4 schools are the state's most struggling schools based on an analysis of four-year trends in absolute achievement, student growth, and academic improvement trends. Level 4 schools are allowed flexibilities to accelerate student achievement and are given priority to receive DESE targeted assistance."

15. Alyssa Haywood, "The Power of Whole Class Reviews."

16. Bowden et al. "Benefit-Cost Analysis," 8.

17. Steve Webb, conversation with Elaine Weiss, December 2017.

18. Vancouver Public Schools uses seven milestone benchmarks, many of which resemble the Say Yes steps: (1) students are ready for kindergarten; (2) third graders are reading on grade level; (3) sixth graders are ready for middle school; (4) seventh graders are ready for pre-algebra or algebra in eighth grade; (5) ninth-graders are ready for high school; (6) tenth graders are passing the High School Proficiency Exam; and (7) students are ready for college and career. Each of these benchmarks has one or more measures or indicators to assist in monitoring progress.

19. Sherryl Kuhlman et al., "Case Study: Say Yes to Education; Guilford and the Application of a Data-Driven Approach," Wharton Social Impact Initiative, July 13, 2016, 5, http://static1.squarespace.com/static/568c19f10e4c114023d2ffb7/t/578e79ce37c5812 5138a630f/1468955088183/WSII-Say+Yes+Case+Study_vf+%287-2016%29.pdf.

20. Gene Chasin, the chief operating officer of Say Yes, notes that school leaders and representatives from community-based partner organizations worked, with help from the American Institutes of Research, to modify and develop the revised postsecondary planning system platform according to key indicators of need.

Chapter 4

1. In December 2017, Elaine Weiss conducted video interviews with several FCRC community partners, including Anne Johnston of Clark County Public Health, who discussed the role of church coffees in scaling up the ISS initiative. See "Community Schools—Anne Johnston," video, posted January 29, 2018, www.youtube.com/watch ?v=d3u1YqLCWqM&list=PLjPW4QfVPysyvnOOB5T-f0EOWAPGRAWHQ&index=2.

2. See, for example, Elaine Weiss, "Bright Futures in Joplin, Missouri," case study, Broader, Bolder Approach to Education, accessed December 5, 2018, www.bold approach.org/case-study/bright-futures-joplin-mo.

3. C. J. Huff, email correspondence with Elaine Weise, September 2017.

4. Steve Patterson, interview with Elaine Weiss, May 2016.

5. Bright Futures Joplin, "School Partners," accessed November 4, 2018, http://bright futuresjoplin.org/school-partners.

6. Dave Sovine, interview with Elaine Weiss, June 11, 2018.

7. Bright Futures USA, Community Engagement Conference, The Power of One, March 1–3, 2017, "Workshops," https://events.brightfuturesusa.org/cec2017/workshops.

8. Emily Younker, "Bright Futures USA to Host Conference Beginning Monday," *Joplin Globe*, October 12, 2013, www.joplinglobe.com/news/local_news/bright-futures-usa -to-host-conference-beginning-monday/article_81e4da2b-ebc5-5baa-a0ec-4af5bbc 889c5.html.

9. "Community Schools—Anne Johnston," video.

10. "Community Schools—Anne Johnston," video.

11. Melissa Baker, assistant principal, Tyner Elementary School, interview with Elaine Weiss, December 7, 2017.

12. Nadine Couch, principal, Big Creek Elementary School, interview with Elaine Weiss, December 7, 2017.

13. Beth Brown, project director, Partners for Education at Berea College, interview with Elaine Weiss, December 7, 2017.

14. Mary Mathew, email correspondence with Elaine Weiss, May 2018.

15. "Community Schools—Anne Johnston," video.

16. Shepherding the Next Generation, home page, accessed October 24, 2018, www
.strongnation.org/shepherding.

17. Faith institutions represented included Catholic Charities, Church of the Brethren,
Evangelical Lutheran Church in America, Islamic Society of North America, the
Reform Action Committee (advocacy arm of Reform Judaism), the Salvation Army,
and the Society of Jesus (the Jesuit order of the Roman Catholic Church). Pastors
and ministers from AME Metropolitan Church and Luther Place Memorial Church in
Washington, DC; the Spring River Baptist Association in Missouri; and the Winchester Church of God also attended, as did leaders from Bright Futures USA, which
works intensively to engage faith leaders as a core part of its ISS work.

18. The Clapham Group (http://claphamgroup.com) describes its work: "Named for a
group of social justice reformers in the late 18th century in England that included
William Wilberforce, who worked to abolish the slave trade in his country, The
Clapham Group represents and consults clients working to address modern-day
injustices and promote the common good. We operate in marketing, think-tank, and
consultation spaces. Whether through social marketing, public relations, or political
and policy consulting, The Clapham Group believes that renewing the culture, con-
fronting injustice and promoting the common good must be undertaken together if
anyone is to succeed in shaping the conversation and, ultimately, improving the lives
of individuals and families."

Chapter 5

1. The others include Native American reservations in the West, Hispanic communities
in the Texas Rio Grande Valley, and a predominantly African American swath across
the Deep South and along the Mississippi Delta. Trip Gabriel, "50 Years into the War
on Poverty, Hardship Hits Back," New York Times, April 20, 2014, www.nytimes.com
/2014/04/21/us/50-years-into-the-war-on-poverty-hardship-hits-back.html.

2. Gabriel, "50 Years."

3. Both of these challenges—lack of jobs and of social service providers—are starkly
illustrated in the documentary film Rich Hill, about a small town in the Ozarks region
of Missouri that was produced in 2014 by a brother and sister team who grew up
in the area and wanted to make such realities less invisible. Tracy Droz Tragos and
Andrew Droz Palermo, prods. and eds., Rich Hill, 2014, www.richhillfilm.com/#top.

4. "Demolitions Beginning to Clear Way for McDowell Teacher Housing," Charleston
(WV) Gazette-Mail, June 6, 2016, www.wvgazettemail.com/news-education/20160606
/demolitions-beginning-to-clear-way-for-mcdowell-teacher-housing.

5. C. J. Huff, interview with Elaine Weiss, September 19, 2017.

6. Tangelo Park is bordered on all sides by major throughways or highways, which cut it
off from Universal Studios, Disney, and other area attractions.

7. Tangelo Park leaders note that by taking advantage of early-childhood specialists and
nurses embedded in the local elementary school, the schools can ensure high quality
while keeping costs comparable to those of other central Florida pre-K and childcare
programs, roughly $140 per week per child.

8. Minnesota Department of Human Services, "Minnesota State Targeted Response
to the Opioid Crisis," Project Narrative, April 2017, https://mn.gov/dhs/assets/mn
-opioid-str-project-narrative-april-2017_tcm1053-289624.pdf.

9. Rob Grunewald, "The Promise of Early Childhood Development in Indian Country," *Community Dividend* (Federal Reserve Bank of Minneapolis), November 17, 2017,
https://www.minneapolisfed.org/publications/community-dividend/the-promise-of
-early-childhood-development-in-indian-country, explains that tribal communities
can also benefit from a relatively recent source of federal funding: "In 2012, the U.S.
Department of Health & Human Services started the Tribal Early Learning Initiative
(TELI), which provided grants to ten tribal communities in the country to develop
and implement strategies to coordinate services across ECD sectors. The grant also
included support for infrastructure to assist with coordination, such as shared data
systems."

10. Launched in 2009, services sponsored by the foundation also include a shuttle to
transport residents to medical, dental, and mental health providers. "Rural Medical
Dental Homes Launch Services," *Telluride Daily Planet*, July 23, 2009, www.telluride
news.com/the_watch/news/article_ce9aa149-57cb-5e66-920e-4b6dc4d53515.html.

11. Elaine Weiss "Appalachian Schools Are Helping Rural Students Go to College: Here's
How," *Talk Poverty*, July 12, 2016, https://talkpoverty.org/2016/07/12/appalachian
-schools-isolated-students-college.

12. Technology can also increase students' social capital by extending their networks and
exposure. See, for example, Julia Freeland Fisher, *Who You Know: Unlocking Innovations
That Expand Students' Networks* (San Francisco: Jossey-Bass, 2018).

13. The National Assessment Governing Board, which oversees the National Assessment
of Educational Progress, produced a set of four short videos that illustrate this work
in four very different schools as a way to explain why its little-known assessment of
U.S. students' skills and knowledge in the arts, and arts instruction in schools, are so
important. National Assessment Governing Board, "New NAEP Arts Infographics and
Arts Education Video Available," 2016, www.nagb.gov/naep-results/arts/2016-arts
-education.html.

14. The low rate of educational attainment in Appalachia is likely related to the region's
workforce participation rate, which is lower on average than the national rate and
dips even further in some of the hardest-hit regions—to 65 percent in rural areas and
just 60 percent in central Appalachia. Appalachian Regional Commission, "Education
in Appalachia, 2012–2016," Data Snapshot, www.arc.gov/noindex/research/ACS
-infographics2012-2016/DataSnapshot-EducationInAppalachia.pdf.

15. Weiss, "Appalachian Schools Are Helping."

16. Reconnecting McDowell partner Shentel Communications played a key part in the
broadband project. See "'Reconnecting McDowell' Is Gaining, Gayle Manchin
Says," *Charleston (WV) Gazette*, December 28, 2012, www.wvgazettemail.com/news
/reconnecting-mcdowell-is-gaining-gayle-manchin-says/article_e2de5814-62ee-5d95
-bc7f-8ac36a03f4e9.html.

17. Berea College has been home to Partners for Education, which began as a new department to manage its Upward Bound program in 1967, for fifty years.

Chapter 6

1. Coalition for Community Schools, "What Is a Community School?," Coalition for
Community Schools and Institute for Educational Leadership, accessed November 4,
2018, www.communityschools.org/aboutschools/what_is_a_community_school

.aspx (emphasis added). The remaining goals are that "students succeed academically; students are healthy—physically, socially, and emotionally; students live and learn in a safe, supportive, and stable environment, and communities are desirable places to live."

2. For example, The Children's Aid Society, *Building a Community School*, 3rd ed. (New York: Children's Aid Society, 2001), www.communityschools.org/assets/1/Asset Manager/CAS_building_a_communityschool.pdf notes, "The community school concept works best when it is developed from the ground up, not laid over some other approach that isn't working. A new building or school isn't necessary, but *a new idea—created, implemented and evaluated by a joint school-parent-agency team—is essential*" (emphasis added).

3. Lisa Seigel, president, Rolling Terrace PTA, interview with Elaine Weiss, May 2017.

4. Vancouver Public Schools, "Strategic Plan: Community's Vision for Our Schools," accessed November 4, 2018, https://vansd.org/strategic-plan.

5. Anne Henderson describes Austin Interfaith as "a collaboration of local faith-based congregations, the teachers union, a dozen public schools, and an electrical workers union." Anne T. Henderson, "Community Organizing to Build Partnerships in Schools: The Alliance Schools Movement in Austin" (a case-study jigsaw activity with facilitator's guide and group readings), Annenberg Institute for School Reform at Brown University, July 2010, www.annenberginstitute.org/sites/default/files/product /199/files/Mott_AustinToolReading.pdf.

6. Richard J. Murnane and Frank Levy, "The First Principle: Agree on the Problem," in *Teaching the New Basic Skills: Principles for Educating Children to Thrive in a Changing Economy* (New York: Free Press, 1996).

7. Kathleen Davis, interview with Elaine Weiss, July 21, 2016.

8. Kathleen Davis, notes from her interview with Elaine Weiss, July 2016.

9. Kavitha Mediratta, Seema Shah, and Sara McAlister, *Building Partnerships to Reinvent School Culture: Austin Interfaith* (Providence, RI: Annenberg Institute for School Reform (AISR) at Brown University, 2009), www.annenberginstitute.org/sites/default/files /product/845/files/Mott_Austin.pdf.

10. Henderson, "Community Organizing to Build Partnerships," 1.

11. Sheila Y. Smalley and Maria E. Reyes-Blanes, "Reaching Out to African American Parents in an Urban Community: A Community-University Partnership," *Urban Education* 36, no. 4 (2001), 518–533.

12. See, for example, the discussion of this issue in Annette Lareau, *Unequal Childhoods: Class, Race, and Family Life* (Berkeley: University of California Press, 2011).

13. Smalley and Reyes-Blanes, "Reaching Out."

14. These two critical factors are among those discussed in Broader, Bolder Approach to Education, "East Durham Children's Initiative, (East Durham, NC)," case study, accessed November 4, 2018, www.boldapproach.org/case-study/east-durham-childrens -initiative.

15. Rochelle Garrett, interview with Elaine Weiss, December 6, 2017.

16. Owsley County elementary school principal Nadine Couch noted that the growing share of grandparents responsible for raising the students in her school has shifted in the past few years to include more than a few great-grandparents. In one family she mentioned, a single grandmother was raising five children ages nine and under.

17. Families and Schools Together (FAST), "How FAST Works," accessed November 4, 2018, www.familiesandschools.org/how-fast-works/program-structure.
18. Sue Christian, interview with Elaine Weiss, December 8, 2017.
19. Christian, interview with Elaine Weiss, December 8, 2017.
20. Rochelle Garrett, interview with Elaine Weiss, December 6, 2017.
21. J. Morgan, interview with Elaine Weiss, December 6, 2017.
22. Ken Zarafis, president, Education Austin, interview with Elaine Weiss, May 16, 2016.
23. Henderson, "Community Organizing to Build Partnerships," 9.
24. Henderson, "Community Organizing to Build Partnerships," 10.
25. The Collaborative for Academic, Social, and Emotional Learning (CASEL) has a web page devoted to describing its successful efforts in social and emotional learning in Austin: CASEL, "Partner Districts: Austin," accessed November 3, 2018, https://casel.org/partner-districts/austin-independent-school-district. And the Austin Independent School District describes its current community school status, with thirteen schools participating, in Austin Independent School District, "Community Schools: Welcome!," accessed November 4, 2018, www.austinisd.org/communications/community/community-schools.
26. Tangelo Park Program 15th Anniversary Report, "Timeline of Events," recorded in Community Advisory Board meeting minutes, as reported by the school principal.

Chapter 7

1. Say Yes to Education, "Our Story" accessed November 4, 2018, http://sayyestoeducation.org/about/story.
2. Tangelo Park Program, "2-3-4-Year-Old Program," accessed November 4, 2018, www.tangeloparkprogram.com/programs/2-3-4; Patti Jo Church-Houle, email correspondence with Elaine Weiss, May 2017 (regarding developmental milestones).
3. Lizette Alvarez, "One Man's Millions Turn a Community in Florida Around," *New York Times*, May 25, 2015.
4. Tangelo Park Program, "Cornell University: Cornell Alternative Spring Break," accessed November 4, 2018, www.tangeloparkprogram.com/programs/cornell-university.
5. Kalamazoo Promise, "Colleges & Universities," accessed November 4, 2018, www.kalamazoopromise.com/ParticipatingCollegesUniversities.
6. Michelle Miller-Adams, interview with Elaine Weiss, December 12, 2016.
7. Michelle Miller-Adams, *Promise Nation: Transforming Communities Through Place-Based Scholarships* (Kalamazoo, MI: W. E. Upjohn Institute for Employment Research, 2015), https://upjohn.org/sites/default/files/WEfocus/promise-nation.pdf. *Dosage* refers to the share of students eligible for the Promise, *intensity* to the level of support they receive, and *saturation* to the proportion of students who end up taking advantage of the commitment.
8. Because Tangelo Park is so heavily poor, the same issue does not pertain; virtually every child would be eligible even if Rosen had made income an eligibility criterion, which he does not. Kalamazoo, in contrast, also houses a number of middle-class and wealthier families, making this an important distinction.
9. Pam Kingery, email correspondence with Elaine Weiss, August 2018.
10. W. E. Upjohn Institute, "About the Kalamazoo Promise," accessed November 4, 2018, www.upjohn.org/about-kalamazoo-promise.

11. Healthy Futures, which was launched in 2003, later merged with two other similar organizations to serve schools county-wide as the Kalamazoo Communities In Schools Foundation.

12. Kingery, interview with Elaine Weiss, December 13, 2016.

13. Michelle Miller-Adams, correspondence with Elaine Weiss, January 7, 2017.

14. Timothy Bartik, interview with Elaine Weiss, November 22, 2016.

15. Miller-Adams, *Promise Nation*, 120–121.

16. Those involved included the then head of United Way, a local interfaith community organizing group (ISAAC), the president of Kalamazoo College, and twenty-five or so leaders from public schools, private preschools, childcare providers, and others, including district superintendents. Bartik, interview with Elaine Weiss, November 22, 2016.

17. It offers half-day or full-day preK classes in Kalamazoo Public Schools elementary schools. The district provides bus transportation from home or childcare (located in the district) to school and back. Children eligible for free- and reduced-price meals receive them in their Prekindergarten Early Education Program (PEEP) as they would at K–12 schools. Kalamazoo Public Schools, "PEEP Pre-K Home," accessed November 4, 2018, www.kalamazoopublicschools.com/Departments/PEEPPre-KHome.aspx.

18. Miller-Adams, *Promise Nation*. The survey was conducted by the Western Michigan University Evaluation Center.

19. Miller-Adams, *Promise Nation*, 69.

20. Timothy J. Bartik, Brad Hershbein, and Marta Lachowska, "The Effects of the Kalamazoo Promise Scholarship on College Enrollment, Persistence, and Completion," working paper 15-229, Upjohn Institute for Employment Research, June 2015, http://research.upjohn.org/up_workingpapers/229, tables 5 and 2.

21. Any postsecondary institution is eligible. According to Miller-Adams, *Promise Nation*, 2, "Even very short-term career and technical programs offered by community colleges, as well as one apprenticeship program and a vocational training school for special needs students, are covered by the Kalamazoo Promise."

22. Bartik, Hershbein, and Lachowska, *Effects of the Kalamazoo Promise.*

23. Noradeen Farlekas, "A New Application of Social Finance Combining Impact Investing with Philanthropy to Increase Positive Educational Outcomes and Reduce Incarceration in Low-Income, High-Crime Neighborhoods" (LPD thesis, Northeastern University, Boston, June 2016), 118.

24. Weiss was inspired by a similar promise made in 1981 by philanthropist Eugene Lang to sixth graders in Harlem, an initiative that evolved eventually into the I Have a Dream Foundation. Callahan, David. "Saying Yes in Syracuse", *The American Prospect*, November 16, 2009.

25. The interactive map at www.whimsymaps.com/view/collegepromise can be searched to find, for example, all Promise programs in a given state. It explains the seven categories of Promises that it includes in this broader description of College Promise programs: Penn Graduate School of Education, "College Promise Programs: A Comprehensive Catalog of College Promise Programs in the United States," accessed November 4, 2018, http://ahead-penn.org/creating-knowledge/college-promise.

26. Both of these issues and others are addressed in W.E. Upjohn Institute, "About the Promise Database," accessed November 4, 2018, www.upjohn.org/promise/database /index.html.

27. Sam Butler, interview with Elaine Weiss, May 4, 2017.

28. Robert Frahm, "The Promise: A Case Study of Say Yes to Education in Buffalo," Principles for Effective Education Grantmaking, Case 15 (Grantmakers for Education, October 2016), 11, http://sayyestoeducation.org/wp-content/uploads/2016/10/Case -Study-Say-Yes-Buffalo-final-2016.pdf. A subsidiary, related issue may be the origins of the donor. The Kalamazoo Promise was launched and will be funded in perpetuity by an anonymous group of local donors who are widely assumed to include member of the Upjohn family, long-standing city corporate leaders, and philanthropists. They know the city and its assets, needs, and culture intimately and have a strong personal stake in its success. And while Harris Rosen is not from Tangelo Park, he intentionally sought out a high-need community in Orlando as a way to give back to the city that made him a wealthy man. Weiss and Say Yes have no innate connections to Syracuse or Buffalo; those cities were chosen for investment because of their commitments to interagency cooperation and to comprehensive school reform, and on state money that was available to supplement the Say Yes per-pupil costs. It may be worth explor- ing whether a Promise donor's connection to the city is associated with effective enactment of, or the ultimate success of, such initiatives, or both.

29. The Tangelo Park Program covers full tuition for any eligible institution to which the student is accepted as long as the youth lived in Tangelo Park for at least the junior and senior years, whereas Kalamazoo covers between 65 and 100 percent of tuition, depending on how long the student had been in district schools before graduation.

Chapter 8

1. Richard Rothstein, *Class and Schools: Using Social, Economic, and Educational Reform to Close the Black-White Achievement Gap* (Washington, DC: Economic Policy Institute. 2004).

2. Bruce Katz and Jeremy Nowak, *The New Localism: How Cities Can Thrive in the Age of Popu- lism* (Washington, DC: Brookings Institution Press, 2017).

3. Elizabeth "Libby" Schaaf, interview with authors' collaborator Lynne Sacks.

4. Jorge Elorza, presentation given at "Poverty Matters: Making the Case for a System Overhaul," By All Means Convening, Cambridge, MA, May 2016.

5. Joseph Curtatone, presentation given at "Poverty Matters: Making the Case for a System Overhaul," By All Means Convening, Cambridge, MA, May 2016.

6. Olivia Allen-Price, "How Many Are Being Displaced by Gentrification in Oakland?," *KQED News*, February 9, 2017; and Christin Ayers, "Oakland Putting Up Storage Sheds as Temporary Solution for Homeless Crisis," *CBS SF Bay Area*, November 29, 2017.

7. Harry Harris, "Violent Crime in Oakland Down 23 Percent Since 2012," *(San Jose, CA) Mercury News*, January 9, 2018.

8. Sam Levin, "Libby Schaaf Announces New Director of Education Position," *East Bay (CA) Express*, June 11, 2015.

9. Oakland Promise, "Oakland Promise Vision," accessed November 27, 2018, http:// oaklandpromise.org/ourvision/.

10. Kimberley Driscoll, mayor Salem, MA, interview with authors' collaborator Lynne Sacks, February 27, 2017.

11. City Connects, "Results," City Connects web page, accessed October 29, 2018, https://www.bc.edu/bc-web/schools/lsoe/sites/cityconnects/results.html.

12. Emily Sandahl, "How Salem Is Reshaping the Role of Education," *Speak United* (blog), October 24, 2017, https://unitedwaymassbay.org/blog/how-salem-is-reshaping-the -role-of-education.

13. Driscoll, interview with Lynne Sacks, September 19, 2017.

Chapter 9

1. See, for example, community-level initiatives by the Collaborative for Academic, Social, and Emotional Learning (CASEL), which instituted practices and policies in schools in eight large urban districts (CASEL, "Key District Findings," Collaborative for Academic, Social, and Emotional Learning, Chicago, accessed November 4, 2018, https://casel.org/cdi-results/), and studies on the importance of social and emotional learning by such high-profile researchers as James Heckman ("Topic: Character Mat- ters/Social & Emotional Skills," Heckman Equation, web page with several links to videos, accessed November 4, 2018, https://heckmanequation.org/topic/character -matters-social-emotional-skills) and Angela Duckworth, who emphasizes, too, the complexity of the concept and measures of it at the student level (Anya Kamenetz, "A Key Researcher Says 'Grit' Isn't Ready for High-Stakes Measures," *NPR*, May 13, 2015, www.npr.org/sections/ed/2015/05/13/405891613/a-key-researcher-says-grit -isnt-ready-for-high-stakes-measures).

2. See, for example, Harvard University's Center on the Developing Child (https:// developingchild.harvard.edu), where neurologist Jack Shonkoff has built on his early work, which was popularized in Jack P. Shonkoff and Deborah A. Phillips, eds., *From Neurons to Neighborhoods: The Science of Early Childhood Development* (Washington, DC: Na- tional Academy Press, 2000), to establish concepts like "serve-and-return" interactions between babies and parents as foundational to the subsequent development of a range of skills, both academic and "noncognitive."

3. The difference is particularly dramatic for young homeless children, who have gar- nered substantial attention in Vancouver Public Schools. Among this most vulnerable subgroup of children, fully half of homeless kids in Vancouver are ready for kinder- garten ("Percentages of Incoming Kindergarten Students Demonstrating Readiness in All 6 Domains" [2017–2018 WaKIDS fall data], table provided by Kelly Mainka, lead early-childhood education specialist, Vancouver Public Schools, email to Elaine Weiss, August 2018).

4. Mawnie Belcher and Chris Morgan, staff members of Readiness Buses, interview with Elaine Weiss, December 7, 2017.

5. This is one component of Vancouver Public Schools' use of a mindfulness, as we ob- served in the schools. Advocated in "Pam," "All About the Brain," *The Mindful Classroom: Taking a Mindful Approach to Teaching, Learning, and Life* (blog), October 8, 2012, https:// themindfulclassroom.wordpress.com/2012/10/08/all-about-the-brain.

6. Jill White, quoted in Broader, Bolder Approach to Education (BBA), "Bright Futures in Joplin, Missouri," BBA, accessed December 5, 2018, www.boldapproach.org/case

-study/bright-futures-joplin-mo; C. J. Huff, "Community Engagement 2.0: A Three-Part Scaffold for Local Schools to Capture the Public's Trust and Build on It for Student Benefits," *School Administrator*, April 2017, 35–37.

7. Tennant Kirk and Natalie Gabbard, interviews with Elaine Weiss, Berea, KY, December 2017.

8. Operation College Bound Facebook page, www.facebook.com/OperationCollege Bound?fref=ts.

9. "Joplin School District Earns Future Ready, Apple Awards," *Joplin Globe*, November 26, 2015, www.joplinglobe.com/news/local_news/joplin-school-district-earns-future -ready-apple-awards/article_76065bbc-12c4-5d5b-88bb-9a7af43ef101.html.

10. C. J. Huff, interview with Elaine Weiss, November 2016.

11. Charlie Davidson, interview with Elaine Weiss, December 8, 2017.

12. Berea College, "About Student Crafts," accessed November 4, 2018, www.berea.edu /student-crafts/. The Craft Program is part of the Berea College Labor Program, which requires all Berea students to "work at least 10 hours per week to further their educational experience and to enable the College to offer an affordable education" (Berea College, "Greetings from the President," accessed November 5, 2018, www .berea.edu/student-crafts/greetings-from-the-president).

13. Scott Balley, email exchange with Elaine Weiss, August 2018.

14. Elaine Weiss visit to McLoughlin Middle School, January 17, 2018.

15. James S. Murphy, "The Undervaluing of School Counselors," *Atlantic*, September 16, 2016, www.theatlantic.com/education/archive/2016/09/the-neglected-link-in-the -high-school-to-college-pipeline/500213.

16. Mark Wreath, director of career and technical education, Vancouver Public Schools, email correspondence with Elaine Weiss, August 2018.

17. The plans list in detail students' assessments, career interests, goals, and activities, among other aspects of their lives, and track their progress on each aspect, helping them build early résumés and college applications.

18. Wreath, email correspondence with Elaine Weiss, August 2018.

19. Elaine Weiss visit to Hudson's Bay High School, January 17, 2018.

Chapter 10

1. Joy Dryfoos and Sue Maguire, *Inside Full-Service Community Schools* (Thousand Oaks, CA: Corwin Press, 2002), 18.

2. Coalition for Community Schools, "What Is a Community School?," accessed November 1, 2018, www.communityschools.org/aboutschools/what_is_a_community _school.aspx.

3. "100 Years of Community School History," College of Education, Health & Human Sciences, University of Tennessee, Knoxville, accessed October 30, 2018, web.utk .edu/~fss/minutes/history.doc. There has been relatively little written about the history of this movement and the evolution of the Coalition for Community Schools. This section of the chapter thus relies heavily on the preceding reference ("100 Years of Community School History") and is supplemented by the authors' interviews with community schools leaders and others.

4. Fran Krajewski and Val Osowski, "The National Center for Community Education: On the Threshold of a New Age," *Mott Exchange* 12, no. 1 (summer 1997). The Mott Inter-University Clinical Preparation Program was staffed with faculty from

seven Michigan colleges and universities. (The program was discontinued after Mott helped establish regional centers to train educators, but many Mott fellows remained in community-school leadership positions.)

5. The film is available for viewing at "Flint Michigan 1962: The Great Community," video, uploaded January 1, 2011, www.youtube.com/watch?v=SrGCpJGyx5E. The film quality is not great, but the content is inspiring. Advocates may want to reconsider how the use of schools beyond the school day could be incorporated into a broader community schools campaign.

6. Anna Maier et al., "Community Schools: A Promising Foundation for Progress," *American Educator*, summer 2018.

7. At one point, as the major provider of training for the 21st Century Schools grant recipients, the National Center for Community Education was training hundreds of people each year about community schools.

8. National Center for Community Schools, "History," accessed November 1, 2018, www.nccs.org/history.

9. Communities In Schools (CIS), "Our History," accessed November 1, 2018, www .communitiesinschools.org/about-us.

10. Bill Milliken, interview with Elaine Weiss, July 17, 2018. The CIS Facebook page (https://www.facebook.com/pages/Communities-In-Schools/109275022425715) describes this evolution: "The last 15 years, meanwhile, have witnessed a profound transformation at CIS: from a visionary, mission-driven enterprise led by a charismatic founder-entrepreneur to a mature, professionally managed, data-driven enterprise that uses research and evaluation to influence and innovate."

11. Coalition partners range from educational associations like AASA (the School Superintendents Association) and both national teachers unions to nonprofit organizations devoted to health (like the American Public Health Association) and to child and family well-being writ large (such as the Child Welfare League of America). It also includes other national organizations that promote different visions for ISS, like the Promise Neighborhoods framework and the Campaign for Grade-Level Reading, as well as civil rights organizations like the National Urban League and the National Council of La Raza.

12. The coalition feels strongly that community schools are a strategy rather than a model, as other organizations in the ISS field sometimes describe them.

13. Coalition for Community Schools, "About Us," accessed November 1, 2018, www .communityschools.org/about/overview.aspx.

14. National Center for Community Schools, "How Many Community Schools Are There in the United States?," accessed November 1, 2018, www.nccs.org/block/how -many-community-schools-are-there-united-states.

15. Dryfoos and Maguire, *Full-Service Community Schools*.

16. On August 14, 2018, for example, Philadelphia mayor Jim Kenny opened an event at the Center for American Progress highlighting the importance and growth of district-level community school work, with coalition director José Muñoz and CIS executive director Dale Erquiaga discussing their collaboration on this front in service of their organization's respective and joint goals to greatly scale up this work.

17. Coalition for Community Schools, "Scaling Up School and Community Partnerships: The Community Schools Strategy; An Interactive Guide," accessed November 2, 2018, www.communityschools.org/ScalingUp.

18. Oyler has since been converted into a preK–12 school (Amy Scott, "How a School Is Transforming Not Only Its Students, But Its Community," Marketplace, *PBS*, June 16, 2015, www.pbs.org/newshour/education/oyler-school). The Coalition for Community Schools produced a scaling-up case study about Cincinnati ("Cincinnati, Ohio: One Brick at a Time; How a Facilities Master Plan Enhanced Collaborative Decision Making," accessed November 1, 2018, www.communityschools.org/resources/cincinnati _ohio_one_brick_at_a_time.aspx). There is another case study: National Center for Community Schools, "Building Community Schools: A Guide for Action," October 2011, www.theoryofchange.org/wp-content/uploads/toco_library/pdf/NCCS _BuildingCommunitySchools.pdf.

19. *Oyler: One School, One Year* (2015) was produced by Amy Scott, the *Marketplace* reporter who spent time in Cincinnati, especially in this preK–12 school, as part of her reporting on the community-schools work there for NPR and American Public Media (www.oylerdocumentary.com). It was featured in multiple film festivals, including the Cincinnati and Austin Film Festivals and the Chicago International Social Change Film Festival, and was an official selection of the American Film Showcase. www .oylerdocumentary.com/home.html.

20. Coalition for Community Schools, "Cincinnati's Community Learning Centers In-Depth Webinar Series: Examining CLCs at the Site-Level," accessed November 1, 2018, www.communityschools.org/assets/1/AssetManager/Webinar2%20final.pdf.

21. Coalition for Community Schools, "School Initiative Information," accessed November 1, 2018, www.communityschools.org/mapdetails.aspx?iid=21; and Toledo Public Schools, United Way of Greater Toledo page, accessed November 21, 2018, www .tps.org/community/united-way-of-greater-toledo.html.

22. By 2018, CIS had dozens of local affiliates, in addition to its twenty-six state (and DC) affiliates (Communities In Schools, "Find Your Affiliate," accessed November 5, 2018, www.communitiesinschools.org/affiliates/.

23. Kristin Anderson Moore et al., *Making the Grade: Assessing the Evidence for Integrated Student Supports* (Bethesda, MD: Child Trends, February 2014), www.childtrends.org /publications/making-the-grade-assessing-the-evidence-for-integrated-student -supports, drew on studies from three initiatives: James Comer's comprehensive school improvement model, Communities In Schools, and City Connects. While CIS and City Connects are both members of the Coalition for Community Schools, they note that their models for delivering ISS are specific and may not apply more broadly.

24. Kristin Anderson Moore et al., *Making the Grade: A Progress Report and Next Steps for Integrated Student Supports* (Bethesda, MD: Child Trends, December 2017), www .childtrends.org/wp-content/uploads/2017/12/ISS_ChildTrends_February2018.pdf.

25. Jeannie Oakes, Anna Maier, and Julia Daniel, "Community Schools: An Evidence-Based Strategy for Equitable School Improvement," National Education Policy Center (Boulder, CO) and Learning Policy Institute (Washington, DC), June 2017, https:// learningpolicyinstitute.org/sites/default/files/product-files/Community_Schools _Evidence_Based_Strategy_BRIEF.pdf.

26. The two institutions created an extensive spreadsheet that includes information from all 148 studies cited in the report. The vast majority fall into ESSA's less rigorous categories of evidence. "Community Schools Research Compendium Live," Google

collaborative document, accessed November 4, 2018, https://docs.google.com
/spreadsheets/d/1xh0STxHsDf1F1A7A8ed6v0RCbj9v2U0M1_d2eGcgDOM/edit
#gid=0.

27. *Comprehensive Services for Children in Poverty: Setting the Research Agenda for Integrated Student Support*, conference report, spring 2018, Boston College, Center for Optimized Student Support, and American Educational Research Association.

28. A few less prominent pieces of legislation have also been passed. The Teaching Fellows for Expanded Learning and After-School Act of 2007 awards competitive grants to eligible entities to recruit, select, train, and support programs for twenty-first-century community learning centers, among others. The Working to Encourage Community Action and Responsibility in Education (WeCare) Act amends Title I of ESEA. And the 2011 Time for Innovation Matters in Education (TIME) Act authorizes the secretary of education to award grants to local education agencies or to partnerships between these agencies and other public nonprofit entities to plan and implement expanding learning time initiatives, especially at high-needs schools.

29. According to Tiffany Miller, CIS vice president of government relations, such legislation has also been introduced, though not yet passed, in Michigan, Indiana, and Pennsylvania.

30. Partnership for the Future of Learning, *Community Schools Playbook* (Washington, DC: Partnership for the Future of Learning, 2018), https://communityschools.futurefor learning.org/assets/downloads/community-schools-playbook.pdf, 3–17.

31. Partnership for the Future of Learning, *Community Schools Playbook*.

32. Center for Popular Democracy, "About the Community Schools Campaign," accessed November 1, 2018, https://populardemocracy.org/campaign/advocating-community-schools

33. Alliance to Reclaim Our Schools, "We Demand," accessed November 1, 2018, www .reclaimourschools.org.

34. Journey for Justice Alliance, "Campaigns," accessed November 1, 2018, www.j4j alliance.com/campaigns.

35. Alliance to Reclaim Our Schools, "About the Alliance," accessed November 1, 2018, www.reclaimourschools.org/about.

36. Alliance to Reclaim Our Schools, "Resources—Community Schools: A Roadmap for Investment and Success," accessed November 1, 2018,www.reclaimourschools.org /resources. In addition to a one-page brief defining and explaining community schools that it developed in-house, the AROS website provides links to the Learning Policy Institute's brief on community schools, the Center for Popular Democracy's 2016 brief on community schools as a school improvement strategy, and a second school "transformation" brief by the Center for Excellent Public Schools.

37. Coalition for Community Schools, "2012 National Forum," www.communityschools .org//2012nationalforum.aspx.

38. Dryfoos and Maguire, *Full-Service Community Schools*, lists the following barriers to implementation that full-service community schools face: lack of space, turf, maintenance, transportation, confidentiality, discipline, need for integration, and sufficient funding. The lengthy list helps explain why more full-service community schools don't exist today.

39. The two organizations' websites perhaps most clearly show these differences. The Coalition for Community Schools website is difficult to navigate and feels dated. Many of the publications, which can be hard to find, are several years old. The site suggests both a lack of consistent maintenance and insufficient funds to do so. The Communities In Schools website, in contrast, is fresh and streamlined and leads with stories about CIS-driven student successes. It is clearly updated regularly, well-maintained, and technologically up-to-date. The site also features multiple examples of data points derived from CIS evaluations. Moreover, the coalition had five staff members, including director José Muñoz, by August 2018 (Reuben Jacobson had just left), whereas CIS employed nine people in its national office alone, with staff in each of its thirteen state affiliates and many times more in its local affiliates.

40. An-Me Chung and Elaine Weiss, email correspondence and telephone conversations, July and August 2018; Joelle Auguste et al., "The Evolution of 21st Century Community Learning Centers: Working to Meet the Holistic Needs of America's Students," Harvard Graduate School of Education, fall 2009, http://a100educationalpolicy.pb works.com/f/21st+CCLC+Comprehensive.pdf.

41. Coalition for Community Schools, *Scaling Up School and Community Partnerships: The Community Schools Strategy; an Interactive Guide*, accessed November 1, 2018, http://www .communityschools.org/ScalingUp.

42. Coalition for Community Schools, "Networks," accessed November 1, 2018, www .communityschools.org/about/networks.aspx.

43. José Muñoz, interview with Elaine Weiss, August 17, 2018.

44. StriveTogether also recently saw a change in leadership. In January 2018, Jennifer Blatz succeeded Jeff Edmonson, who had been StriveTogether's executive director since he founded the network in 2011. Edmonson became managing director of the Ballmer Group, which is providing substantial multiyear financial support for Strive-Together network communities across the country.

45. StriveTogether, "Aligning Networks to Enable Every Student to Thrive," December 2016, www.communityschools.org/assets/1/Lists/Aligning%20Networks%20 Discussion%20Brief.pdf.

46. Dawn Raftery, "10 Communities Will Receive Up to $150,000 Each to Improve Outcomes for Kids," StriveTogether, October 23, 2017, www.strivetogether.org/news/10 -communities-will-receive-15000-improve-outcomes-kids.

47. Shital Shah, email correspondence with Elaine Weiss, August 2018.

Chapter 11

1. Brookings Institution, "The Social Genome Project," accessed November 4, 2018, www.brookings.edu/the-social-genome-project.

2. National Center for Education Statistics, "Public School Revenue Sources," last updated April 2018, figure 2, https://nces.ed.gov/programs/coe/indicator_cma.asp.

3. Emma Garcia, "Inequalities at the Starting Gate: Cognitive and Noncognitive Skills Gaps Between 2010-11 Kindergarten Classmates," Economic Policy Institute, June 17, 2015, www.epi.org/publication/inequalities-at-the-starting-gate-cognitive-and -noncognitive-gaps-in-the-2010-2011-kindergarten-class.

4. For example, Levacic explains the transition among European countries to funding schemes that use per-student costs, building in special education and other metrics of

disadvantage to ensure more equitable funding. Rosalind Levacic, "Funding Schools by Formula," International Conference on Educational Systems and the Challenge of Improving Results, University of Lausanne, Switzerland, September 2006, https://docplayer.net/50968394-Funding-schools-by-formula.html.

5. Funding has increased in several other states in the past few years, so in addition to New Jersey and New York, Alaska ($20,540), Connecticut ($19,297), Vermont ($19,300), and Wyoming ($17,407), as well as Washington, DC ($21,735) devote per-pupil resources at similar levels to that of Massachusetts. National Center for Education Statistics, "Current Expenditure Per Pupil in Average Daily Attendance in Public Elementary and Secondary Schools, by State or Jurisdiction, 2013–14 School Year," table 236.70, https://nces.ed.gov/programs/digest/d16/tables/dt16_236.70.asp.

6. The other two states are Delaware and Minnesota. Bruce Baker et al., "Is School Funding Fair? A National Report Card," 6th ed., Education Law Center, January 2017, https://drive.google.com/file/d/0BxtYmwryVl00VDhjRGlDOUh3VE0/view.

7. The Education Law Center also ranks and grades states on their distribution of funds. These states provide between 95 and 105 percent of the funding to low-income schools that they provide higher-income schools. And two others, Maryland and Texas, provide just under 95 percent, also earning C grades. Baker et al., "Is School Funding Fair?"

8. Other titles within the extensive law are designed to compensate for flaws within state and local funding mechanisms by directing funds to schools and districts that serve students who are disproportionately poor, but the Title I program has by far the largest funding power and, thus, the largest impact on schools and districts.

9. An unintentional flaw in the Title I formula means that larger, but less poor, school districts receive a higher per-pupil Title I allocation, a flaw that disproportionately affects small, rural schools across the country. Elaine Weiss and Noelle Ellerson, "Rich Hill: The Gap Between Student Needs and School Capacity," Broader, Bolder Approach to Education and AASA (School Superintendents Association), April 2014, www.aasa.org/uploadedFiles/Policy_and_Advocacy/files/White%20paper%20Rich%20Hill%2004_24_14_FINAL.pdf.

10. Michael Leachman, Kathleen Masterson, and Eric Figueroa, "A Punishing Decade for School Funding," Center for Budget and Policy Priorities, November 29, 2017, www.cbpp.org/research/state-budget-and-tax/a-punishing-decade-for-school-funding.

11. Michael A. Rebell et al., "A New Constitutional Cost Methodology for Determining the Actual Cost of a Sound Basic Education," Teachers College, Columbia University, September 2016, www.centerforeducationalequity.org/publications/safeguarding-students-educational-rights/Constitutional-Cost-Methodology-final,-09-16.pdf.

12. Education Law Center, "Major Cases, Kentucky," accessed November 2, 2018, www.edlawcenter.org/states/kentucky.html.

13. Brookings Institution, "The Social Genome Project."

14. Kerry Searle Grannis and Isabel V. Sawhill, "Improving Children's Life Chances: Estimates from the Social Genome Model," report, Brookings Institution, October 11, 2013, www.brookings.edu/research/improving-childrens-life-chances-estimates-from-the-social-genome-model.

15. Richard Rothstein, Tamara Wilder, and Whitney Allgood, "Providing Comprehensive Educational Opportunity to Low Income Students: How Much Does It Cost?," Cam-

paign for Educational Equity, Teachers College, Columbia University, October 2011, https://files.eric.ed.gov/fulltext/ED573119.pdf.

16. Rothstein, Wilder, and Allgood, "How Much Does It Cost?," continue: "If these costs were converted to New York State dollars, the lifetime per child cost would be approximately $256,000 and the average annual per child cost would be about $13,900. Assuming conservatively that each child would access 75% of the available services, the New York City annual cost would be approximately $11,800 per child and the New York State cost approximately $10,400."

17. Helen Warrell, "Bond Offers Return for Lower Offending," *Financial Times*, March 19, 2010, https://web.archive.org/web/20100615191522/http://www.ft.com/cms/s/0/d9dca292-32f6-11df-bf5f-00144feabdc0.html.

18. Robert Dugger and Robert Litan, "'Pay-For-Success' Social Impact Finance: A PKSE Bond Example to Increase School Readiness and Reduce Special Education Costs," paper 2012-007, Human Capital and Economic Opportunity Global Working Group, University of Chicago, March 2012, https://hceconomics.uchicago.edu/research/working-paper/pay-success-social-impact-finance-pkse-bond-example-increase-school-readiness. This adapted program is nicknamed PKSE, or Peek-See.

19. "Gates Foundation Failures Show Philanthropists Shouldn't Be Setting America's Public School Agenda," editorial, *Los Angeles Times*, June 1, 2016, www.latimes.com/opinion/editorials/la-ed-gates-education-20160601-snap-story.html.

20. Bill and Melinda Gates, "The 10 Toughest Questions We Get," *GatesNotes*, February 2018, www.gatesnotes.com/2018-Annual-Letter?WT.mc_id=02_13_2018_02_Annual Letter2018_GF-media_&WT.tsrc=GFmedia

21. Dale Russakoff, *The Price: Who's in Charge of America's Schools?* (New York: Houghton Mifflin Harcourt, 2015). In the final chapter, Zuckerberg acknowledges mistakes, including the failure to engage the community in his investment, and he discusses his intent to work differently going forward.

22. See Chan Zuckerberg Initiative, "Initiatives: Bringing World-Class, Cutting-Edge Engineering to Social Change," accessed November 1, 2018, www.chanzuckerberg.com/initiatives.

23. An-Me Chung, email correspondence and telephone conversation with Elaine Weiss, August 2018.

24. Sanjiv Rao, email correspondence with Elaine Weiss, August 2018.

25. John Jackson, email correspondence with Elaine Weiss, August 2018.

26. Mary Deatrick, Harris Rosen's assistant, email correspondence with Elaine Weiss, August 2018.

27. Harlem Children's Zone Fact Sheet, accessed November 5, 2018, https://hcz.org/wp-content/uploads/2014/04/FY-2013-FactSheet.pdf.

28. Bruce Katz and Jeremy Nowak, *The New Localism: How Cities Can Thrive in the Age of Populism*, (Washington, DC: Brookings Institution Press, 2017), 2.

Chapter 12

1. Even as this book goes to press, we see daily news about grants that support ISS work and major providers like Strive (large grant from the Ballmer Group) and Communities In Schools (large grant from AbbVie). See Cassie Walker Burkey, "Chunk of

$55 Million AbbVie Gift Will Go Toward More Counselors in Schools," *Chalkbeat*, November 16, 2018, https://chalkbeat.org/posts/chicago/2018/11/16/chicago-school-counselors-get-boost-from-55-abbvie-donation; "Ballmer Group Pledges $60 Million to StriveTogether," *Philanthropy News Digest*, October 10, 2017, https://philanthropy newsdigest.org/news/ballmer-group-pledges-60-million-to-strivetogether. At the same time, provider partnerships and convenings of various kinds are proliferating.

2. Ralph Smith, Broader, Bolder Approach to Education meeting of national ISS leaders, Washington, DC, September 2016, asserted that a true ISS field does not yet exist, and he emphasized "muscle-building" as an important way to create a field and a meaningful, unified ISS movement.

3. Coalition for Community Schools, "ESEA Reathorization: ESSA Resources," Coalition for Community Schools, accessed November 8, 2018, www.communityschools. org/policy_advocacy/esea_reauthorization.aspx, provides guidance on leveraging ESSA from its various partners. Communities In Schools (e.g., "The Every Student Succeeds Act," CIS, accessed November 8, 2018, www.communitiesinschools.org /policy-corner/policy-initiatives), has developed several useful briefs on the subject; and the Learning Policy Institute, "The Every Student Succeeds Act (ESSA)," Learning Policy Institute, accessed November 8, 2018, https://learningpolicyinstitute.org /topic/essa, provides scholarly guidance for organizations looking to capitalize on ESSA. Most recently, Partnership for the Future of Learning, *Community Schools Playbook* (Washington, DC: Partnership for the Future of Learning, 2018), https:// community schools.futureforlearning.org/assets/downloads/community-schools -playbook.pdf, offers detailed information on the various ESSA provisions that can be utilized to advance community school (and ISS) work.

4. Under the auspices of the creation of a new "Virtual Center on Community Schools" by Bruce Levine at the Washington, DC, office of Drexel University, one of us (Elaine) began to work with two postdoctoral scholars, Todd Brown and Amber Vrain, in the summer of 2017. The objective is to map out resources in the areas of research, messaging and advocacy, technical assistance, and "unusual allies" (noneducation networks collaborating with ISS initiatives or organizations). Although the effort is not complete, it provides a helpful starting point and model for how this work might be conducted comprehensively to help the field take advantage of its collective resources (and build muscle in the process).

5. The team also included Chris Cross, founding partner of education consulting firm Cross & Joftus; Punam Mather, executive director of the Elaine P. Wynn Family Foundation; and Elaine Wynn, chair of the CIS Board of Directors. Punam Mather, interview with Elaine Weiss, July 15, 2018.

6. Punam Mather, conversation with Elaine Weiss, July 12, 2018.

7. Such litigation can also lead to more broad-based school reforms. For example, equity and adequacy litigator Michael Rebell recently filed a federal lawsuit charging Rhode Island's public schools with failing to prepare the state's disadvantaged students to participate in a democratic society. See Alia Wong, "The Students Suing for a Constitutional Right to Education," *Atlantic*, November 28, 2018, www.the atlantic.com/education/archive/2018/11/lawsuit-constitutional-right-education /576901.

8. At the end of 2018, the data-collection effort was nascent and not yet discussed by the coalition, but we hope that it has since evolved and grown.

Appendix
1. Information in this appendix is derived from case studies of these initiatives. Data on school district and student demographics comes from those districts' websites or from websites or reports from the sponsoring ISS organizations. In some cases, these are supplemented with information from state or federal agencies and/or academic reports. Information on funding sources was obtained from each initiative through interviews and email exchanges.

Acknowledgments

Elaine and Paul are grateful to the many individuals and organizations whose work made this book possible. We first want to thank the leaders of the school districts, communities, and partnership organizations whose pioneering work is featured in these chapters. We greatly appreciate their persistent, committed efforts to ensure an excellent and equitable educational experience for every child and for the time they devoted to speaking with us so that we could illuminate their work for our readers. We also thank the Economic Policy Institute for creating the Broader, Bolder Approach to Education and for supporting the development and publication of the case studies, and the Harvard Graduate School of Education for supporting the creation of the Education Redesign Lab and its By All Means initiative.

Thanks, also, to leaders of national organizations advancing integrated student supports on the ground and advocating for policies supporting this work. These include Marty Blank, founder and former President of the Coalition for Community Schools; current president José Muñoz; and Dan Cardinali and Dale Erquiaga, former and current presidents of Communities In Schools. Thanks to Mary Walsh and Joan Wasser-Gish at City Connects; C. J. Huff and Kim Vann of Bright Futures USA; Lisa Cylar-Barrett of the Promise Neighborhoods Institute at Policy Link; Ralph Smith, founder of the Campaign for Grade-Level Reading; Mary Anne

Schmidt Carey and Eugene Chasin of Say Yes to Education; and the former and current leaders of StriveTogether, Jeff Edmondson and Jennifer Blatz.

We also thank several individuals who have contributed in important ways to this book. Elaine is especially grateful to Larry Mishel, former president of the Economic Policy Institute, for his unwavering commitment to BBA and to her work to advance integrated student supports, and to Lora Engdahl, Krista Faries, and Margaret Poydock of the EPI communications team, whose excellent work on the case studies made the stories stronger and more readable. She also thanks her BBA cochairs: Helen Ladd, Pedro Noguera, Thomas Payzant, Joshua Starr, and, of course, Paul Reville, for their guidance and excellent advice. Finally, she thanks Jeannie Oaks for suggesting that the case studies would make for good book material and Josh Starr for his help with the proposal. Gratitude, too, to Emma Garcia for being such a supportive colleague and always available as a sounding board.

Paul thanks Elaine for her conception of this book and hard work on it. He particularly appreciates the wise counsel and committed assistance of his Education Redesign Lab colleagues, notably Lynne Sacks, who collaborated on the By All Means chapter. He also acknowledges the consistent support of this work by the Harvard Graduate School of Education.

We are also very lucky to have supportive families, whose patience made writing this book possible. Elaine thanks her wonderful parents, sister, husband Michael and daughters Kayla and Maya. Paul thanks his wife, Julie Joyal, and his children and grandchildren for being there. Finally, we are grateful for the helpful and wise counsel of Nancy Walser, who has been a guide throughout the process. We are lucky to have her as our editor.

Many other scholars, advocates, community leaders, and educators also contributed in various ways to this book. And others across the country continue to advance integrated student support in a variety of ways. We wish we could name and thank each of them individually. We hope this book does them justice.

About the Authors

Elaine Weiss has been the lead policy analyst, income security, for the National Academy of Social Insurance since January 2019. She was the national coordinator for the Broader, Bolder Approach to Education (BBA) from 2011 to 2017. There she worked with four cochairs, a high-level advisory board, and multiple coalition partners to promote a comprehensive, evidence-based set of policies to allow all children to thrive in school and in life. Major publications for BBA include case studies of diverse communities that employ comprehensive, whole-child approaches to education across the country. She has coauthored two studies with Economic Policy Institute economist Emma Garcia on early achievement gaps and strategies to reduce them. With Don Long, she wrote a 2013 report, "Market-Oriented Education Reforms' Rhetoric Trumps Reality," and she wrote a 2013 Economic Policy Institute paper, "Mismatches in Race to the Top Limit Educational Improvement." In 2014, Elaine worked with multiple educators to write a series of commentaries for *Bill Moyers & Company* on the many links between poverty and education. She has also written dozens of blogs for the *Huffington Post*, the *Washington Post Answer Sheet*, *Talk Poverty*, the *Nation*, and other publications. Prior to her work with BBA, Weiss served as project manager for the Pew Charitable Trusts' Partnership for America's Economic Success campaign. Weiss has also served as a member of a Centers for Disease Control task force on child abuse and as volunteer counsel for clients at the Washington Legal Clinic for the Homeless.

Paul Reville is the Francis Keppel Professor of Practice of Educational Policy and Administration at the Harvard Graduate School of Education (HGSE), where he has been a faculty member since 1997. He is the founding director of HGSE's Education Redesign Lab. Reville served as secretary of education for the Commonwealth of Massachusetts from 2008 to 2013. His career, spanning more than four decades, has combined research, policy, and practice focused on educational equity and reform in Massachusetts and the nation. He has been a top policy-maker, a teacher, a principal, and the founder of a research center and several other organizations devoted to education equity and reform.

During his service as the secretary of education for the Commonwealth of Massachusetts and as Governor Patrick's top education adviser, Reville established a new Executive Office of Education and had oversight of higher education, K–12, and early education in the nation's leading student achievement state. He served in the governor's cabinet and played a leading role on matters ranging from the Achievement Gap Act of 2010 and Common Core State Standards to the commonwealth's highly successful Race to the Top proposal. Before joining the Patrick administration, Reville had chaired the Massachusetts State Board of Education, founded the Rennie Center for Education Research and Policy, cofounded the Massachusetts Business Alliance for Education (MBAE), chaired the Massachusetts Reform Review Commission, chaired the Massachusetts Commission on Time and Learning, and served as executive director of the Pew Forum on Standards-Based Reform, a national think tank that convened leading US researchers, practitioners, and policy-makers to set the national standards agenda. Reville played a central role in MBAE's development of, and advocacy for, the Massachusetts historic Education Reform Act of 1993.

Reville began his career with service as a VISTA volunteer and youth worker. He worked as a teacher and principal of two urban alternative high schools. He founded a local education foundation, which was part of the Public Education Network, where he also served as a member of the national board. He has recently served as cochair of the national Broader, Bolder Approach to Education initiative. He is currently a board member of, and adviser to, a host of organizations such as City Year Boston, BELL, Bellwether, Boston After School and Beyond, and Harvard Medical School's MEDscience program. He is a frequent writer and speaker on education reform and policy issues. He holds a bachelor's degree from Colorado College, a master's degree from Stanford University, and five honorary doctorate degrees.

Additionally, Reville is the education commentator for WGBH's Boston Public Radio. He frequently contributes to *Education Week* and has recently written for *Times Education Supplement, Nature Human Behaviour,* and the publication of the Federal Reserve Bank of Boston. He edited the book *A Decade of Urban School Reform: Persistence and Progress in the Boston Public Schools.*

Index